Joy

A Guide for Youth Ministry

David F. White *and* Sarah F. Farmer
General Editors

Foreword by
Miroslav Volf

Joy: A Guide for Youth Ministry

The General Board of Higher Education and Ministry leads and serves The United Methodist Church in the recruitment, preparation, nurture, education, and support of Christian leaders—lay and clergy—for the work of making disciples of Jesus Christ for the transformation of the world. Its vision is that a new generation of Christian leaders will commit boldly to Jesus Christ and be characterized by intellectual excellence, moral integrity, spiritual courage, and holiness of heart and life. The General Board of Higher Education and Ministry of The United Methodist Church serves as an advocate for the intellectual life of the church. The Board's mission embodies the Wesleyan tradition of commitment to the education of laypersons and ordained persons by providing access to higher education for all persons.

Wesley's Foundery Books is named for the abandoned foundery that early followers of John Wesley transformed, which later became the cradle of London's Methodist movement.

Joy: A Guide for Youth Ministry

Research for *Joy: A Guide for Youth Ministry* was funded by a generous grant from the John Templeton Foundation.

For information regarding rights and permissions, contact the Publisher, General Board of Higher Education and Ministry, PO Box 340007, Nashville, TN 37203-0007; phone 615-340-7393; fax 615-340-7048. Visit our website at www.gbhem.org.

All web addresses were correct and operational at the time of publication.

978-1-945935-73-2

GBHEM Publishing is an affiliate member of the Association of University Presses.

Manufactured in the United States of America

Note: All identifying information and personal names have been changed to protect confidentiality.

Contents

CONTENTS

Foreword

Youth Ministry and the Reasons for Joy

MIROSLAV VOLF

Who would have thought that it would be controversial to focus theological research on joy! Yet there was pushback when, with the support of the John Templeton Foundation, we started a three-year study titled "Joy and the Good Life." This book is one result of that surprisingly controversial intellectual labor.

What could possibly be wrong with studying joy? Is joy, assumed to be superficial and bubbly, not a topic weighty enough for academic inquiry? There were some murmurings to that effect, but that was not it. Was resistance to joy part of some self-contradictory struggle of self-absorbed humans? This idea of a postlapsarian flight from and fight against joy, of which C. S. Lewis wrote in *The Great Divorce*,[1] didn't seem to figure in anyone's pushback. There were three main concerns: two moral ones and a third related to research propensities in the human sciences and humanities. If any of these concerns are in fact justified with regard to joy and research about joy in general, they would also apply to joy and research about joy in adolescents. Let's examine them briefly.

1 See C. S. Lewis, *The Great Divorce* (New York: HarperCollins, 2000), 67–75, 129.

For some of our critics, the main problem was that the time taken to do research on joy and to actually rejoice was time taken away from engaging the pressing problems of the world, the visible and audible signs of which include desolate landscapes and destroyed cities, contorted faces and the tears of the bereaved, the groans of the oppressed and screams of the tortured, the sighs of the persecuted and the blank stares of the depressed. First remove the causes of suffering, they suggested, and then start rejoicing or, if you are so inclined, take up reflection on joy.

True, joy can be complacent and self-absorbed. But it need not be. The labor of alleviating suffering and removing its causes is not an alternative to finding and promoting joy; the two can be done together. More important, joy can light up our faces and make our hearts sing in the midst of suffering. A life in which you can find reasons to rejoice notwithstanding suffering—a life in which you rejoice always, as the Apostle Paul writes in Philippians 4:4, is better than the one that suffering and sorrow have conquered. Finally, joy can be "oppositional," as my colleague Willie Jennings has argued, and therefore a form of struggle against suffering.[2] When joy celebrates true life in the suffering-suffused false life, it enacts hope.

Other critics worried less about the effects of joy on suffering and more about joy's opportunity with regard to human "progress," for joy celebrates the good that is or is about to come. Call it exuberant contentment. But many of us, citizens of the modern world, are uncomfortable with contentment. Some time ago I posted on Facebook and tweeted a statement in praise of contentment. The condemnation was swift and strong (though there was some praise, too, as I recall). Contentment is putting up with things rather than striving to reach goals and realize dreams. Contentment is flaccidity rather than zest. Contentment is

---

2 Willie Jennings, "Joy that Gathers." Work in progress prepared for Yale Center for Faith & Culture consultation on "Religions of Joy?" 2014, https://faith.yale.edu/sites/default/files/jennings_-_joy_that_gathers.pdf.

falling behind rather than keeping up, let alone winning. Time taken to rejoice over what is is time not spent creating what could be.

Discomfort with contentment is not surprising. Indefinite progress and acceleration of change are key features of modernity, and ample dissatisfaction with what we have and who we are is as important to the modern economy as a plentiful supply of energy. The result is a joyless culture. Speaking at Lambeth Palace at the launch of Archbishop Justin Welby's *Reimagining Britain*,[3] I noted the prevailing joylessness of modern societies:

> Our economy is largely joyless. Our education is joyless. Our politics are joyless. Our entertainment, though full of wonderful humor, is joyless. Our pleasures, intense and many, are joyless. In all these spheres, our belief in the perfectibility of the world and our natural insatiability, put into high gear by the competitiveness that marks our societies, undermine our gratitude for and joy in the goods that are already ours.[4]

A joyless rat race is not a compelling image of the flourishing life, as most modern "rats," upon reflection, readily admit. One purpose of research about joy is to think through what it means not to put striving and joy in opposition but rather in positive relation to one another. What would it mean, for instance, to strive for six days—or six hours, or six minutes—out of seven but take that one remaining day, hour, or minute not so much to rest but to rejoice? Would not such joy transform the world?

Finally, in academic work—especially in the social sciences and humanities—there is hesitation about studying positive aspects of human lives. For many years the main interest of psychology, for instance, was mental illness, which is to say the removal of the negative. Though positive psychology, founded in 1998, is thriving, interest in the

---

3 Justin Welby, *Reimagining Britain: Foundations for Hope* (London: Bloomsbury Continuum, 2018).

4 Miroslav Volf, "Public Faith and What Matters Most" (lecture, Lambeth Palace, London, 15 March 2018). https://www.youtube.com/watch?v=PnmCCDP7zz0.

negative still predominates among psychologists. The same is also true of animal studies. Scholars have shown "an overwhelming interest in negative aspects of animal societies," writes Nicholas Christakis in *Blueprint*, "with an extraordinary amount of attention lavished on topics like competition, conflict, manipulation, coercion, deception, and even . . . kidnapping, rape, murder and cannibalism." True, "love, friendship, altruism, cooperation, and teaching" are getting increasing attention, but still the study of the negative holds sway.[5]

In the humanities the predilection for the negative is notorious. Many in the humanities feel that they would fail their moral responsibility if they did not spy out the negative in everything that sets itself up as positive, if they did not interrogate and unmask, trouble and problematize, expose and subvert, demystify and destabilize.[6] For a long time now, great critics have been the royalty of the humanities. As Matthew Croasmun and I have argued in *For the Life of the World*, theology, too, has come to be practiced in the "negative mode" as well.[7] It is as if the obsession with sin of a few centuries ago put on a modern garb. Conservative theologians join other intellectuals in penning jeremiads, bemoaning the devolution of modern societies from some "golden age" in the past. Progressive theologians, in contrast, echoing the critique in the humanities, attack various structures of oppression.

My point is not that modern societies do not deserve criticism or that, all the progress notwithstanding, something important from the past hasn't been lost in them. Losses are real, and criticism is often well deserved. My point is that jeremiads and critiques are compelling only if they are in service of a positive vision. In its absence they tend to degenerate into mere griping.

---

5 Nicholas A. Christakis, *Blueprint: The Evolutionary Origins of a Good Society* (New York: Little, Brown Spark, 2019), 232.

6 For a critique of critique, see Rita Felski, *The Limits of Critique* (Chicago: University of Chicago Press, 2015).

7 Miroslav Volf and Matthew Croasmun, *For the Life of the World: A Theology That Makes a Difference* (Grand Rapids: Brazos, 2019), 35–59.

The dominance of the negative is particularly troubling in Christian theology. For all its talk about sin, the Christian faith isn't primarily about removing the negative (e.g., the stain of sin and our captivity to sin) but about the promise of the positive (e.g., new life in the power of the Spirit of life). Notwithstanding the centrality of the cross in the life of Jesus Christ, the Christian faith is, as Jürgen Moltmann put it, "uniquely a religion of joy."[8] The crucifixion, brutal end to Christ's short life that it was, did not amount to a defeat of the good news, the proclamation of which defined his ministry. To the contrary, it was an enactment of one of its crucial dimensions; the resurrection and the ascension that followed after the crucifixion underscored this.

More than any New Testament text, the Gospel of Luke places joy at the center of what Jesus was all about. The Gospel starts with resounding joy over the birth of Jesus (2:10) and of his forerunner, John the Baptist (1:14). It ends with the followers of Jesus returning to Jerusalem "with great joy" (24:52 ESV) after his resurrection and ascension. In the middle of the Gospel, the three parallel stories about the lost sheep, the lost coin, and the lost son each culminate in rejoicing (15:5–7, 9–10, 32). And between these high points of the Gospel, there is more joy, much more. Joy is one of the red threads in the Gospel of Luke. In other biblical texts, both in the Hebrew Bible and in the New Testament, joy may not be as central as in the Gospel of Luke, but it is surprisingly prominent once you start paying attention.

The abundance of joy in biblical texts is but a consequence of the key biblical conviction, expressed most clearly in the first pages of the Bible, that God is good, that God created a world that is good, and that, notwithstanding the spread of sin and violence in the world, the world's goodness abides. Though brokenness runs like a crack through the entire edifice of the world and the depths of its pain are at times inexpressible, they are secondary. Goodness is primary; it is primordial

8 Jürgen Moltmann, "Christianity: A Religion of Joy," in *Joy and Human Flourishing: Essays on Theology, Culture, and the Good Life,* eds. Miroslav Volf and Justin Crisp (Minneapolis: Fortress, 2015), 6.

and ineliminable. Joy is, therefore, more basic and stronger than its opposite. Our research about joy and the good life has confirmed these convictions.

One of the most remarkable—and troubling—facts about adolescent lives in modern societies is how joyless they have become. Right when life is opening up to them with all its possibilities, a staggering number of them are beset by anxiety and depression.[9] This should not surprise us. Joyless parents living in a joyless culture will have joyless offspring passing from childhood to adulthood: the joylessness of modern culture is magnified in their experience as they try to figure out their place and purpose in the world and the meaning of their lives.

Anxiety and depression and other such maladies are stones in their shoes. Before they can comfortably walk, the stones must come out. But for them to walk with a spring in their step, they will need reasons for joy. My hope is that this book will generate research about joy in the lives of adolescents and help to recenter youth ministry around helping adolescents find reasons for joy—and to rejoice!

---

9 A study in 2001 showed that 28.3 percent suffered from serious depression within the previous year. In 2003, it was estimated that about 13 percent of children and adolescents suffer from anxiety. The Commission for Children at Risk, *Hardwired to Connect: The New Scientific Case for Authoritative Communities* (New York: Institute for American Values, 2003), 72. See recent numbers from the Centers for Disease Control and Prevention: "'Ever having been diagnosed with either anxiety or depression' among children aged 6–17 years increased from 5.4% in 2003 to 8% in 2007 and to 8.4% in 2011–2012. 'Ever having been diagnosed with anxiety' increased from 5.5% in 2007 to 6.4% in 2011–2012." https://www.cdc.gov/childrensmentalhealth/data.html. Accessed 24 April 2019.

Introduction

Joy as a Guiding Metaphor for Youth Ministry

David F. White

Anyone who cares for youth on a regular basis will recognize joy as a feature of adolescent life. A number of years ago, I served as youth minister at a United Methodist Church in California where two sophomore girls, Audrey and Amanda,[1] were as close as two friends could be. They swapped clothing; they finished each other's sentences; they slept at each other's homes on weekends; they took courage from each other to try new things—boyfriends, music, dance classes, track and field, those scary AP classes. Early one fall semester they invited a gaggle of friends to a dance sponsored by our Methodist district at a local gymnasium, an event that I was expected to supervise. I recall the event especially because it was held the weekend following my father's death after his long struggle with cancer. For much of the evening, I watched the dancers from the gym bleachers, too dejected in my grief to join them on the dance floor. After an hour or so of my glum observing, Audrey and Amanda and a throng of about a dozen of their friends came to me in the bleachers and reached out their hands to

1 The names and identifying details of youths in this chapter have been changed to protect the privacy of individuals.

me. Refusing to take no for an answer, they pulled me onto the gym floor and surrounded me in joyful dance—and my morose lumbering slowly turned into a surprisingly happy shuffle (still not quite what could be called dancing, but nevertheless infused by joy at the grace of their gesture). To this day I remain grateful for their love that encircled me in my grief. As impossible as it was to escape their circle, it was even more impossible to comprehend their gesture without drinking deeply from their joy. This is only one example of how those who minister with youth are privileged to witness young people as they embrace joy and offer it as a gift.

I think also of the time when fourteen-year-old Julie mustered her courage to sing a solo with the adult choir only to be received by the congregation with thundering applause—transforming timid Julie into Julie "the singer." I recall watching Charlie and Chris playing a basketball game in which they altered the rules on the fly to make them fair for their younger sibling, to the delight of them all. I recall a late-night conversation with Michael, who wanted clarification about some challenging Bible verse, and his joy at learning new insights. I recall the joy of youths collaborating in creating a liturgical dance for the congregation. I recall Emily's joy in competing at science fairs—joy that eventually led adult Emily with a team of other scientists to a Nobel Prize! Too numerous to count are the stories of young people who discovered joy in romance and friendship.

Early twentieth-century theorist of adolescence G. Stanley Hall observed that adolescence is the "springtime of the heart."[2] He claimed that adolescence is uniquely and wondrously attuned to the plenitude of beauty in the world. Because of this attunement, young people, he claimed, are prone to delight in romance, comradery, religion, and new experiences and discoveries. Hall revealed that adolescent joy and wonder is key to their further study and action. This joyful attunement has

2 G. Stanley Hall, *Adolescence: Its Psychology and Its Relation to Physiology, Anthropology, Sociology, Sex, Crime, Religion and Education*, vol. 1 (New York: Appleton, 1922), 131.

been largely neglected by social scientists, yet those who work with youth often glimpse such joy, even among today's over-pressured youth. Attentive youth ministers appreciate that joy is part of the very fabric of adolescent life—indeed it may constitute one of the gifts they offer to the church and the world.

Youth ministry in the modern era has been guided by a variety of root metaphors (discipleship, friendship, Godbearing, family, adoption, relationships, discernment, etc.) that serve as powerful tools of analysis, enabling us to see some particular claim concerning what is true about youth and ministry as maps enlarging our imaginations concerning what are appropriate activities for youth ministry. For example, when we learn to see youth ministry as "Godbearing," as Kenda Creasy Dean and Ron Foster propose,[3] we discover that our relationships with youths are holy ground; when we see youth ministry as family based, as suggested by Mark DeVries,[4] the scope of our ministry is enlarged to include the webs of family relationships that form youths.

Joy is a root metaphor for youth ministry.

This book explores the possibilities opened for youth ministry when we embrace "joy" as a root metaphor. Taking cues from Miroslav Volf[5] and other Christian theologians, the authors in this volume insist that reclaiming joy for youth ministry may be crucial in light of modern secularism that has, according to philosopher Charles Taylor, evacuated the world of such things as mystery, wonder, grace and transcendence.[6] The modern world urges us to work and consume compulsively; to value its creatures only for their use or to serve our egos. While consumption sometimes yields momentary fun or happiness, only rarely does it yield

3 Kenda Creasy Dean and Ron Foster, *The Godbearing Life: The Art of Soul Tending for Youth Ministry* (Nashville: Upper Room, 2005).

4 Mark DeVries, *Family-Based Youth Ministry* (Downers Grove: IVP, 2010).

5 Miroslav Volf and Justin Crisp, eds., *Joy and Human Flourishing: Essays on Theology, Culture, and the Good Life* (Minneapolis: Fortress, 2015).

6 Charles Taylor, *A Secular Age* (Cambridge, MA: Belknap Press, 2007).

joy. We contrarily assert that to reclaim joy is to retrieve a practicable virtue of the Christian faith, a practice that involves attending to gratitude for God's gracious gifts, which potentially moves us to worship and empowers us for active love of God and neighbor. This introductory chapter provides a brief theological rationale for joy, interprets this secular moment and the urgency of reclaiming joy, reveals connections between adolescence and joy, and previews how our authors view the practices of youth ministry in light of the concept of joy.

But first it will be important to address the elephant in the room. Why joy? Today talk of joy and wonder can seem irrelevant and even cruel in light of the widespread suffering of children and youth. The horrors of the Jewish Holocaust and the church's feeble efforts in the face of such suffering prompted post–World War II theologians famously to vow that theology can now only be credible in the presence of "burning children"—and we might today add school shootings, suicides, depression, alienation, and the general sense of hurt among youth. As theologian Justin Crisp observes, "When we stand in the shadow of the towering wreckage of history, joy fails to stand out as the most obviously promising candidate among possible pivots of theological thinking."[7] Not only does joy seem ethically irresponsible, but is it not also too fickle an emotion to withstand the assault of suffering—would not anger or rage be sturdier? Is joy not simply another opiate of the masses distracting us from the real world? Why should we not resist anything that restrains the discontent necessary to bring real change? These are faithful questions, and not to be dismissed. In this book we hope to counter the popular notion that Christian joy is merely naive or Pollyannaish in its disregard of these concerns. We insist that there are good reasons for acknowledging joy as essential for a Christian faith that is not naive, a resource for confronting suffering.

Why joy now?

7 Crisp, "Introduction: A Bright Sorrow," in Volf and Crisp, vii.

The suspicion that joy may be naive emerges not only from the specter of the Holocaust but also from the limitations imposed by secularism. In our secularized modern age, a misguided scientism renders all things as expected, necessary and predictable outcomes of efficient causes, subject to our complete comprehension and willful manipulation. All things—human consciousness, sexuality, childrearing, nation-building, youth ministry, and indeed our breakfast cereal—can now be explained (or so we imagine) as a chain of physical causes and effects, immanently understandable and controllable. No other kind of explanation is necessary—indeed no other is allowed. For secular people (and to some great degree we are all inescapably secular!) nothing in the world has meaning apart from our mental processes that ascribe it significance. The world beyond our "buffered selves"[8] is seen as inert, semiotically vacant, lacking any purpose in itself; all meaning is constructed by our minds. A world in which all things are reduced to efficient causes thus ceases to flow with spiritual mysteries. Our arrogance in comprehending and engineering the world has exceeded our appreciation for its sacramental depth—as a cosmos created, sustained, and redeemed by God, through which we glimpse God's glory.

Moreover, in a world that holds no intrinsic meaning that we should respect, we presume that we are simply entitled to its goods—and as a sign of our cosmic privilege we grow petulant when things cannot be controlled and consumed without remainder. Joy is rendered extraneous in an era that obscures the fact that the world is given as a gift. Modern life involves an endless struggle to secure what we want by force of ego and will, since these are now the only meaningful forces in the cosmos. While we may experience fleeting happiness when we acquire what we want, joy remains rare, because there is no gift, no

8 Charles Taylor, *Secular Age*, 27–41. Taylor characterizes the difference as one between the world of the "porous self"—an "enchanted world" in which spirits and cosmic forces "could cross a porous boundary and shape our lives, psychic and physical"—and that of the modern "buffered self," in which the boundaries between self and other, as well as between mind and body, are much more evident and firm.

surprise, and no Giver. While we are created in God's image, made for joy and restless in its pursuit, in our modern consumerist world our quest for joy is interrupted by our endless grasp for momentary, transactional, and idolatrous fun.

Examples of modern disenchantment abound. According to Charles Taylor, in a modern world evacuated of mystery we are at risk of losing our tongue and our ear for poetry.[9] If we believe that the world is immanently comprehensible and that words map neatly onto things in the world, then poetry is superfluous, and we grow resentful of poets who should, we imagine, simply say things directly. Taylor observes that language is not merely designative but also constitutive, revealing hidden worlds and creating new possibilities. Poetry, for example, expresses unexpected meanings and hidden mysteries by carefully juxtaposing images and metaphors. In poetry truth resonates rather than argues. Such a view of language demands that we attend more closely to the cosmos, which never ceases speaking in surprising ways. Poets and artists are those who potentially see beneath the modern veil, joyfully behold the world as a gracious donation, and give words to "unofficial versions" of reality. Without poetry we are left with ideologies that claim to entirely map the world.

When the created order is flattened to mere explanatory ideologies, there are also ethical consequences. Instead of being moved by the mysteries that surround us, we must first consult our ideologies for permission or an excuse to feel or act. Taylor recounts the Bible story of the Good Samaritan, in which religious officials ignored the wounded man while the despised Samaritan, moved by kindness, cared for the man.[10] He notes that Jesus's parables seem constantly to be interrupting our various ideologies. The more we are trapped in our fixed ideologies, the less we are likely to perceive the sacramental quality of the world that signals the holy depths in which we live and move. If

9 Charles Taylor, *The Language Animal: The Full Shape of the Human Linguistic Capacity* (Cambridge, MA: Belknap Press, 2016), 56.

10 Taylor, *Secular Age*, 246.

we cannot sense the world alive with grace manifested in the face of a stranger, then we cannot feel compassion. If our rigid ideologies reduce others neatly into our familiar categories, then we cannot see them as bearing joyful witness to God nor imagine the possibility of joy in our communion.

Our reductive language and suppressed compassion are conditioned, in part, by a consumerism that perpetually promises joy but instead renders all things as commodities that reflect back to us our own egos. In the glittering mirror of commodities, we find mostly isolation, resentment, suspicion, and weariness—driving us to the next purchase and momentary relief. The restless self that St. Augustine described,[11] when exploited by the consumerism of late modern society, quickly leads to boredom. And we learn once again the truth of Ecclesiastes 1:2 that "all is vanity," as our strategies of distraction fail to escape the nihilism of the modern world and as the world, now evacuated of its enchantment, features our lonely selves warring with other lonely selves. What our ideologies do not allow is holy mystery. What we cannot perceive is gift. And what we cannot feel is joy.

Unfortunately, even we Christians take for granted such a flattened world and fail to grasp the radical nature of the Christian gospel of joy. While the term "joy" appears in our hymns and liturgies, it has too often become an empty signifier, a word that we mutter mindlessly. Nevertheless joy stands at the very heart of Christian faith and practice. Jürgen Moltmann asserts that "Christianity is a unique religion of joy, expressed in its liturgical feasts, its depiction of God, and the treatment of theodicy."[12] Neglecting joy has left Christians "bereft of a key resource for articulating a compelling vision of the good life capable of pushing against the tide of suffering and of resisting the shifting tides of a culture unmoored from transcendence."[13] Christian joy confronts the

11 "Because you have made us for yourself, and our hearts are restless till they find their rest in thee." Augustine, *Confessions*, 1.1.1.

12 Jürgen Moltmann, "Christianity: A Religion of Joy," in Volf and Crisp, 6.

13 Crisp, "Introduction," viii.

anesthetizing and distracting "fun culture" of the Western world. Perhaps unexpectedly, joy has an activist dimension.[14] Joy motivates dissatisfaction with suffering and constitutes a deep wellspring of abiding hope in God's redemption: "Joy in life . . . motivates us to revolt against the life that is destroyed and against those who destroy life. And grief over life that is destroyed is nothing other than an ardent longing for life's liberation to happiness and joy."[15] According to Miroslav Volf,

> Joy wants something: all emotions do. They project themselves into the future and motivate action. . . . [Joy] simply delights in and celebrates the good that is and proclaims, implicitly, that it is good for that good to continue to be. Joy points to what Aristotle would call "the good" life, but as Christians affirm this is a life not lived as an end in itself, but one ordered by the eternal God. "All joy wants eternity—wants deep, deep eternity," wrote Friedrich Nietzsche. The vision of the good life and hope of life with God elicit a kind of joy that is both the beginning and end of authentic personal, social, and political transformation.[16]

What Is Joy?

It is important to clearly distinguish joy as a concept, especially in a culture that generates spectacular counterfeits—such as happiness, fun, ecstasy, satiation, and success (winning!). These heightened moments have their place in human experience, but they fall short of the biblical notion of joy. For example, happiness is the pleasurable feeling we get when something fortuitous happens to us—when things go well, when we partake in pleasurable activities, when we meet a beloved friend or partner, go for a walk on a sunny morning, or eat some delicacy. Yet the biblical notion of joy is usually marked by a sense that these things are

14 Volf, "The Crown of a Good Life," in Volf and Crisp, 132.

15 Crisp, xi.

16 Volf, "Crown," 132.

gotten not by our own dogged efforts or as accidents of an unfolding universe but as gifts of a gracious Creator.

Joy recognizes the contingency of things; they might not have been given in such radiant goodness, or indeed at all.

In joy our pleasure is heightened by our connection with the Giver—a connection that depends upon our interpretation of the gift as good and unnecessarily given. For Christians the world is not only created ex nihilo by God but is wantonly given in each new moment. Christian joy involves awakening to the invisible cloud of grace that infuses the created order and occasions a sense of gratitude, communion, and covenant with the Giver. When we do not view our fortuity as gift from a Giver, we do not experience joy, communion, or gratitude. When we recognize these gifts, our joy may be deepened by our return response to the Giver overflowing to our neighbors. As our lives are caught up in gratitude, communion, and mutual gift-giving to God and neighbor, we are sustained in joy—and this is the inbreaking of God's kingdom. Joy is the very condition of Christian existence.

"Joy is an emotional attunement between the self and the world—usually a small portion of it—experienced as blessing." —Miroslav Volf, *Joy and Human Flourishing*

Joy is woven into the fabric of the Judeo-Christian tradition and is essential to its story. The ubiquity of joy in the Jewish and Christian scriptures bears witness to God's making and redeeming the world. The Hebrew Scriptures plainly drip with joy: Psalm 16 boldly declares that "in [God's] presence there is fullness of joy" (16:11); the life of Jesus is flanked on one hand by the glad tidings of his birth (Luke 2:10) and on the other by the joy intended for the world as its true redeemed *telos* (Heb. 12:2). Joy is characterized by St. Paul as among the fruits of the Spirit (Gal. 5:22–23), and he famously admonishes the church at Philippi to "rejoice always" (Phil. 4:4). The three parables of Luke 15—the lost sheep, the lost coin, and the prodigal son—all depict God's joy at the redemption of the lost. So pervasive is this theme and so central to Christian thought that joy can be seen as a distinctive virtue of the Christian life. The Bible asserts three primary and overlapping sources of joy: God's ongoing gift of the created order; the present and coming redemption of all things in Jesus Christ; and the practices of the church that bear witness to God's kingdom.

Joy in the Created Order

J. R. R. Tolkien's fantastic creatures of Middle Earth—the sage wizards, ethereal elves, rapacious orcs, soulless dragons, crafty dwarves, and pragmatic hobbits—did not spring into the author's imagination from thin air, nor were they trivially fashioned. Rather what Tolkien expressed in his sub-creation was the fundamental Christian conviction that God's creation is outrageously wondrous, a source of great joy and delight. Tolkien insisted:

> The definition of a fairy-story—what it is, or what it should be—does not, then, depend on any definition or historical account of elf or fairy, but upon the nature of Faërie: the Perilous Realm itself, and the air that blows in that country. . . . Faërie itself may perhaps most nearly be translated by Magic—but it is magic of a peculiar mood and power, at the furthest pole from the vulgar devices of the laborious, scientific, magician. There is one proviso: if there is any satire present in the tale, one thing must not be made fun of, the magic itself. That must in that story be taken seriously, neither laughed at nor explained away.[17]

Tolkien's convictions can be traced to the influence of G. K. Chesterton, who said, "[Fairy] tales say that apples were golden only to refresh the forgotten moment when we found that they were green. They make rivers run with wine only to make us remember, for one wild moment,

---

17 J. R. R. Tolkien, "On Faerie Stories," in *The J. R. R. Tolkien Companion and Guide*, vol. 1. *Chronology*, ed. Christina Scull and Wayne G. Hammond (London: HarperCollins, 2006), 326.

that they run with water"—thus restoring to us a sense of magic.[18] The fairy stories of Tolkien awaken us to the contingencies of the created order, to the world in all of its abundance and shimmering diversity as gift from the Creator.

When we realize that the world is given, we perceive the created order as gratuity, as perhaps children are best suited to recognize. When young children find delight, say, in a game of peekaboo, they seem to never tire of the surprise of seeing the adult's face appear from behind the hand; they insist, "Do it again!" The magic of a suddenly appearing face is not lost on a child. Similarly the Bible speaks of a God who creates the world from joy and delight and who each day with the rising of the sun must surely exclaim, "Do it again!"[19] In Faërie, Tolkien warns, the one thing that we must not mock is magic; and yet in our world it is precisely the one thing we adults have banished. An adult who has learned that the world unfolds of its own accord or by force of human will may forget to feel such things as wonder, joy, or gratitude.

In the Judeo-Christian tradition, there is no nature; there is only creation. We tell the story of a God who creates the world ex nihilo, from nothing and for no reason save playful delight. As Jürgen Moltmann asserts, the excess of "play" that is woven into the created order ("even the birds sing louder than Darwin would allow") reflects God's own delighted play in creating the world ex nihilo.[20] All creation exists in praise of God ("the very stones cry out"—Luke 19:40). All created being exists not by virtue of any necessity but is given in God's sheer delight, rightly perceived by creatures as shrouded in contingency and gratuity, dependent upon its Creator.

According to Charles Mathewes, our joy in the created cosmos is sacramental—"it is prompted by and points to something beyond and before creation, something done to you yet something you manifest,

---

18 G. K. Chesterton, "The Ethics of Elfland," in *Orthodoxy* (Grand Rapids: Regent College Publishing, 1908, 2004), 81.

19 Chesterton, "Ethics of Elfland," 61.

20 Jürgen Moltmann, *A Theology of Play* (New York: Harper and Row, 1972), 5.

express, and participate in; you and not you, now and not yet."[21] This conception of joy resists, on one hand, fundamentalism's threat of judgment and hell and, on the other, liberalism's emphasis on ethical duty—both of which risk reducing Christianity to an instrumental good in service to fear, thus minimizing gift, gratitude, and joy, more fundamental to God's inbreaking kingdom.

Joy points to something essential about our humanity—for what we are created and what we seek.

Joy points to something essential about our humanity, as that for which we are created and which we seek. According to Mathewes, "ecstatic, joyful praise is humanity's end and current glory. The joyful act of praising God—a thankfulness flowing almost spontaneously from recognition of God's gifts—is the central action of the human, the self-transcending act in which we begin to participate in our fullest flourishing."[22] To live rightly as humans is to participate in the endless joyful round of love that is the Trinity. For Christians joy characterizes our life in a "middle voice"—in one sense done for us but in another involving human response.[23]

Joy in the Inbreaking New Creation in Jesus Christ

N. T. Wright traces God's promises in the Old Testament, for a land, progeny, nationhood, deliverance, the law, a king, loving presence, a new heart, and the call to be a blessing to all. In tracing these promissory themes, he observes that while Second Temple Judaism emphasizes hope, the later Christian worldview emphasizes joy on account of God's promises fulfilled in Jesus Christ and the lordship of Jesus over the

---

21 Charles Mathewes, "Toward a Theology of Joy," in Volf and Crisp, 66.

22 Mathewes, "Toward," 65.

23 "Middle voice" is a term that Charles Mathewes employs to describe the reality that joy is at the same time genuinely our response but also a gift that happens to us, something in which we participate. See Mathewes, "Toward," 66.

lordship of Caesar.[24] Christian joy is here more than an opiate or fleeting sentiment; joy is founded in the sturdy confidence in the salvific work of God that is the wellspring of true rejoicing. In Jesus Christ a new creation is inaugurated. Wright points out that the term "joy" is among the most emphatic in the New Testament, second only to "love" in the writings of Paul. For Paul joy can be attributed to the fact that

> the resurrection and enthronement of Jesus, his lordship over the world, has created a new world, and with it a new worldview. The followers of Jesus understand that the rule of Caesar, and all other pagan powers, is a mere sham, a parody of the truth, and that the truth now revealed in Jesus is the truth glimpsed and celebrated in Isaiah and the Psalms. . . . The Creator God has announced the verdict; the world has been put right; the trees in the field will clap their hands. A new world has been launched, even in the midst of the present, old, corrupt, and decaying world. Those who follow Jesus, who are "found in the Messiah," are already part of it. That is why Paul rejoices, and why he summons the Philippians to rejoice with him. And their joy must express itself in the unity of the church as a publicly known fact. (1:27–2:4, coupled with 2:12–18)[25]

In a world so shadowed by the suffering of those oppressed, exploited, marginalized, or alienated, what can be said of joy? Is it possible to rejoice in the midst of suffering? Is it possible to rejoice while others are suffering? Surprisingly yes![26] The biblical and historic witness of the Christian church—including Christ's own suffering and the suffering of his disciples and apostles—insists that it is possible to rejoice

24 N. T. Wright, "Some New Testament Questions and Perspectives," in Volf and Crisp, 40–49.

25 Wright, "Some New," in Volf and Crisp, 54.

26 While this is our affirmation, the reality is more complex. While we can rejoice in the face of our own and others' suffering, we must also acknowledge that such joy is always tempered by our tears as we suffer alongside others.

amid suffering, even when our joy is tempered by our tears. Volf states, "When we rejoice while suffering it is because of some good that is ours despite the suffering (for instance, God's character, deeds, and the promise of redemption) or because of a good the suffering will produce (for instance, a child for a mother in childbirth). Put simply, 'joy despite' is possible on account of 'joy because.'"[27]

Wright suggests that Philippians 3:11 and Romans 8:17–30 contain the greatest outbursts of joy in the New Testament. In those texts we see that suffering is a part of our hope and hence part of the reason for joy. Paul insists on seeing suffering in terms of the crucifixion, resurrection, and ascended lordship of Jesus—but not in some masochistic sense. The suffering of the present time is an indication that the new world and the old are chafing together and that the followers of Jesus are wedged between the two. Feasts and joyful celebrations were intended to be a public and peaceful witness demonstrating the contrast with the violent and powerful lordship of Caesar.[28] Paul was concerned about the right practice of Eucharistic meals because it was central to what he meant by celebration and rejoicing. Marianne Meye Thompson insists that the biblical notion of "joy notwithstanding" remains rooted in "joy because" on account of its being made possible by the eschatological horizon of Christian discipleship. It consists of joy because of God, in terms both of the consolation one enjoys by virtue of God's continuing presence in the midst of one's suffering and the hope one has in God's eschatological redemption of the evils one presently suffers.[29]

Theologian John Milbank suggests that the church envisions a way of life caught up in a joyful rhythm of mutual gift exchange, reflecting the inner life of the Trinity. The life, death, and resurrection of Jesus Christ constitute a single act of joyful worship—as God the Father gives

---

27 Volf, "Crown," 131.

28 Wright, "Some New Testament," 52.

29 Marianne Meye Thompson, "Reflections on Joy in the Bible," in Volf and Crisp, 20.

the gift of creation, so the Son returns the gift of his life and a redeemed creation to the Father.[30] Even a casual gloss of the Gospels reveals that Jesus is tirelessly returning the ordinary gifts of creation as extraordinary gifts of joy—water into wine; infidelity into forgiveness; a few loaves and fishes into food for masses; lost sheep and coins into found treasures; outcasts into friends; death into life. Even those most curmudgeonly among us cannot but recognize the joy that Jesus manifests as the incarnate kingdom of God. In Christian worship we see this paradigmatically manifested as we celebrate God's gifts and return in gratitude our gifts to God, to those joined with us and beyond us—in the liturgy beyond the liturgy. Through such mutual giving we participate in God's own joy.

Joy in the Church's Practices

Miroslav Volf suggests that joy involves three dimensions: agential (the good life is the life that is lived well), circumstantial (the good life is the life that goes well), and affective (the good life is the life that feels good). As we rightly perceive and orient our lives toward the good (a life of flourishing, responsive to God's good creation and God's inbreaking kingdom), then our lives are crowned with joy. In this sense, joy is an internal good of a good life. For Christians this points to a life ordered by historic practices of the church (which are continually being reformed). If joy is characteristic of Christian faith, then the church is that institution that trains our attention to joy's objects and invites our fitting responses as citizens of the joyful kingdom. Churches are those communities

30 John Milbank, "Can a Gift Be Given? Prolegomena to a Future Trinitarian Metaphysic," *Modern Theology* 11, no. 1 (January 1995): 119–61; John Milbank, *The Word Made Strange: Theology, Language, Culture* (Cambridge, MA: Blackwell, 1997), chap. 2; John Milbank, "Gregory of Nyssa: The Force of Identity," in *Christian Origins*, ed. L. Ayres and G. Jones (London: Routledge, 1998), 94–116; John Milbank, "The Ethics of Self-Sacrifice," *First Things*, no. 91 (March 1999): 33–38; John Milbank, "The Soul of Reciprocity. Part One, Reciprocity Refused," *Modern Theology* 17, no. 3 (July 2001): 335–91; John Milbank, "The Soul of Reciprocity. Part Two, Reciprocity Granted," *Modern Theology* 17, no. 4 (October 2001): 485–507.

where joy in the Creator and Redeemer is most intentionally instantiated. As we pray together; pass Christ's peace to one another; bear witness to God in song, proclamation, and testimony; and join at the table of God's presence, we are caught up in an economy of joyful gift exchange, and our hearts and our habits are conscripted in God's universal mission of shalom on behalf of God's world.

Once we distinguish joy in this way, as memory, experience, practice, it is possible to understand the Apostle Paul's admonition to "rejoice" (Phil. 3:1, 4:4–8). Joy is not merely an impulsive longing. Joy is a response to gratuitous circumstance, and joyous persons are those who can perceive the good gifts in which they can rejoice and to which they can respond. So joy is a disposition and a practicable virtue that can be cultivated. Paul's admonition to rejoice can be taken seriously to the extent that Christians cultivate, as a matter of habit, the practice of rightly interpreting God's gifts and responding with gratitude and joy.

Joy is characteristic of the good life.

In the Christian tradition joy does not stand alone but exists amid an ecology of virtues that provides a soil from which it can grow. If joy consists in attending to the good gifts that surround us, recognizing them as from God, surpassing our egoism in gratitude, and habitually returning our gifts to God and others, then we may see that joy's attitudes and practices are characterizing for Christian people. One example, the Christian practice of *hospitality*, illustrates how joy is bound up in a complex of practice and virtue. As Christians practice hospitality in regular encounters with strangers in need of food or shelter, we are reminded of God's providence and humbled by extravagant grace; our hearts are moved in gratitude to God for the good things we have received; our compassion is heightened concerning the needs of others and we are prompted to share God's grace with them; thus our communion is deepened with God and neighbor in the sharing. The practice of hospitality, as one example, and the virtues that it fosters—wisdom, humility, gratitude, kindness, compassion, charity, prudence, and courage—serve as ground from which joy may spring forth in God's inbreaking kingdom. Other Christian practices—worship, prayer, testimony, keeping Sabbath, discernment, honoring the body, forgiveness, healing, singing—have their own internal goods and foster similar virtues. In each of these practices, gifts are received and given even as our lives are crowned with joy.[31]

Sometimes the practices that sustain joy are not prescribed by the church's historic forms but must be improvised in particular emotional and geographic spaces. The work of joy sometimes exists near to the edges of suffering, nihilism, and death, resisting death's desire to take more and more of life, thus launching oppressed bodies into a struggle for flourishing. Theologian Willie Jennings reminds us of the role of blues music in creating sounds and spaces that identify and mock the contradictions of African American suffering amid crushing racial violence and oppression. Jennings observes that "the blues as sonic space . . . parallels a dynamic presented by the body of Jesus in which his suffering is surprisingly and stunningly linked to his joy—his joy sustains him through his criminalization, torture, and murder. . . . Seated at the right hand of the throne of God, the Son makes his joy present in our space and time which he has made his own space and time (Heb. 12:2)."[32] Creating, performing, and participating in blues music has allowed African Americans to narrate their lived suffering while also creating communities of aesthetic enjoyment and mutual care that served to resist suffering and mobilize them for hope for justice and reconciliation. A similar paschal pattern can be observed in hip-hop and spoken word poetry of contemporary youth.

In the historic and improvised practices, we experience a kind of *ec-stasis*—as we transcend ourselves our hearts are enlarged; as we are emptied our egos are decentered in joyful communion. We are reminded anew that Christian selfhood is co-selfhood with God and

---

31 Volf, "Crown," 127.

32 Willie Jennings, "Gathering Joy," lecture at the Yale Center for Faith and Culture, Yale Divinity School, New Haven, CT, July 31, 2018.

neighbor. In the tradition of Dionysius, *ec-stasis* does not cease at the boundaries of the neighbor but yearns for knowledge, union, and joy with all created things and finally with the Eternal God.[33] Augustine insists that our hearts are restless until they rest in God[34]; thus the joy we experience as receivers and givers prevents our dull indifference and urges us ever forward in return to God, where joy will be complete. Joy constitutes a dangerous memory that reminds us for whom we were made, conditioning our responses to the world's deadening influences.

Joy and Youth Ministry

If, as this chapter has argued, joy is an unsung theological virtue and practice, then what difference would it make for youth ministry to reclaim joy? What practices would embody such change? Here are some suggestions.

Reclaiming the Language of Joy

Ludwig Wittgenstein in 1915 remarked: "The limits of my language mean the limits of my world."[35] The term "joy" has all but vanished from common usage, or else it is inappropriately applied to its counterfeits—fun, happiness, and the like. Congregations, families, and youth ministers who wish to enhance joy might first look for opportunities to expand its usage—to explain and properly use the biblical notion of joy—as an experience that acknowledges a transcendent Giver who created a good world and who has begun to restore all things in joyful communion. Language has the ability to create new meanings in our lives and open us to new domains. When our imagination becomes inhabited by

33 M. Rostovtzeff, *Rome*, trans. J. D. Duff (London: Oxford University Press, 1960), 93–94.

34 *Confessions* 1:1.

35 Ludwig Wittgenstein, *Tractatus Logico-Philosophicus*, 5.6, 5.62.

the notion of joy, we may notice and create new spaces for joy to live among us, cultivating joyful attitudes and communal practices. Youth ministry must not only adopt the current idioms of youth; we also have a responsibility to introduce new language to open new worlds, particularly God's inbreaking kingdom of joy.

Joy as Communal Care for Youth

As mentioned earlier, adolescence is a time filled with surprise and joyful delight—a time of new discoveries of the world, new self-capacities, new relationships, and forays into new avenues of personal and social empowerment that can be supported by communities and embraced as gifts. When youth take delight in their discoveries, relationships, and self, they are receiving God's good gifts, as expressions of God's own speech. For adults who may have forgotten to be surprised and delighted in these gifts, our care for youth may also awaken our own wonder and gratitude for God's donation. Communities may support and celebrate joyful discoveries by adolescents by providing attentive care, guidance, and challenge. As adults give care to young people, our hearts may in turn be enlarged in joyful giving. As Eric Erikson saw, communities can be fashioned anew in each generation, shaped by youth's gifts of questioning, challenging, and creativity.[36] Whatever else it may mean to reclaim joy for youth ministry, it must certainly involve reclaiming practices of caring for young people—receiving their gifts even as the gifts of responsive adults are called forth, forging joyful communion. For Christians, practicing life in community is not an accidental good but a practice that participates in God's own Trinitarian community, in which all creation will culminate in joyful communion. As the chapters of this volume reveal, youth ministry that prioritizes joy cannot avoid the hard but joyful work of living in community.

---

36 Eric Erikson, *Childhood and Society* (New York: Norton, 1950).

Joy in Encountering Transcendence

In a sense our modern secular world suffers under the illusion of Nietzsche's critique of Christianity as an escape to some far-off heaven, to which he opposes Dionysius, the Greek god of wine (known by the Romans as Bacchus), symbolizing a lust for life, majesty, splendor, and power.[37] David Bentley Hart challenges Nietzsche's characterization of Christianity as passive and escapist by reclaiming the typology of wine as a metaphor for joy. He writes:

> (Jesus says) "Verily I say unto you, I will drink no more of the fruit of the vine, until that day I drink it new in the Kingdom of God" (Mark 14:25; cf. Matt. 26–29; Luke 22:18)—wine clearly appears here as the perfect and concrete emblem of the beauty of creation and the joy of dwelling at peace in the midst of others: not the wine of Dionysus, which makes fellowship impossible, promising only intoxication, brute absorption into the turba, anonymity, and violence, but the wine of the wedding feast of Cana, or of the wedding feast of the Lamb. The wine of Dionysus is no doubt the coarsest vintage, intended to blind with drunkenness . . . the wine repeatedly associated with madness, anthropophagy, slaughter, warfare, and rapine. The wine of Scripture on the other hand, is first and foremost a divine blessing and image of God's bounty (Gen. 27:28; Deut. 7:13; 11:14; Ps. 104:15; Prov. 3:10; Isa. 25:6; 65:8; Jer. 31:12; Joel 2:19–24; 3:18; Amos 9:13–14; Zech. 9:17) and an appropriate thank offering by which to declare Israel's love for God (Ex. 29:40; Lev 23:13; Num. 15:5–10; 18:12; 28:14; Deut. 14:23); it is the wine that cheers the hearts of men (Judg. 9:13); the sign of God's renewed covenant with his people (Isa. 55:1–3); the drink of lovers (Song 5:1) and the very symbol of love (7:2, 9), whose absence is the eventide of all joy (Isa. 24:11); it is moreover the wine of Agape and the

37 David Bentley Hart, *Beauty of the Infinite: The Aesthetics of Christian Truth* (Grand Rapids, MI: Eerdmans, 2003), 35ff.

> feast of fellowship, in which Christ first vouchsafed a sign of his divinity, in a place of rejoicing, at Cana—a wine of the highest quality—when the kingdom showed itself "out of season."[38]

We and our youth live in a consumer culture that promises that happiness can be purchased at the cash register. It sells its wares by means of a series of endless broken promises to deliver abundant life, by repeating the promises of Dionysius. Although consumerism has colonized the attention of youth (and adults), it cannot finally deliver on its promises. Only "a wine of the highest quality"—the wine of God's joyful kingdom—can address the abundance for which our young people thirst.

While we assuredly find joy in the gifts of God's good creation—including the beauty of youth and their discoveries—for Christians there is a good that stands above all other goods. The inbreaking kingdom of joy is incarnated in Jesus Christ and his church—in the beauty of self-giving love; in his way of peace that opens us to others; and in the church's worship that dramatizes this love in practices that enlarge our hearts for God, each other, and the world. Joy is found in our encounter with God but is deepened and expanded as we participate with God in the giving and receiving of gifts. Joyful youth ministry involves youth in seeking God in worship, prayer, testimony, song, ministries of compassion, and all the historic and improvised ways Christians have encountered God. Joy is the gift of the Spirit that humbly assures us that we have indeed glimpsed God's kingdom opened for us in Jesus Christ, a glimpse that compels us onward in our sojourn to God and the fulfillment of God's kingdom of joy.

By now it no doubt will have occurred to readers that there is nothing very new in this approach. It doesn't prescribe any tricks, tips, or techniques or multiply the size of your youth membership. By reorganizing youth ministry around the biblical notion of joy, this approach reclaims a fundamental distinction between the mysteries of Christian faith and the reductions of the modern secular world. While joy may

---

38 Hart, *Beauty*, 108–9.

seem at first glance to be trivial or, worse, a distraction from the task of building an adult life or a just society, it is precisely joy that grounds and characterizes our life with God. And it is joy that gives the lie to secularity, consumerism, and other specters of Dionysius.

Some of us have been working in youth ministry for many decades, long enough to know that Christian discipleship cannot be simply an appendage stapled onto the edge of a life in a modern secular world—like a hobby or an adornment. Nor can the church flourish by merely opposing the modern world without clearly representing what we affirm—that God is joyfully afoot in the world. Christian discipleship that takes seriously Paul's admonitions to rejoice holds the potential to re-enchant the world, reinvigorate the work of social justice, and restore human creativity and the bonds of human love. Joy cannot endure without the church's practices that provide the oxygen it requires to breathe new life—practices of expressing joy in scripture reading, prayer, testimony, and song; reflecting theologically on joy's place in the Christian story; and joyfully giving gifts of hospitality, care, friendship, forgiveness, proclamation, creativity, and justice.

Book Overview

In this volume our authors, many of whom have served as youth ministers or have personal or research interests in youth, were asked to reflect on the practices that more deeply ground young people in the joy of God. We do not claim that this compilation is in any sense exhaustive, but it may serve as an introduction to a quality of youth ministry to which we hope you, the reader, will contribute. Since the subsequent chapters are written as more or less stand-alone pieces engaging specific practices of youth ministry rather than as a sustained argument, some readers may wish to select particular topics to reflect on and develop as youth ministry emphases. However, Christian practices that foster joy among young people inevitably overlap, implicate, and spill over into each other. So for some there will be value in reading the entire volume, since what is being sketched here is nothing less than a vision of God's kingdom—and a fulsome vision, a way of life, a better way of being young and supporting youth.

In the first chapter Andrew Root and Christian Gonzalez elaborate the Christian notion of *kenosis* or self-emptying love of Christ, which is the heart of Christian ministry and practice. In their view, the idea of kenosis involves *eka-stasis*, or ecstasy, which is core to the notion of joy. They draw on anecdotes from Dietrich Bonhoeffer's biography and his theology to point to the Christian practice of "place-sharing," which mirrors the incarnation in which Christ enters fully into our suffering. The Apostle Paul's account of his conversion provides a portrait par excellence of a ministry of kenosis and joy.

In the second chapter David F. White and John Leedy elaborate a theology in which all creation participates in God's own beauty, as confirmed in Genesis (1:31) by God's proclamation that all things were created good (*tov*, beautiful, harmonious, working as it should). The beauty of creation prepares us to perceive the incarnation of God in Christ (God's art), even as the beauty of God revealed in Christ awakens us to the beauty of the created order. Formation in Christian faith involves teaching us to see the beauty around us as the witness of God and to participate with God in creating beauty in the world. Seeing through the eyes of beauty awakens us to joy in several important ways—in the enjoyment of the created order, in gratitude for God's gift, and in our sharing of beauty with others as a return gift to God.

In the third chapter Wesley W. Ellis and Kenda Creasy Dean point to the theological significance of friendship, especially as it fosters joy. Jesus told his disciples: "I have called you friends, because I have made known to you everything that I have heard from my Father" (John 15:15b, NRSV). Wes and Kenda point to ways friendships are often instrumentalized in a transactional environment, while for Jesus's followers friendships are mutual, enduring, unconditional, and unfolding to the lonely world. Friendship is first founded in God's unconditional love. As Wes and Kenda remind us, it is only out of God's friendship with the world that God goes to the cross in Christ. Jesus said, "No one has greater love than this, to lay down one's life for one's friends." (John 15:13, NRSV). Youth ministry that affirms this kind of unconditional friendship with youth—a desire to be with them—finds joy. Moreover, as Jürgen Moltmann writes, "We experience ourselves for what we are, respected and accepted in our own freedom."[39]

In the fourth chapter Pamela Ebstyne King and Steven Argue claim that young people experience more joy when they have a life purpose. Drawing on recent research, they suggest that joy involves knowing what matters and how we make sense of the world. They state that joy is a virtue unto itself, but it also goes somewhere—toward a *telos.* Joy points us to a more profound way of being and living, where purpose is the fuel for true joy. Joy gives us energy and motivation—it calls out reflection and so drives our purposes.

In the fifth chapter Fred P. Edie and Alaina Kleinbeck point to worship as the paradigmatic context for Christian joy. Drawing on their experience at Duke Divinity School's Youth Academy, they describe the elements of biblical worship, with emphasis on how they are interpreted and re-created by youth at the academy. Fred and Alaina express the Christian view that joy itself is a response to God's gifts of creation and redemption—and joy turns into worship as it is expressed. Moreover, joyful worship inculcates the habit of joy (as well as other practices and virtues) throughout the rest of our lives. They insist that joy becomes an act of resistance to sin and injustice in the world.

In the sixth chapter Anne E. Streaty Wimberly and Sarah F. Farmer remind us that human beings are born to hope—to have expectations or anticipate and wait for a desired good that brings satisfaction and intersects with joy. Adolescents long to place their hope in something or someone. Yet young people wrestle with what it means to hope in the context of increasing political, racial, and religious turmoil. They consider hope as an active, dynamic, life-affirming quality of human flourishing in the multidimensional sojourn of life. Such courageous,

---

39 Jürgen Moltmann, *Church in the Power of the Spirit* (Minneapolis: Fortress, 1993), 115.

joy-filled hope must be empowered and nurtured in the lives of teens in rapidly changing and challenging times. Theological meanings and attributes of the intersection of joy and hope precede a discussion of the role of agents of hope in youths' formation of courageous joy-filled hope followed by pedagogical suggestions.

In the seventh chapter Amanda Hontz Drury argues that the practice of testifying is indispensable to the adolescent experience of joy. When we neglect to create opportunities and space for teenagers to testify, we are robbing them of a means of joy. While not all conversations about God result in joy, she identifies three ways to cultivate this joy in speaking of God: (1) helping our teenagers to see where and how God may be present in their own lives; (2) providing the space and opportunity for teenagers to testify; and (3) recognizing the testimonies shared in a way that offers honor and respect. The practice of testimony provides a regular means of recognizing God's gratuity on our behalf, of naming God's presence and gift, and of creating the opportunity for gratitude and joy.

In the eighth chapter Almeda M. Wright and Nyle Fort explore the concepts of joy and agency, especially within the lived experiences of young people of color. The authors look to black and brown youth activism as a rich site of theology and politics in which joy and agency dovetail. Agency—active and purposeful selfhood—for black youth and others is joyful in that it stands against forces that oppose life and flourishing. Joy happens horizontally in relation to and in mutual exchanges across generations, in community, and with the natural world. It happens vertically in relation to God in response to God's invitation to trust God and step out on God's word. According to the authors, young activists and artists of color such as Bree Newsome and Nova Venerable illustrate the emergent agency of black and brown adolescent life by defying the stereotype that marginalized youth are voiceless and incapable of transforming their lives and broader society.

In the ninth chapter Miroslav Volf argues that through joining and sharing in God's forgiveness, Christians discover the spreadability of joy. In Luke 5:17–26 Jesus shows that forgiveness, to be authoritative and powerful, finds its source in the forgiveness of God. From Christ we receive the power and the willingness to forgive. Christ forgives through us and that is why we can forgive. Secondary theological aspects of this passage incorporate the role of the friends who carried the person who is paralyzed and the wider community that surrounds this instance of forgiveness, healing, and joy. Upon the forgiveness of sins and healing of the person who is paralyzed, we discover that not only is this person full of joy but also that there is evidence of joy among all who witnessed the drama.

In the tenth chapter Stephanie Paulsell and Vanessa Zoltan observe the odd irony of joyful creativity among youth—the Parkland kids, Beyoncé, and youth who embrace the Broadway musical *Hamilton*—in the face of social injustice and violence. Creativity and imagination are capacities that have the potential to generate a deep and sustaining joy—for adolescents and for us all. To be made in God's image is to have within us the capacity for creativity; when we create, we participate in God's own creativity. Jesus opens a space within which we might create our own stories, our own parables. He invites us to look around, to see where the seeds of the kingdom of heaven might be waiting. If we can't imagine what the lives of others are like, if we can't feel reverence for the worlds contained within them, if all we can do is project our own fears and desires onto them, then we become dangerous to them. Joy is often closely associated with dissatisfaction with the way things are, because it is born from the creative work of imagining the way things might be. "People feel joy, as opposed to mere pleasure," as the social critic Ivan Illich has written, "to the extent that their activities are creative."[40]

In chapter 11 Michal Beth Dinkler considers Paul's understanding of *autarkēs*, which, translated from Greek, means "self–sufficient," or "independent." Contrary to our cultural preference for self-sufficiency, Michal Beth reveals that the Apostle Paul learned the "secret" that self-sufficiency comes not from ourselves but from the God who gives us strength, in facing reality in relationship with the Spirit who is love. What's truly radical about God's kingdom is that *everyone belongs*, no matter what. Real freedom—being "content" in the knowledge that our

40 Ivan Illich, *Tools for Conviviality* (Glasgow: Fontana, 1975), 34.

selfhood is sufficient, that our strength comes from the One who created and unites us—facilitates work against injustice. Joy is a deep inner sense of delight and well-being that comes from the knowledge that we are worthy of love and belonging simply because we belong to the God who created us and first loved us. Christians are joyful because we belong to God and to each other.

In the concluding chapter James K. A. Smith and Kyle David Bennett offer a caution about idolatry or false joy. Drawing on the work of St. Augustine, they characterize the soul's longing for rest from anxiety and frantic pursuits as rest in God. Joy is the blissful rest of someone who realizes they no longer have to perform; they are loved. Augustine emphasizes that to be human is to be a lover and to be a lover is to look to something as the source and end of the happy life. All of creation is to be received as an iconic[41] gift that "refers" us to the immortal, infinite Creator.[42] Disordered liturgies, such as those found in cultural practices of consumerism or nationalism, train us to look for ultimate fulfillment from what is only penultimate, to foist upon aspects of creation what only the Creator could return. Most of our disordered liturgies are variations on a theme of self-reliance and fetishizing our own autonomy. If idolatry—disordered loves and expectations—generates anxiety and restlessness, robbing young people of the joy that attends that rest we find in a gracious God, then only a theological and spiritual response will adequately address this inhibitor. This is how and why youth ministry can be a beacon of joy: precisely by retrieving the disciplines of the faith and the liturgical practices of the church and especially welcoming adolescents into the multigenerational body of Christ, learning how to love, and enhancing capacity for joy/rest.[43]

---

41 Jean-Luc Marion's distinction between the idol and the icon can be helpful here. Jean-Luc Marion, *God without Being* (Chicago: University of Chicago Press, 1991), 21ff.

42 For Augustine this "use" is not merely instrumental; it can be attended with its own, rightly ordered/ranked enjoyment or delight (*Confessions*, 1.33.37, 1.35.39).

43 See, for example, Dorothy Bass and Don Richter, eds., *Way to Live: Christian Practices for Teens* (Nashville: Upper Room Books, 2002).

1

Kenosis

A Dead Dog and the Joy of Self-Emptying

ANDREW ROOT AND CHRISTIAN GONZALEZ

I'm (Andy) a big Jimmy Kimmel fan. I have been for years, all the way back to when he was a radio shock jock on KROQ in Los Angeles. "Jimmy the Sports Guy," he was called. I'm such a big fan that I even named my lovable but dense golden retriever after him (R.I.P., Kimmel!). So I'm sure I'm biased, but I thought he was the best host the Oscars has had in years. The 2017 show wasn't an easy one to host; palpable anxiety was everywhere. Just months earlier the iconic Meryl Streep challenged the new president's immigration order during a Golden Globes speech, leading the president (yes, of the United States) to berate her on Twitter. What would happen at the Oscars?

In a stroke of brilliance, Kimmel set the tone of the night by starting with a song: opening the show was Justin Timberlake, singing his upbeat, celebratory hit, "Can't Stop the Feeling!" Message received.

This chapter, particularly its second half, draws heavily from (even adapting at points) Root's *Faith Formation in a Secular Age*. The connection to joy and human flourishing are unique and new contributions (as is seeing Bonhoeffer's letter about Mr. Wolf as an example of these realities). The chapter draws from Root's work with kenosis to move in these new directions here.

This night was going to be fun, a time to relax and laugh. Kimmel had *formed* his audience, transforming their anxiety into joy with one song. One of the most powerful ways to communicate is through music. One of the clearest ways not only to communicate but also to form the human spirit is through singing. Maybe faith formation in youth ministry isn't different.

In the breadth of this project, all the authors are exploring dispositions and practices that enhance or inhibit young people in living flourishing lives. In this chapter we focus on an enhancer—but a weird one! To enhance something is, by definition, to intensify, increase, or further improve it. Yet our focus here is on the biblical concept of *kenosis*, which attends not to intensification but to renunciation, not increasing but emptying, not for improvement but for humility. It is an enhancer that comes by way of negation. According to Paul, Jesus took on this kenotic nature, coming into the world as a servant, in lowliness. Through this kenotic action, we are given life abundant.

I just said "according to Paul," but actually this assertion that Jesus moves in the world kenotically is not original to Paul. Rather in Philippians Paul is "sampling," drawing from another track, from a song all scholars agree is likely the oldest original piece in the New Testament, called the Christ Hymn. In singing this old hymn, Paul has shaped his vision, seeing this Jesus as the one who enters death for sake of life, suffering for the sake of joy. A life of flourishing is made possible only by emptying ourselves, making it so we can enter the life of another—sharing their place—as the tangible experience of sharing in Christ.

If youth ministry has any concern for helping young people live flourishing lives, then following the beats and rhythms of this kenotic song will be insightful. We believe that following the beats and rhythms of Paul's conception of kenosis will lead us to something remarkable—not only life abundant, as Jesus promises, but joy. A youth ministry practice that takes the distinct and, as we'll argue, practical shape of kenosis is one that not only creates space for young people to encounter the presence of the living God, but also gives them a tune of joy that they can't get out of their heads. What we hope to show in this chapter is that this kenotic disposition gives direct shape to our ministries, helping us understand how our relationships with young people shaped by kenosis can be events of joy, inviting young people into flourishing lives.

These are a lot of big concepts, and maybe a case study will help us understand them. To show how kenosis, joy, and ministry are connected, we'll take a journey to Barcelona, 1928, looking in on the youth ministry of twenty-two-year-old Dietrich Bonhoeffer.

A Closer Look

It has been often missed, but one of the greatest theologians of the twentieth century, a man who died in a Hitler death camp for his faith, was a youth minister. At the end of 1927, Dietrich Bonhoeffer had finished his doctoral dissertation at the age of twenty-one. Too young to become a pastor and not qualified to be a professor, he was encouraged to leave Berlin for a year-long pastoral internship in a German-speaking congregation in Spain. After arriving, Bonhoeffer spent his time doing what he did best, reworking the Sunday school and tending to youth ministry.

One of his most interesting experiences in Barcelona happened about halfway through the internship, when a ten-year-old boy came to him on an errand. We have a detailed report of the experience, because just a few days later Dietrich related it to his friend Walter Dress. Bonhoeffer's letter to Dress is filled with compassion, theological depth, and ministerial sensitivity. As one of Bonhoeffer's best biographers, Ferdinand Schlingensiepen, explains, this story, which "only became known in 1999—when a cache of letters that Bonhoeffer had written in 1928 to Walter Dress, his youngest sister's fiancé, was discovered—reveals just how unusual was Bonhoeffer's gift for dealing with children and young people."[1] There is much we can learn from this letter about how kenosis, joy, and the flourishing life hang together.

---

1 Ferdinand Schlingensiepen, *Dietrich Bonhoeffer 1906-1945: Martyr, Thinker, Man of Resistance* (New York: T&T Clark, 2010), 43.

Bonhoeffer starts the letter as far from humility as could be conceived: "Did I answer your letter about [Emil] Brunner? I don't really remember. When you wrote you seemed pretty impressed by the book; I read up to about the last sixty pages, where I gave up because I didn't expect much more after finding the entire book extremely disappointing." He goes on to express his great disappointment in Emil Brunner's book *The Divine Imperative.* Brunner was one of the most famous and respected theologians of the time, but the cocky young Bonhoeffer has no mercy for him. At the start of the letter, we are light years from humility, let alone kenosis. And if poor Brunner were privy to the letter, his response to Bonhoeffer's words would have been far from joyful.

But quickly, the letter shifts in tone, as Bonhoeffer puts aside academic theology and recounts an experience of ministry:

> Today I encountered a . . . unique case in my pastoral counseling, which I'd like to recount to you briefly and which *despite its simplicity really made me think.* At 11:00 AM there was a knock at my door and a ten-year-old boy came into my room with something I had requested from his parents. I noticed that something was amiss with the boy, who is usually cheerfulness personified. And soon it came out: he broke down in tears, completely beside himself, and I could hear only the words: "Mister Wolf is dead," and then he cried and cried.[2]

Bonhoeffer explains to Dress that he placed the boy on his knee. There was no ulterior motive; he simply heard the call to share in the boy's experience and to be present with him as he suffered.

"But who is Mister Wolf?" Bonhoeffer continues. "As it turns out, it is a young German shepherd dog that was sick for eight days and had just died a half-hour ago. So the boy, ill consolable, sat down on my knee and could hardly regain his composure; he told me how the dog died and how everything is lost now." Inside this moment of shared experience, Bonhoeffer cared for the boy by giving him a space to share his

2 Quoted in Schlingensiepen, *Dietrich Bonhoeffer,* 43 (emphasis added).

broken humanity, indeed to have his suffering shared. He felt a temptation to rush to answer, but he paused and opened himself to kenosis, emptying himself of his need to speak as he became aware that to insert his agenda would avoid the call to a ministry of listening.[3] And so in humility, he just bore the boy's sadness by giving his presence.

This takes the practical form of allowing the boy the opportunity to narrate his experience, to just share his brokenness by sharing his story. So Bonhoeffer reports to Dress that the boy told him how "he played only with the dog, each morning the dog came to the boy's bed and awakened him—and now the dog was dead. What could I say? So he talked to me about it for quite a while."[4]

But then Bonhoeffer relays something fascinating; he says to his surprise that the boy stopped crying, turned to him, and said, "Tell me now, will I see 'Mister Wolf' again? He's certainly in heaven." The theological novice was caught up short, saying to Dress, "So there I stood and was supposed to answer him yes or no." Bonhoeffer wasn't sure what to say, and yet he needed to say something—the boy's humanity demanded it. And so the arrogant young theologian who ripped apart Emil Brunner in the first paragraph of the letter searched for an answer, humbled. He was humbled not in the sense of being put in his place, rather by being taken to holy ground. As he took the form of a minister by kenotically putting aside the debates of the theologian, it became possible for Bonhoeffer to share in the deep experience of

---

3 Here I think of Bonhoeffer's line in *Life Together* in the portion where he is speaking of all the different ministries people have, and he speaks of listening. A paraphrase of that passage: The Christian minister often feels the need to say something when in the presence of others, but he often forgets that listening can be a greater ministry than speaking. If one does nothing but prattle in the presence of his neighbor, then one can imagine he is doing nothing more than prattle before God. Dietrich Bonhoeffer, *Life Together and Prayerbook of the Bible, Dietrich Bonhoeffer Works, Vol. 5* (Minneapolis: Augsburg Fortress, 2004), 98.

4 Eric Metaxas, *Bonhoeffer: Pastor, Martyr, Prophet, Spy* (Nashville: Thomas Nelson, 2010), 86.

a ten-year-old boy. He says to Dress, "And there I stood—I who was supposed to 'know the answer'—feeling quite small next to him." Through the humility of sharing the boy's place, Bonhoeffer encountered the presence of Christ. Emptying himself of his indifference and any condescension, Dietrich cleared his throat and said "Look, God created human beings and also animals, and I'm sure he also loves animals. And I believe that with God it is such that all who loved each other on earth—genuinely loved each other—will remain together with God, for to love is part of God. Just how that happens, though, we admittedly don't know." From this kenotic act—willingly putting aside all theological academia and merely sharing in the experience of the death of a boy's dog—springs joy, from the tomb comes abundant life. Bonhoeffer says to Dress, "You should have seen the happy face on this boy; he had completely stopped crying. 'So then I'll see Mister Wolf again when I am dead; then we can play together again'—in a word, he was ecstatic." We could say that the boy was so overjoyed he was coming out of himself (Gk. *ekstasis*) and touching a reality beyond, a reality that leads from wilting to flourishing.

Without a doubt this was a joy-enhancing experience for the boy. This can be seen no more clearly than in Bonhoeffer's final words: "[It was] one of those cases of 'laughter amid tears,' and doubtless a case of the sort that will not recur very frequently."[5] But why was this? What was it about Bonhoeffer's action that led this boy into an ecstatic experience of joy? And what might we learn from this for ministry, our young people, and our identity as youth workers? As we try to answer these questions, we'll need to turn to Paul, exploring how kenosis itself becomes the disposition that leads us into such experience. And this will take us back to music, because, as we said, Paul learns the practice of kenosis (even discovering that kenosis is the shape of God's own being) from singing.

---

5 Dietrich Bonhoeffer, *Barcelona, Berlin, New York: 1928-1931*, trans. Eberhard Berthge, Ernst Feil, Christian Gremmels, Wolfgang Huber, Hans Pfeifer, Albrecht Schoenherr, Heinz E. Todt, Ilse Todt *(Dietrich Bonhoeffer Works, Vol. 10)*, 138.

Now Back to the Music

Just as the boy with Bonhoeffer, so too Paul had a death experience. In Acts 9 we're told that the young man named Saul, ambitious and zealous in every way, is heading to Damascus, ready to live out his destiny as protector of the law. He has imagined an arc for his life, but instead of being fulfilled, it crashes. At first blush this scene can be called anything but joyful. After being knocked to the ground by a light and voice calling itself Jesus, Saul is bedridden, blind, and broken. The ambitious Saul is now lost on the street called Straight, soaking in the bitter water of a death experience. He is as sullen as a boy with a dead dog; he is a man with a dead dream.

Life is anything but flourishing when Ananias visits Paul and becomes his minister, sharing in his confusion with presence and prayer. It took a kenotic act for Ananias to come and minister to Paul. He had to risk his safety and trust in the call of God to go and pray for a man who had come to town to kill him. But Ananias does more: according to Acts 9:19, he takes broken Paul, who once had plans for murder, into community. It's possible, but speculative, that as he does, the disciples in Damascus teach Paul the song of kenosis, a song Paul is ready to repeat after his experience with Ananias.

New Testament scholars seem to agree that the Christ Hymn, a mere six verses in Philippians 2, has its origins in the earliest days of the church, preceding the epistles or Gospels. It doesn't take much imagination to see Paul, with hood over his head, hesitantly but expectantly entering a small house. Ananias leads him, assuring him all is fine, as the atmosphere of the room becomes suffused with anxiety. This small group has been on alert for weeks, knowing that a bloodthirsty man looking to make a name for himself was coming to kill them. But shockingly, they have heard that Ananias has gone to see this man, because the light of Jesus knocked him to the ground as good as dead.

Perhaps the others try not to stare at Paul, but the fear and intrigue make it nearly impossible. But as the singing starts, the anxiety leaves the room, and their voices join in harmony. Those same eyes that just minutes earlier glanced at Paul in fear now spot him struggling to sing along.

It takes Paul a while to get the words, but as he does, he doesn't so much learn them as recognize them. This song is the very soundtrack to his experience, given a new story of God's action itself, inviting Paul, in the midst of this community, to hang the flesh of his own experience on it. Together they sing,

> [Because] he was in the form of God,
> [he] did not count equality with God a thing to be grasped,
> but emptied himself,
> taking the form of a servant,
> being born in the likeness of [humanity].
> And being found in human form
> he humbled himself
> and became obedient unto death,
> even death on a cross.
> Therefore God has highly exalted him
> and bestowed on him the name which is above every name,
> that at the name of Jesus
> every knee should bow,
> in heaven and on earth and under the earth,
> and every tongue confess
> that Jesus Christ is Lord,
> to the glory of God the Father. (Phil 2:6–11 RSV)[6]

---

6 I've placed "because" in brackets at the beginning because, as I'll describe below, New Testament scholar Michael Gorman thinks that "because" is a better translation than "although," connecting this hymn further to the shape of divine action itself. The other two uses of brackets are to make the hymn more readable. These bracketed words are not in the RSV. I've also used the poetic form of presentation. This is also something the RSV does not do, however, the NRSV does. I chose to put it in this form to give it the more songlike quality it seems to possess.

Paul is told that this hymn encompasses the reality that the crucified Christ brings forth. And he recognizes it because it squares with both his experience on the dusty road and his encounter with Ananias. Ananias has embodied the hymn in his coming to Paul as a humble minister, embracing him through his death experience. This humility to be another's minister mediates the new reality of God's own being—as, to his surprise, Bonhoeffer experienced when he took the boy on his knee and shared in his big questions. Jesus comes to Paul in the death experience of this community, emptying himself to take the form of a servant, the form of a minister.

Paul recognizes that the state of Jesus's own being is kenotic, self-emptying. But what is more radical about this hymn, and what must have been deeply transformational for Paul, is that this kenosis (this self-emptying and self-humiliating) is revealed as the state of God's own being. Paul had imagined that the cross was the smoking gun that eliminated this Jesus of Nazareth from messianic consideration. But now in this community, singing this hymn over and over again, he sees that the cross is not the unavoidable discontinuity between God's being and Jesus's own. Rather Christ's cross is the decisive revelation of what God's self-emptying, self-giving love looks like in human flesh. The cross reveals that kenosis is the shape of God's being. As New Testament scholar Michael Gorman says, "If on the cross Christ conformed to God, then God 'conforms' to the cross. The cross is the interpretive, or hermeneutical, lens through which God is seen; it is the means of grace by which God is known."[7]

Changing the "Although" to "Because"

To make this point clearer and help move us further in seeing how a ministry shaped by kenosis can lead to joy, we need to get a little

---

7 Michael J. Gorman, *Cruciformity: Paul's Narrative Spirituality of the Cross* (Grand Rapids: Eerdmans, 2001), 17.

nerdy—just for a second, so hang with me. Most often when translating Philippians 2:6, the word *hyparchon* is seen exclusively as "although," giving kenosis a sense of slumming it. Too often in youth ministry, particularly, we intuitively translate Philippians 2:6 as something like "*Although* Jesus is in the form of God," which means he's rich, powerful, sexy, and super awesome (because that's who God is); he wasn't cocky about it but was down-to-earth, even going to the cross to help us out, possibly even in jeans and a Hawaiian shirt—because he's just *that* chill. But there has been a strong movement within New Testament scholarship to translate *hyparchon* in the causative sense, meaning that the lyric that captured Paul's imagination by interpreting his experience is not "although" but rather "because."[8] Jesus humbles himself to the point of death on the cross, not *despite* being in the form of God but rather *because* he is in the form of God. The cross is the revelation of God's own being; it is the very shape of divine action itself. The cross is not a unique outlier to God's own act and being but is rather its very core. The Son takes on humanity as the ultimate act of kenosis *because* this is the constitution of the Father's own being. God as Trinity exists as the communion of Father, Son, and Spirit in and through kenosis, just as this triune God acts in creation by taking the form of kenosis, seeking to be humanity's minister in and through the cross.[9]

Paul recognizes through his own experience and the formative singing of this hymn that "God . . . is essentially kenotic, and indeed

---

8 Gorman says, "We would be right, therefore, to join the line of interpreters that runs from Moule to Wright, Hawthorne, Bockmuehl, and Fowl and render Philippians 2:6a as 'precisely because' Christ Jesus was in the form of God and equal with God, he emptied himself." Gorman, *Cruciformity*, 29.

9 T. F. Torrance adds, "The Pauline concept of kenosis was not interpreted in any metaphysical way as involving a contraction, diminution or self-imitation of God's infinite being, but in terms of his self-abnegating love in the inexpressible mystery of the tapeinosis, impoverishment or abasement, which he freely took upon himself in what he became and did in Christ entirely for our sake." T. F. Torrance, *Trinitarian Faith: The Evangelical Theology of the Ancient Catholic Faith* (London: Clark, 1991), 153.

essentially cruciform. Kenosis, therefore, does not mean Christ's emptying himself of his divinity (or of anything else), but rather Christ's exercising his divinity, his equality with God."[10] As orthodox theologian John Behr writes, "By his most human action, an action which expresses all the weakness and impotence of our created nature, Christ shows himself to be God. The profundity of this puts one at a loss for words."[11]

Yet while the causative of *hyparchon* reveals the connection between the kenosis of the Father and the Son, showing the state of the triune being as kenotic, *hyparchon* nevertheless still encompasses a sense of "although"—although in freedom Jesus could have opted to be something other than a minister, he conformed to the kenotic being of the Father, becoming a servant and *the* minister to humanity by taking on the being of humanity, sharing in it fully, even to the point of death on the cross.

Paul, maybe here in this small house with Ananias and the community but for sure in the years that followed, discovers that the structure of this hymn has a practical form. There is an actual pattern we and our young people can live out, making possible the kind of transformational encounters that Bonhoeffer experiences with the boy—those that lead to joy! Gorman says it like this: "The story of Christ crucified is sung, preached, and reenacted, not simply in words and not merely as the means to personal salvation, but as the modus operandi of daily life in this world."[12]

The Pattern of the Disciple

Philippians 2:6–11, as the soundtrack to Paul's own encounter with the living Jesus, provides him with a structure that frames his ministry. The

10 Michael J. Gorman, *Inhabiting the Cruciform God: Kenosis, Justification, and Theosis in Paul's Narrative Soteriology* (Grand Rapids: Eerdmans, 2009), 28.

11 John Behr, *The Mystery of Christ: Life in Death* (Crestwood: St. Vladimir's Seminary Press, 2006), 32.

12 Gorman, *Cruciformity*, 385.

structure that Paul sees in the hymn is "although [x] not [y] but [z]." Gorman, who has brilliantly fleshed out this structure in Paul's thought, connects it back to Philippians 2 when he says, "As the obedient suffering servant who behaves in the pattern 'although [x] not [y] but [z],' Christ displays not only true divinity but also true humanity. Unlike Adam, he does not exploit his status as God's image-bearer or disobey God the Father. Rather, he acts in obedience to the Father in a way that serves not himself but others, bringing about their redemption from sin."[13]

This catchy chorus of "although [x] not [y] but [z]"[14] ("although/because he was in the form of God [x], he did not count equality with God a thing to be grasped [y], but emptied himself, taking the form of a servant, being born in the likeness of [humanity] [z]") becomes the narrative shape of ministry and the practice of kenosis that delivers a tangible experience of joy. Because God's being is found in God's story of cross and resurrection, those formed in faith must take on this story as well. Faith formation—indeed a flourishing life—is performing the "although [x] not [y] but [z]" narrative by being a minister. The process of faith formation is to allow this kenotic chorus, "although [x] not [y] but [z]," to structure your life, calling you to be a minister in the world. Gorman explains further:

> When Paul describes himself as an imitator of Christ and calls others to be imitators of him and thus of Christ (1 Cor. 11:1), he is speaking, not about an option, but about a nonnegotiable

---

13 Gorman, *Inhabiting*, 31–32.

14 Gorman provides a little more texture to the "although [x] not [y] but [z]" structure. He says, "This text is famous for the phrase 'emptied himself,' referring to Christ's utter abandonment of self in service to God and others that theologians call 'kenosis,' from the noun form of the Greek verb 'to empty.' The italicized connecting words in this text from Philippians (though . . . did not . . . but) present a common pattern in Paul's letters that indicates the essence of self-emptying, 'kenotic,' or 'cruciform' (cross-shaped) love: although [x] not [y] but [z], meaning although [x] one possesses a certain status, one does not [y] exploit it for selfish gain but [z] acts for the good of others." Michael Gorman, *Reading Paul* (Eugene, OR: Cascade Books, 2008), 84.

> mandate in which one does not deny but rather exercises one's true identity as an apostle (and one's true apostolic freedom), or, more generally, one's identity (and true freedom) as a "Christian." Imitatio Christi (or, better, conformation Christi) is nonnegotiable because those whose freedom is defined by being in Christ must be conformed to Christ, as Philippians 2:5 suggests. . . . Thus when Paul or the Corinthian community performs the narrative "although [x] not [y] but [z]," this performance is also a matter of "because [x] not [y] but [z]."[15]

Putting our ear to Paul's epistles, we can hear this vibrating chorus of "although [x] not [y] but [z]" everywhere. "Paul adopts and adapts this narrative pattern on numerous occasions," Gorman observes, "not only to tell the story of Jesus, but also to describe his own apostolic life and to exhort others to share in the story of Jesus, too."[16] In other words "although [x] not [y] but [z]" fuses both the process and object of faith. We hear this particularly in the kenotic chorus in 1 Thessalonians 2, where Paul says,

> Though we might have made demands as apostles of Christ [x and y] . . . we were gentle among you, like a nurse tenderly caring for her own children [z]. So deeply do we care for you that we are determined to share with you not only the gospel of God but also our own selves, because you have become very dear to us. You remember our labor and toil, brothers and sisters; we worked night and day, so that we might not burden any of you while we proclaimed you the gospel of God. (1 Thess. 2:7–9 NRSV)

It then appears again in Philippians 2:1–4, when Paul says,

> If then there is any encouragement in Christ, any consolation from love, any sharing in the Spirit, any compassion and

15 Gorman, *Reading Paul*, 23.

16 Gorman, 157.

> sympathy, make my joy complete: be of the same mind, having the same love, being in full accord and of one mind. Do nothing from selfish ambition or conceit [x and y], but in humility regard others as better than yourselves [z]. Let each of you look not to your own interests [y], but to the interests of others [z]. (NRSV)

This chorus can be seen in many other places as well. Paul uses "although [x] not [y] but [z]" in relation to food sacrificed to idols (1 Cor. 8–10): although one is free [x] to eat such meat, don't [y], for the sake of ministering to the weak [z]. Or in 2 Corinthians 8–9, Paul says, "although you are free to not give money to the church in Jerusalem [x], put away that privilege [y], and partner with me in ministry by giving generously [z]."[17] Or Paul says to Philemon, "You have every right to punish your slave Onesimus [x], but I ask you to abandon that right in the name of Christ [y], and instead embrace Onesimus in a ministry of friendship [z], for he is Paul's son in the faith" (paraphrase of Philem. 1:10).

"Although [x] not [y] but [z]" is the structure of kenosis, the shape of ministry that enters into death experience with new possibility (that, in turn, delivers joy). Bonhoeffer took on the "although [x] not [y] but [z]" form: although he was not sure why the boy was crying and was not even on the clock [x], he put aside his right to tell the boy to go home [y] and entered into his experience [z]. Or although he was a highly credentialed theologian [x], having all the test scores to prove it, he put that

---

17 Gorman discusses further how even Paul's decision to be a tentmaker was a living out of the structure of "although [x] not [y] but [z]": "Tent making was normally done by slaves or freedmen recently released from slavery; the artisans worked hard but usually remained poor, and their social status was very low. For Paul, who as an educated Roman citizen came from a significantly higher social class, the decision to work as a tent maker was an act of self-enslavement—deliberate socioeconomic self-abasement, self-humiliation, and status renunciation. Some at Corinth, particularly the few but influential wise, powerful, and noble (1 Corinthians 1:26), would have viewed Paul as a slave engaged in the most humiliating work and worthy of no respect." Gorman, *Cruciformity*, 183.

aside [y] and as minister answered the boy's question about his dead dog [z]. Taking this practical form, Bonhoeffer lived out the kenotic nature of God. He and the boy were transformed: the boy's crying turned into joy because he experienced a ministry that entered his death experience in this kenotic shape, and Bonhoeffer tasted the flourishing life because he had been truly human in the likeness of God. Both were given flourishing life in Christ, because both were given Christ through this kenotic practice of "although [x] not [y] but [z]." This is the very constitution of God's free being. The "although" *acts* of humility are bound in the "because" *being* of God. This becomes the way to seek for divine action, the way to experience a flourishing life in Christ, a life that blooms forth from the act of dying to oneself and living for others. Kenosis leads to joy because it encompasses the fullness of cruciform love.[18]

A big part of faith formation in youth ministry, then, is inviting young people to try on the practice of "although [x] not [y] but [z]," to take on this structure and be a minister, for as we have seen, to minister is to be truly human in the likeness of God. We invite young people to live out in their daily lives "although [x] not [y] but [z]" as the song that moves us through the cross to joy of new life. But this self-emptying pattern is not automatic, not something that comes easily for human beings. This is why Jesus so frequently reminds us that if anyone would follow him, he must "deny himself and take up his cross and follow me" (Mark 8:34 ESV), that "if anyone wishes to save his life, he will lose it, but if anyone loses it for my sake and for the gospel, he will save it" (paraphrase of Matt. 16:25), and that "whosoever wishes to be first in my kingdom, must be last" (paraphrase of Matt. 20:26). More often, than not, however, we seem to find ourselves more like the "sons of thunder," the ones who wish to sit at Christ's right and left,

18 Gorman points further to the places in the Pauline epistles where this chorus of "although [x] not [y] but [z]" is played as a song of love. "Paul applies the principle of cruciform love to the most mundane of situations and disputes, such as two female church leaders not getting along (Phil. 4:2–3), believers taking one another to pagan courts (1 Cor. 6:1–11)." Gorman, *Reading Paul*, 158.

to be exalted with him; but he reminds them, and so reminds us, that the path to exaltation with Christ is that of kenosis, of drinking the cup of voluntary crucifixion for another.

A ministry that is devoted to forming young people into the likeness of Christ, a likeness that *is* the fullness of what it means to live a joyful and flourishing life, must be devoted to practicing kenosis for the sake of preparing young people to share in the hypostatic when the moment demands it. As Bonhoeffer reminds us, too often we feel the need to rush to speak when someone is suffering, often because their suffering makes us uncomfortable. The youth ministry that is dedicated to forming youth to be hypostatic ministers through the kenotic will deliberately take up practices that give youth opportunities to "rehearse" kenosis as it becomes a disposition. Such a youth group may focus on the spiritual discipline of silence, giving youth the chance to get used to feeling comfortable when there is simply nothing to say. It is the kind of youth ministry that will instill in young people a sense of the value of fasting, as young people get used to not getting what they want all the time. They become accustomed to the sense that what they want isn't the most important thing, allowing them to step outside of themselves and focus on the needs of others around them. Kenotic youth ministries exist to make the "although [x] not [y] but [z]" pattern habitual for young people, as it is this pattern that leads to a truly joyful, flourishing life.

So although you're busy with exams and college dreams, and don't have time to hear your classmate's story [x], you decide to see her in person, putting aside the task [y] to share her place and be her minister [z]. Although you are nervous of social status and find it easy to ignore the lonely lunch eater [x], you put that aside [y] and sit down, providing a small act of friendship [z]. Although you can't wait to watch the new season of your favorite show after working all day and you come home to your roommate's dishes in the sink, which he has continually promised to clean himself [x], you put Netflix on hold [y] and do the dishes yourself as an act not of passive aggression but of love [z]. Indeed the opportunities for kenotic ministry, for self-emptying love, are endless, if only we can step outside ourselves long enough to see the possibilities around us.

Summing It Up

This narrative chorus of "although [x] not [y] but [z]" is transforming, bringing an encounter with joy because it is the song of God's own being. To take on the kenotic acts of "although [x] not [y] but [z]" is to be a person in the likeness of the image of God—Jesus himself. This is to say, to be a person in the likeness of the image of God is to be *truly human.* A flourishing life is not one that we think of in contemporary terms as being "fully alive" but rather is one that is manifest as self-emptying love, as death of the self for the sake of another. For Paul we are conformed (and deeply formed) to Christ not when we manifest some spiritual power or even do some great thing (Paul chooses not to boast of these in 2 Corinthians 11) but when we are humble enough to enter the personhood of our neighbor and be his or her minister, answering questions about a dead dog or giving a small act of friendship.

"Although [x] not [y] but [z]" is not do-goodism; it has no ambition through human action to change the world for good or for God. It has no ambition to meet a goal that would swallow the personhood of another. Rather "although [x] not [y] but [z]" is only the moving chorus that invites us to enter the death experiences of the persons around us, to share in their very being by emptying ourselves of our own discomfort and humbling ourselves to experience their personhood. It is a humble act but a powerful one, because when the death experience is shared by practical form of "although [x] not [y] but [z]," it creates a union that turns what is dead into life; it infuses the broken narrative of death experience with a story of new possibility. The boy is beside himself; joy has been born within him, because he has found a minister who shared in his being by hearing his story, bearing his loss, and embodying a new story of hope and possibility. The joy is the reality of finding your death experience remade into life. And it is remade by the power of the crucified God, who sends a minister in God's kenotic form—practicing the "although [x] not [y] but [z]."

2

Beauty

The Light of Joy

David F. White and John Leedy

One of my (David) first memories, from around the age of three, is of peering through a rusty screen door onto a tree-lined gravel driveway as the late afternoon breeze gently stirred the autumn leaves in the golden light of the setting sun. The path of translucent stone chippings set aflame by the red Mississippi clay beneath it snaked from the edge of the unpainted wooden steps below my naked feet to the widening horizon. This is not only my very first conscious memory but also my first recollection of astounding beauty. Even now the scene stands out as extraordinary in my faded reminiscence. Something about it—its brilliance, complexity, or depth—commanded my attention. According to my parents, I pressed against the screen door each day and played endless hours in the stone chips under that sky and under those trees, enveloped by a sense of wonder, an intuition of a mystery. I suspect that we all have such experiences, however deeply buried in our memories.

My Mississippi childhood was filled with such moments of being "caught" by epiphanies of beauty—by dust motes dancing in sunbeams, languid lakes and rippling streams, noble black dogs, cooing doves, and chirping crickets; my mother's ruby red lipstick and my father's beard stubble tickling my face. I found beauty in the soulful twang of my uncle's country singing; my church's a cappella harmonies; the lustrous paintings of my middle school art teacher, Mr. Quinn; the adorable girl in my seventh-grade class; and, somewhat obviously, in a well-thrown curveball. As an adult I came to perceive beauty in the faces of children and nurturing mothers, the selfless work of teachers, and the bravery of civil rights heroes, and I am oddly haunted by the beauty of the story of God's self-giving love in Jesus Christ.

Since the dawn of modern youth ministry in the late nineteenth century, churches have relied upon didactic instruction intended to lead young people along a path of conceptual logic to evident conclusions and intellectual assent, followed by their will and consequent behavior. Today youth ministry finds itself suffering an erosion of confidence in such rational truth alone. Postmodern thought reveals reason as contextual, fluid, and indeterminate—what we perceive as true is conditioned by our gender, ethnicity, class, and relation to power. The prominence of fake news, political talking points, partisan press releases, and hyperbolic advertising renders truth anything but transparent. Truth turns out to be more slippery than we imagined. Sociologist Christian Smith has observed that many young people today are left with little more ethical language than the notion of "banal tolerance"—if truth is indeterminate, all that remains is for us to tolerate each other's experimental pronouncements about what is true "for us."[1] No one can be allowed to speak definitively about truth—and certainly not for others.

Advertisers, parents, teachers, and churches that try to argue a young person into truth know that it is a losing proposition; youths seek something more. They seek a more trustworthy form of truth that touches their soul. Such yearning is, from the perspective of Christian theology, not coincidental. Christian truth speaks of transcendent mysteries that cannot be fully captured by concepts or intellect but in which all being participates. As St. Augustine knew, we are who we are not by virtue of what we know but because of what we desire.

---

1 Christian Smith, *Lost in Transition: The Dark Side of Emerging Adulthood* (Oxford: Oxford University Press, 2011), 25–27.

In this book our authors recommend joy as an important Christian virtue that should be reclaimed by youth ministry. In this chapter I argue the somewhat obvious point that beauty elicits great joy but also the not so obvious point that beauty and joy are inseparable aspects of how Christians know, and, finally, the unthinkable: that such beauty and joy are features of adolescence and as such are parables of God. Before exploring how joy and beauty are implicated in youth ministry, we must first inquire as to the nature of beauty. What is beauty, and what are its features? How does it relate to joy?

Beauty's Singularity

Throughout history a chorus of voices across all cultures has acknowledged the importance of beauty. Although today we tend to think of beauty as an effervescent rarity found in extraordinary places—in great art, movie stars, fashion models, an astonishing sunset, or in the visage of a romantic partner—the ancient Greeks and early Christians perceived beauty in everything, as a feature of sheer being. For those who can see, beauty appears on the vastest scales (as the amazing photographs taken by the Hubble telescope of our beautiful blue earthly orb show) and the most minute (as in a floating dust mote in a sunbeam).

Beauty is also mysteriously singular among human experiences. Beauty has impressed many throughout history as essential, restorative, and even redemptive. Navajo tribes long used beautiful sand paintings to restore the sick to harmony with the universe. Albert Einstein once remarked, "I have deep faith that the principle of the universe will be beautiful and simple."[2] Fyodor Dostoevsky once said that "man can live without science, he can live without bread, but without beauty he could no longer live."[3] Alexander Nehamas observes that beauty mani-

---

2 "Albert Einstein Quotes," Quotes.net, STANDS4 LLC, 2020, accessed February 3, 2020, https://www.quotes.net/authors/Albert+Einstein+Quotes.

3 Quoted by Pope Benedict XVI, "Meeting with Artists," Sistine Chapel, Vatican City, 21 Nov. 2009.

fests a hope that life would be better if the object of beauty were part of it.[4] For theologian David Bentley Hart, "Beauty seems to promise a reconciliation beyond the contradictions of the moment, one that perhaps places time's tragedies within a broader perspective of harmony and meaning, a balance between light and darkness; beauty seems to absolve being of its violences."[5] Beauty appears in quality and abundance far greater than is necessary for natural selection. Dutch biologist F. J .J. Buytendijk states: "To put it simply, the birds are singing much more than Darwin permits."[6] Whatever we make of beauty's significance, we ought to at least be intrigued by its qualities.

The Joy of Beauty

Many Christian theologians have understood beauty as an aspect of the goodness (the Hebrew term is *kavod*, which connotes something like "dripping with glory") bestowed in God's act of creation (Gen. 1:1–31) as analogue to the perfections of God who is beauty—corresponding to what the psalmists describe as God's sensual holiness ("taste and see that the Lord is good"; Ps 34:8). Such created beauty is glimpsed in a spectacular sunset, a child's face, a painting, or an occasion of sacrificial giving—all of which involve a lingering moment of delight (or en-JOY-ment).

Simone Weil insists that beauty requires us to "give up our imaginary position at the center" of the world.[7] British novelist Iris Murdoch tells of a day when she was anxious, resentful, and brooding, preoccupied with

---

4 Alexander Nehamas, *Only a Promise of Happiness: The Place of Beauty in a World of Art* (Princeton: Princeton University Press, 2007).

5 David Bentley Hart, *The Beauty of the Infinite: The Aesthetics of Christian Truth* (Grand Rapids, MI: Eerdmans, 2003), 16.

6 Quoted by Jürgen Moltmann in *Joy and Human Flourishing: Essays on Theology, Culture, and the Good Life*, eds. Miroslav Volf and Justin Crisp, (Minneapolis: Fortress, 2015), 5.

7 Elaine Scarry, *On Beauty and Being Just* (Princeton: Princeton University Press, 1999), 111.

her problems; but upon seeing a beautiful kestrel flying above her, all of this fell away.[8] All of the space formerly in the service of protecting, guarding, and advancing the self was now free to be in the service of something else. Harvard aestheticist Elaine Scarry observes that "in the moment we perceive beauty, we are absorbed into the world, joining the community of beauty."[9] As others in this volume observe, joy is an experience that decenters and enlarges our sense of self (*ekstasis*). And beauty is a prime example of joyful *ekstasis*.

Joy, like beauty, is completed and continued when shared.

Beauty's authority is manifestly a public announcement, not a gnostic secret for only a few scholars or mystics. As witnessed by endless Facebook arguments, reason is subject to endless charges of subjective bias, while beauty remains surprisingly objective. We may quibble over how to interpret it, but we cannot doubt its existence or quality.

Importantly, beauty does not remain closed in upon itself or leave us isolated. Our joy at encountering beauty is completed and continued in sharing it with friends and strangers. According to owners of galleries or museum gift shops, one of the most common responses to beautiful art is a postcard or phone call to a loved one expressing sentiments such as "The impressionists are breathtaking; I wish you were here! Come as soon as you can."[10]

Our connection and joy with others is deepened when we respond to beauty by gratefully duplicating and sharing our gifts with them. When we experience beauty, we want to bring replicas into being for others to see. "The philosopher Wittgenstein," Scarry notes, "says that when the eye sees something beautiful, the hand wants to draw it."[11]

---

8 Iris Murdoch, "The Sovereignty of Good," in *Studies in Ethics and the Philosophy of Religion* (London: Routledge, 1970), 369-371.

9 Scarry, *On Beauty,* 113.

10 Scarry, 6.

11 Scarry, 3.

Such encounters with beauty make us want to reproduce it—to draw it, paint it, take photographs of it, or describe it to other people. Sometimes this imitative impulse of beauty crosses sensory modes, such as when the smooth cheek of a child prompts a caress or inspires us to play with or care for them. This crisscrossing of senses prompted Augustine to love God when he touched something smooth and pleasant; and Dante, inspired by the beautiful Beatrice, to write sonnets of the landscape of God's salvation in which all things are finally caught up in the beauty of God.

Childhood theorists believe that prior to the age of three, before the onset of language, all children perceive stimuli cross-modally—synesthetically crossing two or more senses. The warmth and color of a sunbeam alive with dancing specks is felt globally in our infant bodies and senses—only to be later reduced by the onset of language to the mere term "sunbeam." Daniel Stern observes that "child-directed speech" by which parents communicate with infants involves aesthetic, rounded, affect-laden words, such as "helllll-ooooo—bayyyyy-beeee."[12] Such singsong words offer a musical embrace that invites the infant's attention and draws it near. Child-directed speech can be seen as a response to the fragile beauty of the infant, joyfully connecting parent and child. Recently researchers at a university ran an endless loop in a special screening room of a video recording of Chinese mothers cooing to their infants. Those conducting the experiment were surprised to find that stressed-out graduate assistants came to sit in the room to listen and comfort themselves. The infants' beautiful faces evoked the mothers' beautiful cooing, which even in an unknown (to the students) dialect traversed fields and crossed modes, affecting the weary hearts of the graduate students.

Recently, in my church, as I listened to a sermon by one of my pastors, I felt my whole body relax and my spirits lift. I realized that she was speaking in rounded, singsong words that mysteriously spoke to my

---

12 Daniel Stern, *The Intersubjective World of the Infant: A View from Psychoanalysis and Developmental Psychology* (Grand Rapids, MI: Baker Books, 1985), 138–41.

weary heart. Only later did I remember that she was a new mother and that her speech was surely conditioned by the child-directed speech she employs habitually with her daughter. As I scanned the congregation, their softening eyes revealed that others were also affected by this boundary-crossing beauty.

According to Elaine Scarry, when we encounter beauty, we experience a surplus of aliveness, a wake-up call to the plenitude of life: "Beauty quickens. It adrenalizes. It makes the heart beat faster. It makes life more vivid, animated, living worth living."[13] In beauty's many forms, we find ourselves inexplicably caught in a state of joyous grace. We take pleasure in created things—their form gives us delight. Beauty is a tangible and joyful reminder that the world cannot be reduced to its efficient causes or reasons, that all things exist within an invisible nimbus of gratuity—given as gift and calling forth our own gift giving.

This brief sketch points to the uniqueness of beauty and how it evokes certain virtues and values—joy, connection, community, *poiesis*—which, even at first glance, hold theological significance but which should also make us curious about the role of beauty in Christian thought.

Theological Clues to Beauty

The beauty of God's delighted and delightful act of creation reflects God's own inner joy and splendor that marks the Trinity. As David Bentley Hart states,

> God's beauty is delight and the object of delight, the shared gaze of love that belongs to the persons of the Trinity; it is what God beholds, what the Father sees and rejoices in in the Son, in the sweetness of the Spirit, what Son and Spirit find delightful in one another, because as Son and Spirit of the Father they share his knowledge and love as persons.[14]

13 Scarry, *On Beauty*, 24.

14 Hart, *Beauty of the Infinite*, 177.

God's inner beauty and delight does not remain closed upon itself but opens out into God's creation. Genesis tells us that God created the world out of sheer nothingness, as a deliberate act of artistry, an invention of delight, an expression of love, a gift of grace. In this doctrine the world's beauty is revealed as gift, for it might very well not have been this way—or any way at all. Beauty announces God's glory and creation's goodness with equal eloquence in each moment. Beauty is there, abroad in the order of things, given again and again in a way that resists description and denial with equal boldness. The Bible declares that created beauty is the delighted vision of what is other than oneself—of difference, created by the God who differentiates and pleasing in the eyes of the God who takes pleasure. According to Hans Urs von Balthasar, created beauty speaks as a pleasing form but also in each case shines as a light from the depths of being, drawing us in wonder toward God.[15]

God's inner beauty and delight joyfully open out into God's creation.

In Christ, God uses created being to fashion an image, an expression or exegesis of God's self. The light of God's surprising beauty blazes especially from the cross of Christ bathed in the light of resurrection. There we witness the plenitude of God's self-emptying love reunited with creation. For Balthasar love is the highest form of beauty. In the form of Christ, he saw aesthetic values of proportion, balance, and harmony everywhere—in the relationship between the Son and the Father; the distance of humanity and the nearness of the Son; the relationship between servant and lord, exaltation and humiliation; the relationships between promise and fulfillment, judgment and grace, master and disciple. Each of these seems irreconcilable, but in the Christ image they are objectively harmonized to the eyes of faith.

For Balthasar the epitome of beauty in the world is Jesus Christ, who is the form of all forms, the measure of all measures. This can be

15 Hans Urs von Balthasar, *The Glory of the Lord: A Theological Aesthetics III Studies in Theological Style* (San Francisco: Ignatius, 1986), 118.

seen in the many biblical terms for Christ—shepherd, physician, vine tender, light, living water, peace, truth, word, prince, deliverer, gate, friend, way, among others. All created things find their perfect measure in the beauty of Jesus Christ. Christ, as God's supreme beauty, therefore restores and reveals the truth of creaturely beauty by making the beautiful yet more beautiful and the exceedingly beautiful more beautiful still. For Hart, Christ's miracles "repeat God's gift of creation by imparting joy in the good things of the world—food and wine, fellowship and rejoicing, life and vision and health—to those in whom such joy is lacking," and thus testify to his nature as the "creative Word who can command and restore all the words of creation."[16]

Theologian John Milbank suggests that, as God's creatures, we are, like God, made for a pattern of mutual "gift giving."[17] As opposed to commercial transactions, where the gift and the return are specified and predictable, for Christians gift giving and receiving are unpredictable, joyful responses to one's own resources and the beautiful other. As opposed to a transaction in which the exchange is mandated, the gift truly given is thoughtful and surprising and timely. Exchange in capitalist arrangements operates by expectations of quid pro quo, while Christian gift giving deepens our mutual connection by means of gratitude. Milbank suggests that we and all creation are gifted by God, whose Trinitarian nature is gracious giving. And we are created for such gift giving sociality in patterns of joyful feasting and friendship that connect us to each other and God. The Eucharist is foundational and emblematic of the kind of gift exchange that is key for restoring Christian community in joy and love.

If God's gift to us is the beauty of created being, then our appropriate response is to craft our gifting expressions in surprising and artful

---

16 Hart, *Beauty of the Infinite*, 18.

17 John Milbank, "Can a Gift Be Given? Prolegomena to a Future Trinitarian Metaphysic," *Modern Theology* 11, no. 1 (January 1995), 119–61; John Milbank, *The Word Made Strange: Theology, Language, Culture* (Cambridge, MA: Blackwell, 1997).

forms—as our worship and our practices. Jesus Christ—God's *poiesis*—was the paradigm for such expression, since in Jesus created being was beautifully crafted and offered back to the Father as gift. In the incarnation, Hart holds, God brings about a return of the gift that He has given in creation, by Himself giving it again, anew, "according to the Trinitarian dynamism in which donation and restoration are one."[18] If Christ was the firstborn of the new creation, then we, the later born, are called to participate with God in *poiesis*—returning to God our lives crafted in response to God's own beauty.

Joy is our grateful response to God's beauty.

We must acknowledge that the true significance of Jesus Christ can only partially be articulated in words, concepts, or logic—and never comprehensively. Artful or liturgical expressions of beauty seem more suitable for communicating the Incarnation and creation's glory, since they reveal what is true alongside what is mystery. The church is squarely within its scriptural logic to respond to God's created and incarnated beauty by crafting its own forms of beauty in joyful response—as liturgies, paintings, sculptures, music, and the lovely practices of the church's life.

Secular Flattening

If there are theological reasons for reclaiming beauty, there is also a crying cultural need. Modern secularity has served to disenchant the Western world. Beauty, mystery, and joy have been supplanted by technical reason, which reduces God's creation to usable objects—as calculations of usable economic advantage, as raw materials, bosses, consumers, or competitors. Such disenchantment has prompted alienation, incivility, and environmental degradation. Philosopher Charles Taylor observes

18 Hart, *Beauty of the Infinite*, 325.

that since the late medieval era, the secular Western world has suffered a diminishment of our "palette of such points of contact with fullness."[19]

Among the most troubling losses, according to Taylor, is the systematizing of ethical codes, prompting a kind of distancing from our embodied ethical feelings. Taylor points to the biblical parable of the Good Samaritan, in which a traveler is beaten, left by the roadside, and ignored by religious officials, but ironically cared for by a Samaritan—a people commonly thought to be immoral and untrustworthy. Taylor insists that in Jesus's telling of the story what is emphasized is not an ethical category or idea but the gut reaction of compassion by the Samaritan. Taylor thinks that by rationally codifying our ethics, we miss what is most important—that is, contact with the good via the flesh. He observes that the New Testament calls for a return to our "gut"—an enfleshed response to an enfleshed situation. The Samaritan's charitable response is not a better ethical conception but instead a response of the heart. He perceived the stranger as more than a negative category—as one whose beauty was violated, to whom he responded with gut immediacy in a beautiful act of care and reconciliation.[20]

Additionally, according to Taylor, we have lost the capacity for poetic language, a genre nearer to our embodied experiences. Poetic verse no longer sits easily on our tongues or in our ears. Instead we imagine that all things in the world are directly mappable onto our language as nouns. Hence we grow impatient with poets who could, we imagine, say things more directly but instead speak coyly in obscure circles. Poet Billy Collins says that too often the poem is like a prisoner captured by modern readers: "All they [the readers] want to do is tie the poem to a chair with rope and torture a confession out of it."[21] Such a reduction misses entirely the point of poetic truth, which is much more

---

19 Charles Taylor, *A Secular Age* (Cambridge, MA: Harvard University Press, 2007), 729.

20 Charles Taylor, "Foreword" in *The Rivers North of the Future: The Testament of Ivan Illich As Told to David Cayley* (Toronto: House of Anansi Press, 2005), x-xiv.

21 Billy Collins, "Introduction to Poetry" from *The Apple that Astonished Paris* (Fayetteville: University of Arkansas Press, 1996), 58.

paradoxical and mysterious and felt more deeply than the intellect. For example, the breed of new atheists views biblical literature as nice but untrue stories—as botched pieces of social science. We should be offended not only as theists but also as people who understand the revelatory power of language and good literature. Poetry makes our enfleshed experiences articulable by crafting new words and resonant phrases drawn from creation's plentitude and mystery. Poetry opens up new paths: it sets free new realities and allows for an ontological indeterminacy that is, for mystery, wonder, and paradox. As such poetry exceeds the limits of instrumental reason and broadens our affirmation of ordinary life. Poetic language allows us to see new and astonishing things and new aspects of old things. Taylor argues that language does not merely designate objects already recognized in the world but also has the power to create new realities and new worlds.

In a modern world disenchanted and evacuated of poetic and ethical fullness, joy is impossible. We and our young people must reclaim our vision for the beauty of God's gifts, our ears and tongues for poetic fullness, and our gut responses of compassion. Only in such a renaissance will the modern world learn to rejoice.

Youth and Beauty

What precisely have beauty and joy to do with adolescence? A moment's reflection will reveal that youths throughout history have played poetic roles—in crafting new genres of music, fashion, poetry, and language. While scholars theorizing adolescence commonly emphasize young people's growing cognitive capacities, observers who live with or minister to youths know that they are not driven by mere cognition. Young people are also naturally inclined to wonder and joy. In fact, prior to the late nineteenth century, youth was seen as a stage uniquely attentive to beauty. The Romantic poets of the eighteenth and nineteenth centuries observed youth as a stage of wonder and discovery. In 1904 G. Stanley Hall, the first theorist of adolescence, observed adolescence as the "vernal season of the heart"—the springtime of the heart when "life glistens and crepitates."[22] He held that adolescents are caught up in the wonder of all creation—peer friendships, created things, culture, art, God, and the world unfolding around them, now opened before their hearts in beauty. He saw adolescents as ready to be recruited by epiphanies or encounters with the good creation that serve to prompt them toward future vocation. He traced the success of famed scientists, artists, professionals, politicians, and businesspeople back to the wonder and romance of their adolescence.

Today adolescence is a complex and contested status that often involves confusion, alienation, and pain—and it is risky to over-romanticize. Nevertheless those close to young people observe in youth a resilient hunger for wonder and joy. Their affinity for imaginative fantasy literature such as the Harry Potter series or Marvel movies and their many imitators, for example, suggests that young people somehow know that things are fraught with magic and perhaps a bit of joy. Their fittingness for wonder can also be seen in their endlessly creative efforts in music and art, language, love, religion, and social justice. Even as young people find joy in these endeavors—the church's affirmation is that their search finds its fitting end in Jesus Christ, God's *poiesis*.

Adolescence is the springtime of the heart.

We can affirm that the joy of youth—in their intellectual and bodily discoveries; newfound connections to God, the created world, and beloved friends—constitutes a vivid parable of Christ's joyous redemption of ordinary things. When we truly see young people, we see God's own beauty refracted in them; we catch them on their way back to God, God's perfections, and their true *telos*. Churches that long for life with God do well to draw alongside their young people, who in their beauty and joy point toward God.

---

22 G. S. Hall, *Adolescence: Its Psychology and Its Relations to Physiology, Anthropology, Sociology, Sex, Crime, Religion, and Education*, 2 vols. (New York: Appleton, 1904), 131.

For these reasons—beauty's theological significance, its sociocultural evacuation, and young peoples' fittingness for beauty—beauty may helpfully be a part of our approach for forming youths as joyful Christian disciples. Below is an outline suggesting particular ways congregations might engage young people with beauty as a source of wonder and holy mystery, to which they are invited to joyfully respond. I suggest three different modes of aesthetic pedagogies for youth.

Beauty in Creation: Lingering in *Tov*

> "And to every beast of the earth and to every bird of the sky and to every thing that moves on the earth which has life, I have given every green plant for food"; and it was so. God saw all that He had made, and behold, it was very good. (Gen. 1:30, 31, NASB)

Genesis tells us that God created the world and called it good (Tov, translated beautiful, in harmony with God). If theologians are right that creation, in its beauty, speaks of God—not exhaustively or literally but poetically—then congregations engaging youths in Christian formation cannot ignore the created world, view it as inert, or allow young people to escape into a mere digital existence. If, as suggested above, the created world is an expression of God and the source of our own *poiesis*—a gift to which our only response is giving gifts of our words, images, songs, or work—then Christians must attend to its speaking. If, as Charles Taylor states, our sense of the world has been flattened by technical reason, then the way forward must involve restoring our palettes for fullness—by reconnecting our created being to the goodness of God's world. Educators have long known the importance of experiential learning that begins with encounters with the created world, including wilderness education, art and narrative therapies and pedagogies, and praxis pedagogies. Historically, contemplative practices have involved, as Walter J. Burghardt suggests, "a long, loving look at the real."[23] Of course, this is rarely easy when our vision is consistently clouded not only with busyness but also with our fear, anxiety, anger, and despair. Contemplative practices help to clear away the fog of such distortions in order to see the glory of God's creation and the beam of holy light that shines from beyond it. Here are some of the questions that a curriculum of beauty in created being must attend to.

- Where do we see ordinary and surprising beauty in the created world?
- How does such beauty speak to us? What does it say to us?
- How does this beauty recruit us to wonder?
- How does it spark our imaginations about the possibilities for human and creation flourishing?
- How does our encounter with the beauty of creation allow for unexpected reversals in our assumptions about the world? God? Ourselves?
- Where and how do we find joy in observing, working, and playing in and with created beauty?

The Beauty of the Christ Form: Seeing the Light Come into This World

> And the Word became flesh and took up residence among us, and we saw his glory, glory as of the one and only from the Father, full of grace and truth. John testified about him and cried out, saying, "This one was he about whom I said, 'The one who comes after me is ahead of me, because he existed before me.'" For from his fullness we have all received, and grace after grace. For the law was given through Moses; grace and truth came about through Jesus Christ. No one has seen God at any

---

23 Walter J. Burghardt, "Contemplation: A Long, Loving Look at the Real," *Church*, no. 5 (Winter 1989): 14–17.

> time; the one and only, God, the one who is in the bosom of the Father—that one has made him known. (John 1:14–18, LEB)

Christ, in the perfectly meaningful, expressive unity of his significant form, discloses the nature of the divine Artist. The unity of his form emerges from the scriptures, from a multiplicity of perspectives and authors. He is the image, icon, or artwork of God—the "characteristic qualities" of his actions reveal a particular "style," which in turn shows his relationship to the Father. He discloses the infinite, ungraspable mystery of God's (Trinitarian) love. In Jesus Christ we do not find a set of rational principles or a universal ethical system. Christ incarnate is a form given to us upon the canvas of creation—more like a story or a song or a painting than a system of principles. In Christian faith the captivating force of the artwork that is Christ takes hold of our imaginative powers; we enter into the painterly world that this discloses and, entranced by what we see, come to contemplate the glory of the sovereign love of God in Christ as manifested in the concrete events of his life, death, and resurrection. So entering his glory, we become absorbed by it; but this absorption sends us out into the world in sacrificial love, emulating his beauty, giving and receiving God's gifts, finding joy in communion with God and neighbor.

Representing the Christ form in its eternal brilliance must involve more than reading scriptural accounts, which can become flattened over time into simple portrayals. Throughout history, painters, sculpters, musicians, playwrights, and poets have provided glimpses of the art of God in Christ. Paintings by El Greco, Leonardo da Vinci, Peter Paul Rubens, and Paul Gauguin; music by Wolfgang Amadeus Mozart, Ludwig van Beethoven, and Johann Sebastian Bach; plays such as *Jesus Christ Superstar*, *Godspell*, and *Cotton Patch Gospel*, as well as *Les Misérables*; and movies such as *Jesus of Montreal*, *The Last Temptation of Christ*, and *The Robe* all represent glimpses into the art/truth of the Incarnation. Moreover reading Gospel accounts in contemplative ways allows for deeper insight, which may be supplemented by young people's crafting their own art—poetry, paintings, drama, and music.

In this way the significance of Incarnation does not become flattened to routine interpretations, but through artifice wonder is allowed to do its work of speaking beyond our reason or intentions. Here are some of the questions that a curriculum of beauty focused in the Christ form must attend to.

- How do we perceive beauty in the form of Jesus Christ portrayed in scripture?
- Since over time traditions have a tendency to flatten the fullness of the Christ form by endless and same interpretations of texts, what ways can we find to see the texts afresh and the Christ form with new eyes?
- What new meanings and questions arise in fresh readings?
- How have artists through history portrayed Jesus Christ in art, sculpture, drama, and song? What can we learn by studying these renditions?
- How do fresh readings prompt reversals in how we think of the world? God? Ourselves?
- What new artistic forms can we envision to portray mysterious and unnamed aspects of the Christ form?
- How do we find joy in new expressions of Jesus Christ?

Liturgical Beauty: Offering Our Gifts

> When he came near the place where the road goes down the Mount of Olives, the whole crowd of disciples began joyfully to praise God in loud voices for all the miracles they had seen:
>
> "Blessed is the king who comes in the name of the Lord!" "Peace in heaven and glory in the highest!"
>
> Some of the Pharisees in the crowd said to Jesus, "Teacher, rebuke your disciples!"
>
> "I tell you," he replied, "if they keep quiet, the stones will cry out." (Luke 19:37–40, NIV)

Christian faith is rooted in a holy mystery in which God's beautiful gifts of creation and incarnation are given. By this we mean that we—along with the very stones (Luke 19:40)—are liturgically shaped for receiving God's gifts and returning unto God our worship in grateful emulation of Christ's and the world's beauty. Worship does not only involve the formal acts we perform in the sanctuary on the Lord's day. As D. E. Saliers has said, worship involves the liturgy *and* the liturgy beyond the liturgy—those responses to God's gift that we live out in our relationships, at work, in leisure, at home, and in public.[24] This too is worship. Rightly understood, Christians live in a joyous cycle of repeating in our own creativity the gift of God's beauty, bringing more beauty for each other on behalf of God.

As we have indicated, the capacity for *poiesis*, for example, in language, art, fashion, and social action, can readily be seen in young people. The key to forming youth for beauty in this mode is engaging them in joyful response to God's gifts of creation and the incarnation, without which we risk perpetuating a kind of autarky that is the essence of sin. True relationships thrive only if all participants are receiving and offering their gifts. Only in such gifting are our hearts enlarged and the Spirit of God shed abroad in the world.

We live in a time in which young people are socialized as passive consumers—of parental care and nurture, education, entertainment, material provision, and market commodities. Even youth ministry has too often assigned roles for them to passively consume youth talks, lock-ins, concerts, pizza, and unilateral adult attention. Key to this gift-giving mode of youth ministry is finding ways to encourage young people to give their own offerings of beauty—offerings of art, music, liturgy, relationships, and ecclesial responsibility, of practice and action. This is another way of acknowledging our lives as liturgically ordered by God's own gifts. The questions that give shape to this mode of youth ministry for beauty are such as these:

---

24 D. E. Saliers, "Liturgy and Ethics: Some New Beginnings," *Journal of Religious Ethics* 7, no. 2 (Fall 1979): 173–89.

- What are the gifts of God that surround me? What would my world be like without these gifts?
- What new feelings or thoughts emerge with recognition of these gifts?
- How can I give words to my own responses of gratitude? What other ways can I imagine for expressing my responses to these gifts?
- How does receiving God's gifts prompt me to give gifts to others?
- What can I do to facilitate the flow of gifts between others, myself, and the world beyond?
- How can we together joyfully celebrate the giving and receiving of gifts and the love they foster?

The Christian life, according to Jürgen Moltmann, is to be envisioned not as a purpose-driven life but as a game of delight in the God who creates and redeems the world for nothing.[25] Hence the church as Christ's body can only convincingly speak of Christ as Lord not by our words alone, but only if our beauty resembles his—if our palette for fullness is enlarged to include empathy for the wounded traveler, tongues and ears hungry for poetry, and grateful hearts for gift giving and receiving in friendship and feasting.

In conclusion, this chapter argues that joy might be restored to youth ministry in considering new possibilities for engaging young people in the beauty of God's world and the Christ form, and in giving their own gifts of art. Thus they might participate with God in crafting a joyful new creation of beauty, goodness, and truth where God will be all in all.

25 Jürgen Moltmann, Sam Keen, Robert E. Neale, David LeRoy Miller, *Theology of Play* (San Francisco: Harper Collins, 1972), 18.

3

Friendship

The Joy of Befriending Youth

Wesley W. Ellis and Kenda Creasy Dean

I've (Kenda) said it too, with the best of intentions. I remember taking a deep breath and putting on my grown-up-youth-leader pants to say it: "Kim, I love you, but I am your youth leader, which means I can't be your friend. I'm sorry."[1]

We were in the hallway outside my office, standing under a spluttering fluorescent ceiling light. All these years later, I still remember the look on her face. I wasn't sure what emotion flickered across it—was it hurt? Confusion? Disbelief? Betrayal? I do remember one thing: I wondered if I would ever see Kim again.

The written advice against youth worker friendship with adolescents is sizable. A quick Google search is all it takes to find some:

- A blogger writes: "Students don't need youth workers to be their friends, they need adults who will lead them to God and invest in their lives. Unfortunately, many of us have bought into the lie that we need to be 'friends' with our students in order to have influence in their lives."

1 Names of youths in this chapter have been changed to protect their identities.

- A whole training session titled "Friend vs. Youth Worker" is available to "help your adults move from friendship to being effective youth workers."
- An online author (whose byline says he "reeks with passion") calls befriending youth one of the top mistakes youth leaders make: "Students don't need any more 'friends.' They actually really don't want your friendship. They need adults passionately following Jesus."[2]

All these admonitions assume a definition of friendship that is an undifferentiated peer relationship of equals, in which all friendships are the same, in which "equals" implies equal maturity levels, equal power of authority, equal access to information, equal levels of affection, and so on. These definitions also seem to imply that a caring adult who spends time with an adolescent while maintaining his or her role and status as an adult is not a friend.

All these assumptions are false.

Leaf through your high school yearbook, and you'll recall that, in practice, you never defined friendship this way. You were friends with people in different grades. You shared some information with some friends but not with others, simply because the nature of your friendship shaped the kind of conversations that were appropriately shared. You enjoyed Anton more than you enjoyed Greg, and you shared your deepest secrets with Tamar but not Michelle—yet Anton and Greg and Tamar and Michelle were all genuinely your friends. Friends come in all sorts of flavors, with different norms and expectations governing each relationship. That is why, as an adult, you can be friends with

---

2 Phil Bell, "Youth Ministry Leadership: Friend or Leader?" (March 13, 2012), http://philbell.me/2012/03/13/youth-ministry-leadership-friend-or-leader/; Doug Franklin, "Friend vs. Youth Worker," https://www.leadertreks.org/store/friend-vs-youth-worker/; (both accessed April 29, 2017); Jeremy Zach, "9 Mistakes Made by Youth Pastors," *ChurchLeaders.com* (n.d.), http://www.churchleaders.com/youth/youth-leaders-articles/146054-9-mistakes-made-by-youth-pastors.html (accessed October 30, 2016).

your neighbor, your spouse, and your sister, but you don't mix them up (without serious consequences).

For far too long we youth workers have—either by distortion or conscious decision—withheld our friendship from young people. We have entered into friendship under the false assumption that we need to be like a young person to befriend a young person (thus distorting friendship). Or, under the same assumption, in order to avoid the distortion, we have consciously withheld friendship from young people. The problem is that, in withholding our friendship, we're also missing out on the joy of youth ministry. More important, the young people closest to us miss out on joy as well, for in a world haunted by transactional relationships and bound by an obsession with achievement, there's perhaps nothing young people need more from us than our free and joyful friendship. We need to restore friendship in youth ministry because we need to restore joy to youth ministry!

The Theological Necessity of Christian Friendship

Let's be clear at the outset that no adult who acts like an adolescent should be working in youth ministry at all, for reasons that include and go well beyond the potential to misunderstand Christian friendship. It's not because there's anything wrong with adolescence or acting young, as such; it's just that an adult who cannot bear the responsibilities adults have toward young people should not be given those responsibilities. An adult who acts like an adolescent fails to discern roles properly—a key sign of the inability to know when one's own needs are getting in the way of making decisions based on the needs of others. I understand the motivation behind the scores of web pages advising against becoming friends with adolescents, because I share their concerns—concerns about appropriate boundaries, unhealthy need fulfillment, immature decision making, and flat-out failure to launch among youth workers who are often young, inexperienced, and eager to please.

These are crucial concerns that we must take seriously. The problem is that they have nothing to do with friendship—in fact advising youth workers to avoid befriending youths demonstrates a serious misunderstanding of Christian friendship that is both theologically deficient and pastorally ill-advised. The fact is that compelling data underscores the importance of appropriate, faithful, nurturing friendships between adults and young people for adolescent faith formation, including friendships between teenagers and their pastors.[3] Furthermore none of these concerns take into account the theological necessity of Christian friendship: to follow Christ is to extend friendship to one another, as Christ extended friendship to us.

The issue, of course, is that what often passes for friendship in our culture is not friendship at all—it's a transactional, tit-for-tat, self-interested relationship that, at best, turns young people into relational consumers and exhausts youth workers who try to deliver the most flashy and relevant youth ministry program possible. Even Jesus recognized this transactionalism as a substitute for friendship, not as the real thing. This surrogate friendship has no place in youth ministry. On the heartbreaking evening before his arrest, Jesus told his disciples: "I have called you friends, because I have made known to you everything that I have heard from my Father" (John 15:15b, NRSV). The Greek word for friend in that sentence is *philos*, a word used to connote someone who is dearly loved, suggesting a relationship brimming with personal affection. In Matthew 26:50, however, Jesus says to Judas, just before his seizure: "Friend, do what you are here to do" (NRSV), using the much less common Greek word *hetairos*, or "supposed friend," someone acting in his or her own interest. These kinds of friendships are transactional,

3 Teenagers mentioned with special affection their relationships with their pastors. The more supportive, faithful adult-teen relationships a teenager had during adolescence, the more likely he or she was to have durable and highly devoted faith. Cf. Christian Smith and Melinda Denton, *Soul Searching: The Religious and Spiritual Lives of American Teenagers* (New York: Oxford University Press, 2005); Christian Smith and Patricia Snell, *Souls in Transition: The Religious and Spiritual Lives of Emerging Adults* (New York: Oxford University Press, 2009).

useful—limited by how much I might benefit another and vice versa. Such friendships must be constantly earned. They're exhausting and dehumanizing, and they wind up being a form of entrapment, like a genie in a bottle—a relationship based on wish fulfillment, not love.

We don't need to eliminate adult-youth friendships in youth ministry; we need to understand and enact them in light of Jesus's friendship toward us. Christian friendships honor the uniqueness—including (in youth ministry) age, role, and life experience—of the persons involved. Jesus befriended the disciples without relinquishing his divinity or his salvific role toward them; the disciples loved Jesus without fully comprehending the nature of his love for them. Their friendship was a mutual, loving relationship between people who were not equal in the sense of being peers or even in the sense of what they brought to the relationship, but they were—astonishingly—equally loved by God. Friendships that stand in the tradition of Christ honor difference while maintaining the equality and humanity of all persons in the eyes of God. In the context of a robust theology of friendship—one that honors and celebrates the uniqueness of each person in a relationship as an embodiment of God's love in Jesus Christ—youth ministry should encourage youth worker–young person friendships and find ways to cultivate them creatively, appropriately, and robustly.

"You Ain't Never Had a Friend Like Me"

I (Wes) was seven years old when Disney released its classic film *Aladdin*, but I can't remember a time when it didn't exist. For my generation it seems to be just one of those movies, like *Cinderella* or *The Wizard of Oz*, that you can't imagine the world without. I remember watching it as a kid and feeling like Aladdin was a friend of mine. After all, his story is not unlike every kid's story in his struggle to become something more and his deep conviction that we are or should be more than meets the eye, a diamond in the rough. I remember that magical moment when Aladdin meets the genie. Having been abandoned by the one who promised him liberation, stuck in the Cave of Wonders with no way out, he accidentally summons the genie from a lamp. The genie wastes little time before marketing himself to Aladdin in the classic song "Friend Like Me."[4] The genie, voiced by the late Robin Williams, lays before Aladdin a smorgasbord of appealing possibilities in a spectacular display of attractions. "Can your friends do this? . . . You ain't never had a friend like me!"

I've always loved this song and the magic of that moment. I think just about everyone who has watched *Aladdin* has been enchanted by the relationship between the genie and Aladdin. But only recently did it occur to me that there is a tragic irony in their relationship. Despite the song's title, the relationship between the genie and Aladdin is anything but a friendship. Good humor and kindness aside—and even though a friendship does eventually unfold (more on that later)—the genie is essentially enslaved to Aladdin, not befriended by him. He is bound to Aladdin in a relationship of necessity. The genie's whole purpose, his very existence, depends on his ability to produce, create, offer something nobody else can, and ultimately help Aladdin achieve a respectable adulthood.

When Aladdin meets the genie, he is a diamond in the rough, shouldering the weight of social pressure to find his place in life, to ascend out of his deficiency, and to become somebody. In other words, he's an adolescent. He's gotten himself into some trouble and is in obvious need of help. But rather than help Aladdin realize that he, in fact, does not need to become something or someone else in order to be fulfilled, the genie comes along and says, "Look what I can do! Certainly, I can help you!" It turns out that Aladdin needs the genie, and the genie needs to be needed.[5] And that need turns out to be the true basis of

---

4 Howard Ashman, lyricist, and Alan Menken, composer, "Friend Like Me" on *Walt Disney Pictures Presents Aladdin: Original Motion Picture Soundtrack*. Burbank, CA: Walt Disney Records, 1992.

5 In this, in a sense, the genie truly represents the "generativity" that has traditionally defined adults in relationship to young people. As Erik Erikson has written, "mature man needs to be needed, and maturity is guided by the

their relationship. It's not a friendship; it's a transaction, a contractual partnership. They are bound to one another and (quite literally for the genie, who wears shackles on his wrists) shackled by necessity and obligation rather than liberated by joy.

Youth Worker Genies

As youth workers most of us can relate to the genie. We find ourselves doing all sorts of stunts to get young people to realize how much they need us and our ministries. Of course our tricks aren't as cool as the genie's; we can't really do magic. But we've got camps and worship bands and T-shirts with our church logo on them (that's still cool, right?) and evangelistic rock concerts and even a Facebook page (oh yeah!). Thankfully it seems that the "attractional" approach to youth ministry is on its way out,[6] but we often replace it with what Andrew Zirschky has referred to as the "moth myth"—the myth that young people, like moths, are drawn to any flashing screen. Zirschky writes, "The notion that youth, like moths, are attracted to things that plug-in and light up is truly a myth. None of these approaches are relevant to the heart cry of contemporary teenagers."[7] The temptation to become a youth worker genie lurks behind the moth myth as well: the illusion that if we can just be cool enough and flashy enough, young people will flock to us.

Youth cry out for faithful friendship, which they learn by someone putting faith in them.

---

nature of that which must be cared for. *Generativity*, then, is primarily the concern for establishing and guiding the next generation." Erik Erikson, *Identity: Youth and Crisis* (New York: W.W. Norton & Company, 1968), 138.

6 Mark Ostreicher, *Youth Ministry 3.0* (Grand Rapids, MI: Zondervan, 2008).

7 Andrew Zirschky, *Youth Ministry for the Connected but Alone Generation* (Nashville: Abingdon, 2015), 13.

We've mostly discovered that there's really no point in trying to compete with Snapchat or a Katy Perry concert, and we're learning that we shouldn't want to, either. Young people don't really want tricks or flashy gimmicks—at least not in their heart of hearts.[8] Relationship is the "heart cry" Zirschky is talking about. Young people need enduring relationships that aren't just about rewards and benefits. They are crying out for friendships that demonstrate what developmental psychologist Erik Erikson called fidelity.

Fidelity Failure

Fidelity is the ability to be faithful to something or someone. It's the vital strength, believed Erikson, that adolescents "need to have the opportunity to develop, to employ, to evoke—and *to die for*" (emphasis added).[9] According to Erikson, "'the cornerstone' of adolescence [is] the strength of being utterly true to oneself and others amid competing and contradictory value systems."[10] He wrote, "The adolescent looks most fervently for [people] and ideas to have faith in, which also means [people] and ideas in whose service it would seem worthwhile to prove oneself trustworthy."[11]

But there's a catch. As a teenager you don't wake up one day and decide to put your faith in someone. You only learn fidelity from someone who has put their faith in you. For young people to establish their own fidelity—for them to commit themselves to something or someone—they need first to experience the faithfulness of others. In other words young people need people to demonstrate unconditional

---

8 Of course, because of the reality of sin, we are all drawn, from time to time, to that which glimmers. But in our experience, when young people are given the chance to reflect on it, they have confessed that they really want something more than just a flashy screen.

9 Erik Erikson, *Identity: Youth and Crisis* (New York: W.W. Norton & Company, 1968), 232–33.

10 Kenda Creasy Dean, *Practicing Passion: Youth and the Quest for a Passionate Church* (Grand Rapids: Eerdmans, 2004), 76.

11 Erikson, *Identity: Youth*, 128–29.

relationships that endure in the face of whatever may come. Fidelity is the "even if" kind of relationship.[12] To establish their own fidelity and to construct identity, young people are looking for relationships of fidelity, people who will be true to them even if all others fall away.

Largely society does not seem to be meeting young people's need for fidelity. As I've written elsewhere, "many contemporary young people simply have not experienced enough fidelity on their behalf to acquire it themselves."[13] As a society we have become so bent on progress, achievement, and accomplishment that our social structures tend to demand fidelity from young people without demonstrating it to them. The upshot is that American young people shoulder the weight of a culture that values them for their potential to become full human beings (namely, adults) and generative participants in economic and social life but not for who they are as young people right now. Since the dawn of the industrial age, when we learned to see life as a linear progression on a scale of improvement and to view time as a commodity in the service of progressive achievement,[14] we have viewed children and young people as in transition and on their way to adulthood.[15] These conditions gave rise to stage theories of human development and eventually to the social construction of adolescence as our chief descriptor of young people's experience.[16] In other words, as the ideal of industrial progress

---

12 "For Erikson, fidelity is an unflagging commitment to an ideology that transcends the self and brings about genuineness, sincerity and a sense of duty to others." Jack O. Balswick, Pamela Ebstyne King, and Kevin S. Reimer, *The Reciprocating Self* (Downers Grove: IVP Academic, 2005), 179.

13 Kenda Creasy Dean, *Practicing Passion*, 77.

14 See John Swinton, *Becoming Friends of Time* (Waco: Baylor University Press, 2016).

15 See Chris Jenks, *Childhood*, Second Edition (New York: Rutledge, 2005), 8.

16 We consider "adolescence" a social construct, despite recent attempts to destabilize this theory. For instance, Crystal Kirgiss has shown us that the term "adolescence" was not a post-industrial invention, as some have suggested, nor is the social distinction of youth between childhood and adulthood an exclusively modern Western phenomenon (Crystal Kirgiss, *In Search of Adolescence: A New Look at an Old Idea* (San Diego: Youth Cartel, 2015). In our view,

and achievement captured our imagination in the West, it captured the way we imagined human development, too.[17] Because we were captivated by the idea of progress in the markets and in society, we began to interpret human life likewise—as proceeding through stages "from simplicity to complexity of thought, from irrational to rational behavior."[18]

North American young people are thrust into this process, pressured to achieve adulthood but often stuck in the Cave of Wonders. We expect them to become adults but afford them few adequate resources to fulfill this expectation.[19] As adults in society, we are still wrestling with how best to aid our young people in this transition and guide them through it. Unsure of what else to do, because of our penchant for progress, we hold maturity out like a carrot on a stick. It is all about improvement and expediency. What has developed through all of this is what we might call a culture of achievement and a perpetual search for affirmation. As Amy Jacober describes it, "The identification of adolescents as feeling first lost and then the almost palpable feeling of being abandoned drives them into a frenetic push for affirmation,

---

Kirgiss' historical work helps recontextualize the use of the term "adolescent" but does not refute the social construction argument sufficiently enough for us to abandon it. We maintain that youth, like childhood or any other social identity in the life course, serves as an interpretive framework and not just a nominative category, and in fact that "adolescence" began to operate as a distinctly modern interpretive framework in social science (especially developmental psychology) in the early twentieth century (Allison James and Alan Prout, eds., *Constructing and Reconstructing Childhood: Contemporary Issues in the Sociological Study of Childhood* (New York: Routledge, 1997); Jenny Hockey and Allison James, *Social Identities Across the Life Course* (New York: MacMillan, 2003); also see Andrew Root, "Adolescence and The Secular Age of Unbelief," *Perspectives* (https://perspectivesjournal.org/blog/2017/01/09/adolescence-creation-secular-age-unbelief-2/ accessed 3/8/2017).

17 See Erica Burman, *Deconstructing Developmental Psychology* (New York: Routledge, 2007), 15.

18 James and Prout, *Constructing and Reconstructing* (London: Routledge, 2015), 9.

19 See Chap Clark's concept of "systemic abandonment." Chap Clark, *Hurt* (Grand Rapids: Baker, 2004).

loyalty and solid relationships."[20] Almost every young person in America has this in common: whether they are successful or not, whether they embrace it or not, they are all responding to the enormous pressure of achievement and affirmation. Many of them, like Aladdin, find themselves stuck in the dirt with no way to achieve what is expected of them . . . until along comes a genie. Or, in our case, youth ministry.

Why Can't We Be Friends?

Youth ministry, of course, is not immune to our culture's progress/achievement narrative, and most of us have unwittingly done our share to fuel young people's (and our own) search for affirmation. Congregations tend to support youth ministry as a recruitment op, a means of ensuring that another generation of well-formed church members will one day populate the pews. Youth ministers have been infamously accused of abusing relationships with young people as a means to their own social fulfillment. But even at our best, as Andrew Root has convincingly shown, youth ministry often instrumentalizes friendships, teaching youth workers to make our relationships with teenagers a means to an end—for example, a way to earn trust until we have earned the right to ask teenagers to do something we want them to do, like come to church or youth group, or, more subtly, until we can convince them that they should become more like us. In so doing we sever the relationship between fidelity and friendship in youth ministry, making friendship in youth ministry look like relationships in so many other parts of our culture: transactions, relationships of expectation and necessity.[21]

The concept of fidelity should come naturally to the church. After all, we confess faith in a God who is there whether we "ascend to heaven" or "make [our] bed in the depths" (Ps. 139:8 NIV), a God who will never

---

20 Amy Jacober, *The Adolescent Journey: An Interdisciplinary Approach to Practical Youth Ministry* (Downers Grove: IVP, 2011), 88.

21 Andrew Root, *Revisiting Relational Youth Ministry: From a Strategy of Influence to a Theology of Incarnation* (Downers Grove: IVP, 2009).

leave us nor forsake us (Heb. 13:5 ESV) and promises that "neither death, nor life, nor angels, nor rulers, nor things present, nor things to come, nor powers, nor height, nor depth, nor anything else in all creation, will be able to separate us from the love of God in Christ Jesus our Lord" (Rom. 8:38-39 NRSV). With this core conviction, we should be different! The church should offer an alternative to the culture of achievement.

But instead of offering an alternative, youth ministry—like the genie—often markets the church as the next best way to achieve the goal. In discovering young people's need for adult relationships (and longing for professional legitimization), youth ministers got a little too excited about our own generativity, our neededness. A quick scan of the youth ministry literature of the last thirty years reveals how thoroughly we latched onto our own importance as contributors to young people's development;[22] youth ministers could be helpful mirrors through which teenagers could see their future selves and maybe (on our best days) a glimpse of Jesus to boot. So we marketed adult-youth friendship in youth ministry as a means to an end, a path to adulthood, a way for young people to get what they need. With the best of intentions, we offered teenagers the transactional bargain of a lifetime: if you (metaphorically) sign our church's contract, meet our expectations, come on our mission trips, become the people we want you to be—the church will be there for you. Ta-da! Fidelity!

As a result, rather than offering an escape from the pressure to achieve, youth ministry often became a set of new achievements that

---

22 While we believe we have overemphasized young people's developmental need for adult relationships, we acknowledge the importance of this move in helping us see our shortcomings in meeting the needs of young people and we are indebted to those who have highlighted them. The examples are too numerous for thorough citation. But see, for example, Duffy Robbins, *The Ministry of Nurture: (how to build real-life faith into your kids)* (Grand Rapids: Zondervan, 1990); Richard R. Dunn and Mark H. Senter III, ed., *Reaching a Generation for Christ: A Comprehensive Guide to Youth Ministry* (Chicago: Moody Publishers, 1997); Jim Burns and Mike DeVries, *The Youth Builder: Today's Resource for Relational Youth Ministry* (Ventura: Gospel Light, 2001); and Wayne Rice, *Generation to Generation: Family Process in Church and Synagogue* (Cincinnati: Standard, 2010).

purpose-driven young people could pursue. And for a set of young people (the purpose-driven ones), it worked. But as youth ministers themselves have slowly realized—and as less driven young people, who were essentially driven away from youth ministry, have always told us, in so many words—young people in our achievement-driven culture do not need another achievement to conquer. What they need, and what they long for, is friendship—relationships with people who genuinely delight in them and thereby help them discover and enjoy God's delight (*philos*) in them.

No one in youth ministry would disagree that young people—especially in our culture of contractual, conditional, and fleeting relationships—desperately need free, unconditional, and enduring human bonds. We call those relationships friendship. Since these are the kinds of relationships Jesus offered his friends, we're going to go out on a limb and suggest that they should set the bar for the kinds of relationships the church offers to young people. What's more, we're pretty sure these are the kinds of relationships most youth workers long to offer teenagers (even when they're critiquing friendship as the way to do it). So what would it look like to get our terms straight and call these relationships what Jesus called them—friendships?

The Joy of Friendship: Minimizing Distance, Not Difference

Some philosophers and theologians have constructed a view of friendship exclusively around the concepts of mutuality and reciprocity. These are important dimensions of friendship, but on their own they produce a definition of friendship bound to what John Swinton calls "the principle of likeness"—the idea that mutuality and reciprocity in friendship must mean the abolition of difference.[23] Even though his contributions

23 John Swinton, *From Bedlam to Shalom Towards a Practical Theology of Human Nature, Interpersonal Relationships, and Mental Health Care* (New York: Peter Lang, 2000), 79.

to our understanding of friendship can hardly be limited to this, we owe Aristotle for this idea. In Aristotle's view, because of the centrality of mutuality and reciprocity, friends must be equals—"two good people serving to actualize the virtue of goodness within their friendship relationship."[24] This would mean that young people cannot really be friends with adult youth workers. Youth will be youth and adults will be adults, so likeness is impossible. The difference will never really go away. And it is precisely when we have tried to resolve or minimize this difference that we have run into some real disasters in youth ministry. As an adult you have distinct responsibilities toward youths, just as they have their own respective responsibilities. If there is no room for difference in friendship, then adults certainly can't be friends with youths without putting their adult responsibilities at risk. But mutuality and reciprocity are not all there is to friendship. Difference is to be expected in friendship, not excepted from it. It's not social difference that must be minimized but social distance.[25]

So mutuality and reciprocity need to be oriented around another, more fundamental concept in friendship: freedom. Part of what makes friendship special is that it is freely and voluntarily chosen.[26] This freedom, in fact, is why friendship is so closely linked to joy, because joy also has freedom at its heart. Joy is essentially about delighting in God and, more important, enjoying God's delight in us. As we see it, friendship is what joy looks like in the form of a relationship. It is enduring because it is rooted in delight and, therefore, necessarily noninstrumental.[27] This

---

24 Swinton, *From Bedlam*, 83. Also see Hans S. Reinders, *Receiving the Gift of Friendship: Profound Disability, Theological Anthropology, and Ethics* (Grand Rapids, MI: Eerdmans, 2008), 358-62.

25 Erin Raffety creatively applied this distinction in academic research with children, but we find the distinction equally helpful for thinking about youth ministry. See Erin L. Raffety, "Minimizing Social Distance: Participatory Research with Children" in *Childhood* 22, No. 3 (2014): 409-22.

26 Reinders, *Receiving the Gift*, 5.

27 As Aelred of Rievaulx, the great Cistercian abbot wrote, "spiritual friendship, which we call true, should be desired, not for consideration of any worldly advantage or for any extrinsic cause, but from the dignity of its own nature and the feelings

goes all the way back to creation itself. Creation is God's free and voluntary act of making something instead of nothing—not to achieve anything but just to delight in it. Creation is not an act of necessity. Creation is an act of joy! But if we were to ask "Why did God create the world?" from the perspective of our culture of achievement, we would probably be asking, "What was God trying to achieve, or what did God want to accomplish, by creating the world?" When our mode of self-understanding is so instrumental, it makes sense that we would assume creation to be an instrument of achievement rather than an act of joy.

But if our perspective is one of freedom—if we believe that God really was free to create the world for no good reason other than the fact that it delighted God to do so[28]—then, as theologian Jürgen Moltmann reminds us, "our existence is justified and made beautiful before we are able to do or fail to do anything." The act of creation, as God's free act of joy, is the act of God befriending the world.[29] As Hans Reinders has put it, "Our being, at every moment of existence, originates from the gift of God's friendship."[30] This is the relationship that makes human and divine passion possible. It is only out of God's friendship with the world that God goes to the cross in Christ. Jesus said, "No one has greater love than this, to lay down one's life for one's friends . . . I do not call you servants. . . . I have called you friends"[31] (John 15:13,15 NRSV).

---

of the human heart, so that its fruition and reward is nothing other than itself." Aelred of Rievaulx, *Spiritual Friendship* (Notre Dame: Ave Maria, 2008), 41.

28 As Moltmann points out, this is the position of the Westminster Catechism (1647): "What is the chief end of [humankind]?" ". . . To glorify God and enjoy [God] forever." Jürgen Moltmann, *Theology and Joy* (London: S.C.M. Press, 1973), 42.

29 "[God's] freedom . . . lies in the *friendship* which he offers men and women, and through which he makes them his friends." Jürgen Moltmann, *The Trinity and the Kingdom* (Minneapolis: Fortress, 1993), 56.

30 Reinders, *Receiving the Gift*, 320.

31 As John Swinton writes, "Sacrificial friendship is the definition of love." John Swinton, *Resurrecting the Person* (Nashville: Abingdon, 2000), 43.

Striving for Joy—or Not

We want to suggest that all this makes a practical and not just a theoretical difference in the way we approach ministry with young people. If God's joy in creation is expressed through friendship, then grounding our relationships with young people in a theology of friendship ought to free us from doing somersaults to create joy in youth ministry and allow us to enjoy young people instead—and help them to enjoy one another and, especially, to name and experience God's delight in them. When we spend all our time and energy striving to achieve joy, accomplishing friendships, helping young people achieve adulthood, investing in an endless stream of antics designed to win young people's allegiance, affection, and loyalty to the church, we obscure and miss out on God's presence in the actuality of young people's concrete and lived experience.[32] We fall into a kind of works-righteousness youth ministry—which is seldom joyful and almost always exhausting. In such ministry the adult-youth friendship becomes just another professional tool that we leverage to get the job done, the way Aladdin used the genie to escape the Cave of Wonders.

But if it is true that "identity is ours by redemption, not by development,"[33] then we need a radical change of trajectory—from our orientation toward God to God's orientation toward us. Human flourishing is grounded in God's joyous action toward us, not our actions that lead to joy.[34] God's friendship offered to us, and God's love for us "does not depend on the desirability of its object," to use the words of

---

32 Andrew Root has described the theological turn in youth ministry as seeking "to share in the concrete and lived experience of young people as the very place to share in the act and being of God." Andrew Root, *Bonhoeffer as Youth Worker* (Grand Rapids: Baker Academic, 2014), 7.

33 Kenda Creasy Dean, *Practicing Passion*, 84.

34 This trajectory shift relates closely Moltmann's distinction between *futurum* ". . . what will be . . ." and *adventus* " . . . what is coming" and the eschatological shift from the progress of history to the coming of God in the world. See Jürgen Moltmann, *The Coming of God* (Minneapolis: Fortress, 1996), 25–26.

Thomas Merton, "but loves for love's sake."[35] It is the kind of relationship that is not grounded on our need for a relationship. As Swinton puts it, "The commitment to the other . . . is not enforced by obligation, custom or law, but by a desire to be with the other."[36] In other words friendship brings joy to life, undermines the culture of achievement, and refuses to be merely an instrument of pragmatic purposes—even Christian ones. Through friendship creation is revealed as God's creation and we are revealed as persons. "In friendship," Moltmann writes, "we experience ourselves for what we are, respected and accepted in our own freedom."[37]

Genie, You're Free

That's why we think Jesus grounded his ministry in friendship—and it's why we believe friendship in youth ministry is not just allowed but (ironically, perhaps) necessary. In friendship both the youths and the adults in youth ministry are invited to get beyond just trying to escape the Cave of Wonders—we are liberated from the vicious cycle of moving from one achievement to another. Remember that in Aladdin's story, real friendship isn't really revealed through the genie's tricks and gimmicks, no matter how much the song-and-dance routine portends otherwise. In the end it is Aladdin who demonstrates true friendship to the genie, not by binding the genie to himself in mutuality and reciprocity but by setting him free. Just one wish away from achieving his wish fulfillment, Aladdin chooses instead to set the genie free.

The genie responds, having anticipated exactly where the path they have been following should lead, "One bona fide prince pedigree coming up. I—what?"

---

35 Thomas Merton, "The Good Samaritan" in Thomas P. McDonnell, ed., *A Thomas Merton Reader* (New York: Doubleday, 1989), 349.

36 Swinton, *From Bedlam*, 79.

37 Jürgen Moltmann, *Church in the Power of the Spirit* (Minneapolis: Fortress, 1993), 115.

"Genie, you're free!"

At that a transformation begins. The genie's shackles fall from his wrists; the lamp that once imprisoned him falls to the ground.

Disbelieving, the genie tests his luck. "Quick, quick," he says to Aladdin. "Wish for something outrageous. Say 'I want the Nile.' Wish for the Nile. Try that!"

"I wish for the Nile."

"No way!!" The genie exalts in his new self-determination. "Oh, does that feel good! I'm free! I'm free at last! I'm hittin' the road. I'm off to see the world!"

After a somber benediction, the genie leaves his new friend. Ironic, isn't it? No sooner does the friendship begin than they part ways.[38] This does not mean that friendship always means leaving one another, but this is a symbol of what sits at the heart of true friendship. As Moltmann notes, "Friends open up free spaces for one another. . . . One element in this free human relationship is that we can also leave each other in peace. We do not constantly need to assure ourselves of our friendship. . . . What friends do for us are not services that have to be paid back."[39] In other words only through friendship can we rightfully call youth ministry a ministry by participating in God's self-giving in the world: a self-giving offered out of joy, free of charge.

Setting Our Own Genie Free

So what might youth ministry look like if the church offered young people friendship with no strings attached? What would youth ministry be if youth workers did not have to accomplish joy—if we did not need to achieve anything through our relationships with young people but

38 Not to draw too strong a connection here, but it's reminiscent of the story of the road to Emmaus in Luke 24:13-35. Just after he's revealed to his friends "in the breaking of the bread," the resurrected Jesus disappears from their sight.

39 Jürgen Moltmann, *The Living God and The Fullness of Life* (Louisville: Westminster John Knox Press, 2015), 119.

rather could approach the church as a community where young people experienced God's delight in them and could practice God's delight in others? Here are a few steps that might help us start sowing fidelity.

If Friendships Matter, Measure Them.

It's been said that you measure what matters, or what matters is what you measure. If you're the kind of person who likes clear goals and outcomes in youth ministry, friendship may seem like a counterintuitive objective. We're all for clear outcomes and metrics that help assess the success and failure of ministry programs (we use them too). We suggest adding a metric for friendship into your goals for youth ministry. But instead of asking a linear question like "Am I creating mature Christian adults in my youth ministry?" (which is another way of saying, "Am I getting these young people from point A to point B?"), we can simply ask, "Where are young people in this ministry experiencing friendship: the friendship of God? The friendship of adults? Friendships with their peers?" To be even more precise, we can ask, "Are these young people experiencing and enjoying God's delight in them?" This metric helps us remember to include the all-important relational dimension when measuring success in youth ministry, without suggesting that those friendships need to move them toward a certain goal.

Include Other People's Youths in Youth Ministry.

If youth ministry is going to help young people experience and enjoy God's delight in them, it means that we can no longer limit this opportunity to youths in our own churches. If divine joy and friendship truly stand at the beginning and not just the end of our work, then membership cannot be our criteria for inclusion in ministry. All youths need to experience God's delight in them—maybe especially those who aren't churchgoers (which, if we're honest, is most of them).

There are two exciting, growing edges of youth ministry right now. One is youth ministry in church communities overflowing with young people (yes, there are many): immigrant churches, new Christian communities, Southern Hemisphere churches—all of these, largely off the radar of North America's dominant youth ministry culture, are our next teachers of ecclesial vitality and adolescent mentoring. On the other end of the spectrum are inventive-mission churches where young people are altogether absent. These congregations also have the potential for vital youth ministries; the youths they serve just might not belong to anybody in the congregation. For churches accustomed to paying youth workers to serve congregants' children, this is a perplexing scenario—but for the majority of youth workers who are volunteers, we suspect that this is already happening, and naming it is a liberating reality.

Every youth worker can think of dozens of ways to befriend young people that demonstrate God's delight in them. If we stretch to include young people beyond our congregations, youth ministry expands to include things like adopting a school or a team, celebrating those in our community who work with young people, and taking congregants to cheer and support Sunday soccer players (instead of complaining that they're not in worship). After-school programs, bus stop hot chocolate stands, community-based SAT prep courses, pop-up cafes for studying during final exams—the list is endless for ways the Body of Christ can champion young people in our communities, extending the hand of Christian friendship to them. The point is that reaching beyond young people in our own congregations expands not only the youth roster but also the possibilities for the practice of friendship in youth ministry as well.

Make the Church a Playful Space Where God's Wonder and Delight Can Be Experienced.

Sometimes we treat play and playfulness as pesky things we have to do to keep kids interested before we do the real ministry. But if joy and friendship really motivate ministry, then church should be playful. Play is itself ministry (after all, in its most ancient form, worship was a play performed for the gods). By definition play creates a space where the only expectations are created by the game itself, which is why we get lost in games, lose track of time in a good conversation or a good book, or forget our feet in the joy of the dance. We're not performing to meet others' expectations—we are simply delighting in the play itself. When youth ministry is truly playful, it liberates young people from the need to be useful, from the need to worry constantly about status, from the constant pressure to improve and mature. Instead youth ministry invites young people to come before God in the worthlessness of free joy and friendship with the God who is joyful in God's very being.[40]

Make Church a "Practice Field" for Delight-Filled Intergenerational Friendship.

At our little church in Kingston, New Jersey, a beautiful thing happens every week. One of the families of our church opens their barn loft, which they've converted into a fully operational woodworking shop, to anyone who wants to come create things with wood. They provide the tools, support, and even the wood itself. All you have to do is come with an idea, and the Kane family helps you see it to completion. It's actually a fairly low-key activity and might sound a little mundane. But what has happened there is incredible. Each week young people gather alongside older adults. There are snacks and conversations. Together people create picture frames, peg shelves, lazy Susans, cutting boards, wooden spoons. They even break for a short devotional. And, most important, everyone enjoys each other's company. All it took for this beautiful ministry to happen was for one family to share what they love with some young people in their church.

Rethinking friendship in youth ministry frees youth workers to delight in youth as God delights in them, recognizing differences and boundaries while extending fidelity.

40 For a more extended treatment of this topic, see Wes Ellis, "Youth Ministry Games: Play as Ministry," *Kindred Youth Ministry* (November 3, 2016): http://kindredyouthministry.com/youth-ministry-games-play-as-ministry/ (accessed March 18, 2017).

Many adults are convinced that they don't know enough to work with young people. But the stuff of friendship is sharing what we love, not what we know. Churches are one of the few intergenerational communities left where young and old naturally intermingle. It may not be woodworking—maybe it's cooking, quilting, or gardening—but cultivating spaces where adults practice intergenerational friendships by sharing their passions with youths not only expands youth ministry, but it also begins to sow relationships of fidelity throughout the congregation.

Conclusion

For the record, Kim—that young person with whom I thought I couldn't be friends—did come back. In fact she remained a key member of our group until she graduated. But what I wish I would have said was not "I can't be your friend" but "Because I'm your friend, we're going to take some boundaries seriously—because you're sixteen, and I'm not. Having some rules will free us to be the people God brought together in this relationship: a young person and an adult. And that is a beautiful thing." Rethinking the practice of friendship in youth ministry not only gives young people a way out of the culture of achievement's Cave of Wonders, but it also frees youth workers to stop using our relationships with young people as means to accomplish certain goals and frees us to delight in youth as God delights in them, recognizing our differences while extending fidelity to them. There are rules to the game—especially in a world that has been so broken by sin and injustice—and we need to take them seriously. But we are invited to play. We are invited to stop instrumentalizing our relationships, instrumentalizing ourselves, and start delighting in young people, inviting them to delight in the joy of God's friendship with them. Friendship is not a mistake. Friendship—true friendship—is the heart of youth ministry.

4

Purpose

Finding Joy in Life Direction

PAMELA EBSTYNE KING AND STEVEN ARGUE

You have undoubtedly noticed that teenagers come to dread a particular question that adults ask with increased frequency and intensity the closer teens come to the end of their high school careers: "What are you doing after graduation?" Even graduation ceremonies seem to rush through any celebration of accomplishment toward giving advice about "what's next." I (Steve) recently spoke at one of these ceremonies. I told the students that perhaps the well-meaning comments adults make evoke different meanings for them:

> "I'm proud of you" sounds like "Don't ever disappoint us."
>
> "You've worked hard" is heard as "You think high school was hard? Just wait until college, military, and work!"
>
> "You can be anything you want to be" feels like a warning: "You can be anything—as long as you remain the best."
>
> "You did it!" acts like a demand: "And . . . you . . . must . . . keep . . . doing it. You can never stop or rest."

What surprised me were the visceral responses I heard from the student section—groans, nods, and wide-eyed stares at each other. Somehow I managed to name the elephant in the commencement room, and perhaps the teenagers were happy that an adult saw it too. It makes us wonder if we adults spend more time asking teenagers about their life's purpose without considering their life's joy. Emphasizing purpose without joy seems to put teenagers into pressure cookers that they all feel deeply.

What if we were to ask teenagers instead "What brings you joy?" This question is not a typical conversation starter with youths—or anyone, for that matter. In fact rather than launching a conversation, it is more likely to elicit blank stares or verbal fumbling. We don't think it's because people don't have an answer. It's just hard to name. It's a challenging question, especially if you cannot articulate what matters to you.

One way for young people to understand what matters at a practical level is for them to identify a purpose in their life. We are not necessarily talking about their grand, existential purpose in life (though we will talk more about this below); we are referring to an actual and achievable goal or aim that informs how one lives, how one spends their time, and what one believes in. So if you ask "Got joy?" we would respond, "Got purpose?"

For clarity let's make sure we are clear on the difference between happiness and joy. Happiness is well recognized for being a pleasant or positive feeling in response to something that occurred. We feel happy because we experienced something or something came to mind that we deem good.

Joy = feeling + reflection

Joy is a bit more complicated, as it is more than an emotional response. Joy involves a "cognitive appraisal" (that's geek-speak for when we reflect on an experience that moves us). It is a positive feeling that involves conscious or unconscious reflection on what matters. As a result one can experience joy not only in experiences that bring happiness but also in the face of suffering or loss. For instance a teenager might feel disappointment over not making a team but still be able to find joy that a friend made the team instead. In this case joy involves reflection or reframing.

Understanding that joy combines both feeling and reflection helps us appreciate Paul's reminder to the Jesus followers in Rome: "And not only that, but we also boast in our sufferings, knowing that suffering produces endurance, and endurance produces character, and character produces hope" (Rom. 5:3–4 NRSV). Through the lens of happiness, this statement sounds dreadful, depressing, even masochistic. Feelings alone will make us flee this moment. Through the perspective of joy, Christians' beliefs frame a richer picture where feelings are not the end but the beginning of a transformative moment. If our hearts our broken, might we become more compassionate? If we are hurt by someone, might it teach us to forgive? If we are disappointed, might it teach us to be even more diligent? Christians are more than naive spiritual optimists. But hope and joy are rooted in the gospel of love, grace, and redemption.

As you might guess, joy doesn't usually come naturally, but we can cultivate it—on purpose. It takes practice. Just as we work out and train our bodies at a gym, we can train and cultivate "joy muscles." Now the religious things we do in and through our faith communities start to make more sense. Prayer, worship, participating in other spiritual disciplines and Christian community are forms of working out—they are exercises that enable us to see things more clearly and consistently through the eyes of Christ. In this way our interpretive responses become more natural—like a golfer who has perfected her swing, the birdwatcher who knows where to look, or the artist who instinctively grabs the right brush. Our joy muscles or instincts know what to do, where to look, and how to reflect.

Even though the goal is for joy to become natural, it doesn't always come naturally. It takes discipline, time, and consistency for it to become a habit. Young people are starting to learn discipline, navigate time, and establish habits, so it is up to adults to help them by establishing a frame that allows them to grow in joy. Joy, then, is no longer an abstract or isolated idea but becomes part of our everyday practice, thinking, and outlook. Thus #joyonpurpose is like a life-hashtag (mantra) that shows up in our choices, our relationships, and our aspirations.

Because of the interpretive aspect of joy, we need to know what matters and how we make sense of the world. No doubt we offer young people the frame of faith—the gospel narrative; the story of crucifixion and resurrection; life, death, and new life; our basis for hope. But in a teen's daily life experiences of brains bursting with growth, bodies bursting with hormones, and buddies bursting or bruising friendships, such abstract and lofty ideals of faith are often too far afield to make a difference. But when faith gets applied or translated into a practical, achievable purpose that has more immediate implications for how a young person lives or plans their days, weeks, and months, then having a purpose can provide a more immediate and practical sense of what matters. In the following section, we discuss specifically what we mean by this kind of purpose.

Even though the goal is for joy to become natural, it doesn't always come naturally.

Joy on Purpose

The title of this chapter has two meanings. Not only can we be purposeful about cultivating joy (#joyonpurpose meaning number 1), but also young people can experience more joy when they have a purpose (#joyonpurpose meaning number 2). Youth purpose is actually a burgeoning area of study within developmental psychology.[1] Research clearly reveals that having a sense of purpose is associated with higher

1 People leading this research include William Damon, the director of the Center on Adolescence at Stanford University; Kendall Cotton Bronk at Claremont Graduate School; and Ben Houltberg at the Thrive Center for Human Development at Fuller Theological Seminary.

grades, good health, and greater sense of well-being.[2] As my (Pam's) fourteen-year-old would say, purpose is "lit"! But it's important to note that not all life goals have such benefits. In particular purpose refers to a "stable and generalized intention to accomplish something that is at the same time meaningful to the self and consequential for the world beyond the self."[3] We point out four specific points in this definition. A purpose is

1. stable and enduring;
2. intended to accomplish something;
3. meaningful and relevant to an individual young person; and
4. constructive and contributes to the world beyond the young person.

Purpose Is Stable and Enduring.

This does not mean that it is lifelong, especially in the case of an adolescent, but that the purpose has a meaning significant enough to endure mild fluctuations of interest or obstacles. For something to count as a purpose for young people, it has to be compelling enough to keep them committed, even in the face of challenges or distractions. Interests might change and be more fleeting, but purposes captivate and are longer lasting.

Purpose Involves a Specific Aim to Accomplish Something.

We are not just talking about having a sense of meaning in life; a purpose actually involves a goal of achieving something tangible. When asking youths about their purpose in life, kids give a variety of answers. Some have no idea. Some may say something general like "to glorify God," and others will describe something more specific such as raising

---

2 See K. C. Bronk, *Purpose in Life: A Component of Optimal Youth Development* (New York: Springer, 2013).

3 W. Damon, *Path to Purpose: How Young People Find Their Calling in Life* (New York: Free Press, 2008), 33.

awareness of global poverty levels or raising money to provide water wells for African children. The most effective and transformative purposes are those that are more concrete and attainable.

Purpose Is Meaningful and Relevant to an Individual Young Person.

Accordingly the goal aligns with the youth's interests and abilities. Purposes arise out of emerging lifelong desires. Although adolescents often do not know their vocation or calling, they have some awareness, or with some encouragement and affirmation can become aware, of their deep yearnings. For example a young person who is passionate about cooking might pursue a purpose involving nutrition or food. Whether or not this becomes a vocation only time will tell, but it still reveals something meaningful to them.

Purpose Is Constructive and Contributes to the World beyond the Young Person.

William Damon describes this kind of purpose as "noble purpose."[4] Goals or aims that do not further the social good at some level do not count as a purpose. So in the latter example, a young person passionate about cooking and food might work to provide meals for the homeless in their community or raise money for an international organization that plants nutritious indigenous crops.

Attempting to tie this all together, we suggest that pursuing a purpose is living out what matters. To take another example, Audrey, an extremely gifted runner, has a deep desire to help kids in poverty. Given her interest in running and connections with local schools and track clubs, she develops a specific purpose: to send shoes to children in developing nations. She finds an organization that will distribute shoes in Africa, and she leverages her connections and has other teens donate used athletic

---

4 William Damon, *Noble Purpose: The Joy of Living a Meaningful Life* (Philadelphia: Templeton Foundation Press, 2003).

shoes that she collects, cleans, and gives to the organization that ships and distributes them. Based on Audrey's interests and capacities, she identified a specific and actionable goal that she could work toward.

Telos: The Place #joyonpurpose Takes Us

A critique of what we have presented up to this point may be that all this talk of joy and purpose sounds like self-absorption. As Christians the gospel calls us toward God and toward each other. Sanctification makes us both more holy and more human. We believe that we find purpose and joy as we move toward God and one another and become more fully who God created us to be. To emphasize this point, we add one other aspect of joy and purpose to our understanding that frames the panoramic picture we hope you will see. One way of understanding what matters is to draw on that biblical concept of *telos*. *Telos* is Greek for "purpose" or "goal" and conveys a sense of ultimacy. Theology uses it to refer to God's purposes or goal for humankind. So human *telos* refers to God's intention or goal for humanity.

As a developmental psychologist, when I (Pam) think about the point of human development or wondering what people are growing or maturing toward, I often ask what is the goal or purpose of human development from God's perspective.[5] We Christians often default to important but esoteric statements like "glorifying God" or "loving God and loving others." These theological phrases can be inspirational, but they rarely help Jesus followers in their everyday lives. We hope these guidelines on purpose can help you encourage young people you know to identify a specific purpose that points them toward a meaningful way to glorify God in their lives.

Let's explore what this might mean by considering the four elements of purpose. Stable and long-lasting purpose reminds us that

5 See J. O. Balswick, P. E. King, and K. S. Reimer, *The Reciprocating Self: Theological Perspectives on Development*, 2nd ed. (Downers Grove, IL: IVP Academic, 2016).

the things we do that matter can have a developmental trajectory that grows with us. Purpose takes time, coaching, development. Through this pursuit one finds her or his unique voice and contribution. As Christians we recognize this process as sanctification. Drawing on the doctrine of the image of God, we become like Christ, which means following Jesus into the unique creations that God has created us to be (Ps. 139), to use the gifts God has given each of us (1 Cor. 12–14). Thus the Christian view of *telos* as conformity to Christ does not mean uniformity to Christ. We are each called to become like Christ as our unique selves.

Purpose with a goal or aim to accomplish something shows us that our efforts point to something about the way we make sense of ourselves, God, and the world. Achievements along the way do not always come easily or predictably. Instead they evoke internal and external challenges that transform and expand our view of self, God, and others. The Bible tells us that Jesus is the perfect image of God (Col. 1:15). Becoming more like Jesus is part of our goal (or *telos*) and a means of glorifying God. This work inspires us to live into who God sees us to be, while also trusting that God promises to complete the good work God has started in us (Phil. 1:6).

Purpose, now, becomes meaningful and relevant. It draws from something deeper in people where, no matter the work or even the outcome, working toward their purpose is "worth it." In seeking to understand adolescent spirituality, Christian Smith and Melinda Lundquist Denton observe that young people's views of the world shape the way they see meaning in their decisions.[6] Those who believe we live in a "morally insignificant universe" see moral commitments, decisions, obligations, and actions as having little impact beyond their own lives. On the other hand, those who hold to a "morally significant universe" see their lives connected with something bigger where their actions affect others beyond themselves. They identify a *telos* where their lived

6 Christian Smith with Melinda Lundquist Denton, *Soul Searching: The Religious and Spiritual Lives of American Teenagers* (Oxford: Oxford University Press, 2005).

lives contribute to an ultimate goal. The Christian narrative's *telos* frames for young people what matters in a meaningful context and trajectory.

Purpose is constructive and contributes in a socially meaningful manner. Our pursuit of what really matters is more than a self-focused exercise; it expands people's view of how their efforts connect with others' efforts and challenges around them. Purpose becomes no longer atomized but finds its context in a larger narrative that connects people with something bigger than themselves. For Christians this means that purpose becomes about more than "me"; it also becomes about "we." Humans grow toward their ultimate purpose, becoming more Christ-like as their unique selves and contributing to the greater world. Figure 1 illustrates this threefold sense of *telos*—that involves becoming more like Christ as one is uniquely suited and as one discovers a meaningful contribution to the world around them.

This threefold *telos* depicts a way that a young person can understand a sense of purpose. Pursuing a purpose should always take Christians deeper into discipleship; it should always draw us further into the ways—the character and actions—of Christ. A young person's purpose

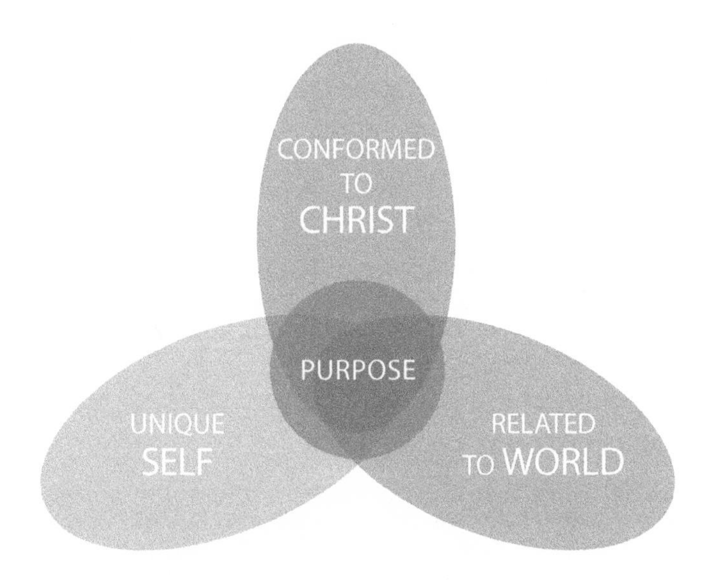

Figure 1: Purpose in light of a threefold sense of *telos*

should always be consistent with their passions and personality. It should delight them and motivate them—not be drudgery or a dreary duty. Lastly a purpose is not just about bettering oneself or becoming more oneself; it is not just self-serving or about personal satisfaction. Rather it is about service to others, contributing and making a difference.

So How Do You Get Purpose?

Given that purpose is "lit"—such a promising source of joy—how does a young person get purpose? Dr. Belle Liang and her colleagues at Boston College agreed that purpose sounded great for kids, but they were suspicious. Sure, this is fantastic, they thought—for those who have the luxury of having and pursuing a noble purpose. But what about kids from less privileged backgrounds? What about kids who might be more oriented toward surviving than thriving? In short they looked at purpose among ten less advantaged youths in a College Bound program and found that they also described having purpose in their lives.[7]

In their study the researchers identified four interrelated themes around the development of purpose. Conveniently they all start with *p*. They are known as the four P's of purpose: (1) people, (2) prosocial benefits, (3) propensity, and (4) passion.

People

The young people in the study described the way adults in their lives, like parents, teachers, and coaches, played an important role in inspiring, affirming, and supporting them in finding and refining their purpose. For example one youth described how their mentor noticed them in a group of thirty kids and suggested that the student be placed in

---

7 B. Liang, A. White, A. M. DeSilva Mousseau, A. Hass, L. Knight, D. Berado, and T. J. Lund, "The Four P's of Purpose among College Bound Students: People, Propensity, Passion, Prosocial Benefits," *Journal of Positive Psychology* 12, no. 3 (2017): 281–94.

an honors program. In another study a boy talked about how an adult from a church would drive him to worship band practice so he could pursue his passion of leading worship.

Prosocial Benefits

The youths in this study were motivated to pursue their purpose because it benefited others. In the case of this study, youths talked about helping various family members. For example, one student talked about wanting to be able to help his mom buy a house. Another said, "I know there's a lot of kids that really need help, but they don't know where to go for it. So I want to be that person to help them."[8]

Propensity

Students' explanations also included their excelling in competencies and skills important for attaining their purpose. In addition youths were aware that they had personalities suited to their particular purpose. For example, one student described why she had what it takes to become a nurse practitioner by elaborating on several personal qualities: "I definitely am a good student academically . . . school's very important to me. I'm very outgoing. I like to try new things, meet new people, very kind and caring, determined and ambitious about my goals and my future."[9]

Passion

In addition these kids had a passion for what they were pursuing. They deeply enjoyed the activities associated with it. Their deep interest in the area propelled and sustained their commitment to it. One student explained that she wanted to be a child psychologist " 'cause I'm really interested in how the mind works and how kids develop."[10] She realized that there were many children in the world in need of help—including

---

8 Liang et al., "The Four P's," 6.

9 Liang et al., 8.

10 Liang et al., 8.

a childhood friend—and she decided she wanted to make a difference for such children.

These four themes break into two major dimensions: influences on purpose (i.e., capability and motivation) and sources of such influences (i.e., intrinsic and extrinsic). These categories are not intended to capture opposites but rather to identify resources that shape purpose. In particular purpose is shaped by capability and motivation, which in turn can be intrinsic or extrinsic. For example people are an external resource, whereas propensity is an internal resource. Being motivated by benefiting another person (e.g., prosocial benefits) is an external motivator. Passion is an internal motivator.

Young People, Their Faith, and Their #joyonpurpose

When youths live and serve out of an authentic and meaningful expression of themselves, they experience the significance of their own passions and their effectiveness, and this is deeply empowering. When kids have an identifiable sense of purpose that they can effectively pursue, they gain a clear and immediate sense of what matters. This becomes an excellent frame for joy! In the ebb and flow of life—decisions, friendships, emotions, wins and losses, highs and lows—they will have a frame through which to view these experiences. A lived purpose incorporates beliefs, values, hopes, desires, and passions; offers a more immediate reference for interpreting emotions and what matters; and ultimately enables kids to thrive and experience joy.

As adults (especially ministry leaders and parents), we want this for our young people. The challenge comes in how we might create environments to teach and encourage joy on purpose.

See Purpose Framed in Faith as a Joy Booster

No doubt purpose is not the only resource of joy available to youth, but it is an especially effective source of joy, because pursuing a purpose concentrates important joy boosters in a young person's life. Purpose framed through faith serves as a means for activating young people's ideals in their daily living—translating beliefs and values into actions with an enduring commitment. Purpose framed through faith equips young people to identify and pursue that purpose by helping them develop (1) an awareness of what's important—one's beliefs and values; (2) a social network of people that are aligned with one's purpose; and (3) a sense of transcendence or being a part of something bigger. In this way purpose serves as a joy booster by providing young people with clarity about what matters to them, a community of like-minded people, and a deeper connection to God.

Encourage Purposeful Choices to Help Young People Discover Their Values and Beliefs

Although purpose does not require clearly articulating one's complete worldview or writing one's own personal rule of life, it can serve as the way a young person puts a stake in the ground on what matters to her or him. Purpose consolidates and activates what is significant to young people. This puts a whole new spin on their choices and schedules as they discover that they cannot do or be everything and that making a choice often means saying yes to one thing and no to another. Do I

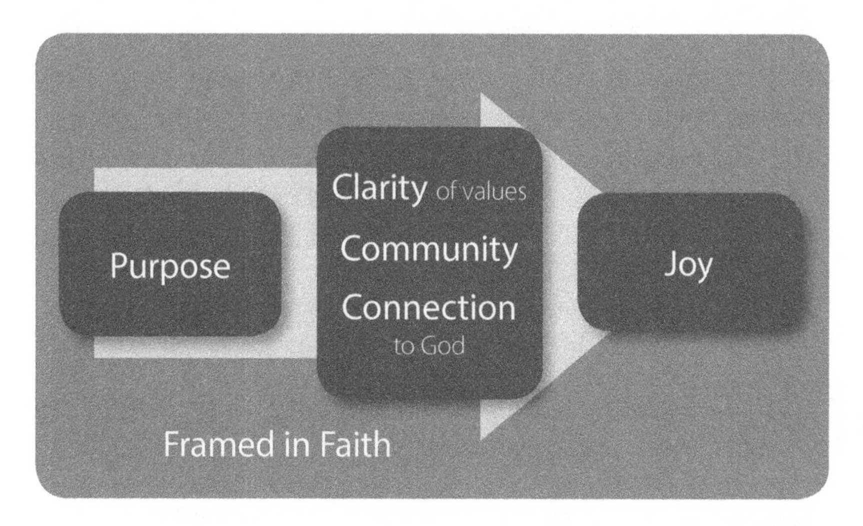

Figure 2: Purpose framed through faith

stand with my friend and endanger my popularity? Do I go to church even though I have tons of homework? Do I volunteer or search for a job that pays something? Do I risk getting involved or not? Certainly young people will make good and bad choices along the way. If adults can see their choices beyond goodness/badness and instead use these opportunities to talk with young people about what really matters to them, these events can turn into meaning-making moments.

Leverage Purpose for Connection and Support

Research shows that youths who pursue a purpose end up with high levels of social capital.[11] The activities in which youths participate in order to carry out their purpose engage them with adults and peers who hold similar interests. This results in increased opportunities to be surrounded by positive peer and adult influences. Additionally individuals who share deeply held interests have increased chances of having meaningful and highly trusting relationships. Thus pursuing a purpose is a great way to make really positive and strong friendships and be surrounded by supportive and caring adults.

There is something significant to consider here. Often in congregations we group people by age and/or gender. Might it be even more effective to group people based on their purposeful interests? What if the artists in the congregation met to encourage each other's' projects? What if the businesspeople joined with business majors to talk about faith, ethics, entrepreneurialism, or the triple bottom line? What if teachers gathered to explore pedagogy? What if those who

11 Social capital refers to benefits that a person has access to through relationships. In this case, several studies have demonstrated that pursuing purpose connects youth to like-minded and supportive adults and peers. See Belle Liang and S. G. Ketcham, "Emerging Adults' Perceptions of Their Faith-Related Purpose," *Psychology of Religion and Spirituality* (2017); doi:10.1037/rel0000116. For further information on social capital and religion, see Pamela E. King and James L. Furrow, "Religion as a Resource for Positive Youth Development: Religion, Social Capital, and Moral Outcomes," *Developmental Psychology* 40 (2004): 703–13.

have particular interests in race relations, homelessness, or immigration gathered to implement next practical steps? What if all these groups shared their conversations with the whole community? Purpose could be a more compelling force by joining people by similar passions rather than by demographics.

Keep an Eye on Transcendence and Fasten Your Seatbelts

Furthermore, pursuing a noble purpose as we have described in this chapter provides youth with the experience of connecting with something beyond themselves. For young people of faith, following a purpose is usually their faith in action—and then they experience their purpose as a part of something much bigger than themselves. For instance, a young person's effort to care for animals at an animal shelter is part of their efforts at tending to God's creation. They can experience their actions as more significant than just acting on their affection for furry creatures but as part of God's work on earth. "When you know the story to which you belong, and when you know your role in that story, you have a profound sense of purpose. That is what we are invited into: The ultimate story—God's ongoing work in this world. When we find ourselves contributing to a greater story, we thrive."[12]

In addition when young people make a recognizable impact on the broader world around them, they are deeply affirmed and experience a sense of their own efficacy. When kids get a taste of their ability to make a difference, it enlivens and encourages them. Even if the impact is small and only affects their family, kids who recognize that they are contributing to someone or something beyond themselves realize that they are an active part of a world and reality that are bigger than themselves. Contribution and connection provide a sense of transcendence and continue to motivate young people to grow into thriving adults.

---

12 P. E. King, "The Reciprocating Self: Trinitarian and Christological Anthropologies of Being and Becoming," *Journal of Christianity and Psychology* 35, no. 3 (2016): 15–32.

Whether for believers or for nonreligious youth, purpose serves to identify and activate one's values, engages young people in meaningful social networks, and allows youths to experience that they are part of something bigger. In this way purpose becomes a means to lived faith. It is a great means of exploring what matters. It often puts people on the pathway to vocation. In a world where so much is about competition and consumption, it's a great antidote to focusing and worrying about oneself and also a promising source of joy.

Creating Ecosystems for #joyonpurpose

As much as we adults are tempted to, we cannot pick our young people's purposes for them. They undertake this process, and it is our role to create environments and opportunities for them to discover and live into their purposes, which will bring them joy. Further if the Christian life is all about ensuring good behavior in our young, we short-circuit their process of discovering and embracing who they are as people created in the image of God, uniquely connected to something bigger than themselves, where their gifts, talents, and purposes can bless their communities and even the whole world. Adults are tempted to try to control this process, but it is better for them to create environments or ecosystems that allow young people to grow into their joy on purpose.

Know Christ . . . Know Your Purpose

The Apostle Paul makes a quite compelling appeal in his letter to the Philippian believers. In chapter 3 he admits that he wants to "know Christ" and seems to want his readers/listeners to join him in that pursuit. This concept of "knowing" (*ginōskō*) is closely connected with the Hebrew word *yada* found in Psalm 46:10, which appeals to the reader to be still and "know" God. This "knowing" has a quality of bringing together theoretical understanding and the actual experience of something. "Knowing" forms the intersection.

Good learning theory recognizes that people are not blank slates ready to be filled with knowledge. Nor do people always live out what they know. Rather people sometimes have experiences that they can't articulate. Or they live their way into understanding. This is important and, perhaps, a challenge to ministry leaders and parents. Adults default to giving their young people information. Are you sad? Read this Bible verse. Are you doubting? Read this book. Are you behaving badly? Listen to this sermon. This is not enough for young people, and it doesn't seem to be enough for Paul, either. He is exhibit A for holding plenty of knowledge that was not transformative until he encountered the resurrected Christ. But that seems to have changed him forever. His purpose then became to know Christ in the fullest sense.

Content and Context: An Ecosystem for Knowing Christ

In light of Paul's declared purpose, how might we cultivate such vision for our young people? While we can't dictate their knowing or prescribe their purpose, we can create an ecosystem where knowing Christ and their purpose can grow. This ecosystem resides in the knowing intersection of knowledge and experience. We cultivate an ecosystem for knowing by being committed to excellent content embedded in nurturing contexts. By content and context, we mean the following.

Content refers to the curricular scope and sequence that have been developed to ensure theologically sound and developmentally appropriate teaching and learning. For ministry leaders this includes weekly programming, small group resources, and retreat materials that help young people understand the Christian narrative of which they are part. For parents this includes regular dialogue with your kids about life, faith, and the Christian story your family desires to live within. Great content invites students to connect their stories to God's story. Great content needs great teachers, and the best teaching starts with the learner in mind, as the teacher artfully evokes their imaginations and connects concepts with their experiences. As Christians we believe we have a great story. We need to be great storytellers! It is the responsibility of the ministry leader to faithfully tell this good story, which is rooted in the faithful teaching of Christianity's narrative theology.

The term *context* indicates relational environments that are safe and nurturing, which young people need. Like learning to be great teachers, adults must learn to be great environmentalists. Are the relational spaces at church, youth group, and home safe, nurturing spaces? Do our young people feel comfortable enough to share what they really feel, offer what they really think, ask their real questions, or doubt something they think they're supposed to believe? If content is about teaching the Christian narrative well, context is about creating space for young people to live into the Christian narrative through their thinking, doubting, feeling, and acting.

When adults prioritize content and context, they create an environment where it is possible for a young person to know Christ, pursue their purpose, and experience joy. This is good news to a young person.

Content and Context in Motion

Content and context assume something we have hinted at throughout this chapter. They assume that young people often discover their purpose more than deliberate on this pursuit. Purpose is rather abstract, and young people's shorter, less experienced lives affect how they reflect on their purpose. Still, as we have suggested, they have interests and passions and frequently choose what matters most to them. Adults who create environments that emphasize helpful, age-appropriate content and context provide space for young people to discover their purpose. Table 1 on page 108 lays out a way to consider content and context for those ages twelve through their twenties.

Broadly speaking, table 1 reminds adults that because of human development, seeking purpose is "in motion." Thus parents and ministry leaders must constantly be working to nurture the best environments (through content and context) to encourage young people to discover their purpose. Finally note—at the very bottom—that adults cannot attempt this from a distance. We are not fixing young people or ensuring that they grow. Any of our attempts to encourage our young people to know Christ and know their purpose invite us to reflect on our own knowing. We share in this attempt together, owning with them the beautiful and scary discoveries about God's own calling on our lives.

Igniting Sparks in an Environment Full of Surprises

The late Peter Benson, former president of Search Institute, described youths as sparks waiting to be ignited. He challenged adults not to think of them as vessels waiting to be filled but rather sparks that deserve to be lit and fanned into major flames.[13]

From a Christian view, Benson's words ring true and remind us, as adults, that one of the best things we can do for our young people is not to try to control their faith, their purpose, or their joy but to call out the sparks in their lives. Young people need adults to do what they often cannot do for themselves: speak to their image-bearing-ness. Let's catch them doing things right; let's point out the qualities we see in them; let's celebrate their talents; let's join them in working through the brokenness they see around them; and let's remind them that they are made in the image of God. They are good, they have value, and they have purpose.

Don't let these thoughts on purpose end as aspirations. Make them happen—on purpose. We offer a fully scripted lesson that we hope you will find inspiring, that sets the stage for thinking about #joyonpurpose, and that provides the opportunity for young people to begin to identity their purpose. This exercise is based on the threefold understanding of *telos* presented above in figure 1. Feel free to copy the diagram or make your own version that youths fill out to begin to identify their gifts and passions; the places and ways they enjoy making a difference; and how they feel God is calling them to be more like Jesus as a way of identifying their purpose. In addition have your teens or young adults identify five steps necessary to accomplishing their purpose—including what

---

13 Peter L. Benson, *Sparks: How Parents Can Help Ignite the Hidden Strengths of Teenagers* (San Francisco: Jossey-Bass, 2008). Peter L. Benson, "Sparks: How Youth Thrive" (April 22, 2011), https://www.youtube.com/watch?v=TqzUHcW58Us

Table 1: Content and Context Ecosystem for Young People

	Middle School Adolescent [ages 12–14]	**High School Adolescent [ages 14–18]**	**Emerging Adult [ages 18–20s]**
Content	**Learning the story of God** Encourage questions of content by inviting them into the story. For example: What's going on? What do you see? How would you feel? What's cool? What's strange? **Great content here** teaches them the Christian story and shows them how this narrative is unfolding; it is not random. **Avoid** moralism that reduces teaching to demanding behaviors. The goal is discovery, not behavior modification.	**Practicing the story of God** Encourage questions of congruency by inviting them to "walk out" the Christian story. For example: You believe in forgiveness; who do you need to forgive? What does compassion look like for the students in your school that are the least popular? Is generosity possible—and how—when you don't feel like you have very much money? **Great content here** teaches them to consider how the story frames their life perspectives. It calls them to bring their believing and their living of faith closer together. **Avoid** giving quick answers. The best teaching here is patient and willing to let young people discover what following Jesus can mean, what it might cost them, and what they might discover.	**Extrapolating the story of God** Draw out questions of meaning. Often it is the emerging adult who now brings questions to the Christian narrative. With their lives now being more specialized and diverse, faith must be extrapolated. There is less a "right answer" and more a "faithful next step." **Great content here** acknowledges nuance and offers room to challenge, doubt, and create new ways forward in their faith journeys. **Avoid** controlling the conversations. Curate their comments and learn to speak back to them what they are processing. Tap into biographies of people who have searched for purpose in their own lives. Ask how they resonate with stories, movies, or novels.

Table 1, cont.

	Middle School Adolescent [ages 12–14]	**High School Adolescent [ages 14–18]**	**Emerging Adult [ages 18–20s]**
Context	**Space to explore and experience** 1. Be sensitive to the development of middle school students and their need for space to learn, understand . . . and learn and understand! 2. Recognize that play, fun, and adults who are interested in them make these spaces meaningful.	**Space for honesty about fears and doubts** 1. There are few spaces where high schoolers feel like they can be their real selves. Encourage an accepting environment where they can ask honest questions and express real doubts. They need this space to make their faith their own. 2. Create space where you can celebrate with them in the good times and walk with them in the hard times.	**Space for dialogue and creativity** 1. Emerging adults need more than calls to conformity. The spaces they need will hold differing views, encourage thoughtful dialogue, and point them toward "third way" solutions. 2. Create space that values their relational (often beyond church or home) rather than programmatic participation.
Environment Killers	An uninteresting environment (faith/formation matters in daily life).	An unsafe environment (questioning faith is essential, expected, and encouraged).	An undynamic environment (their faith looks different from that of parents and needs community).
	For all of these periods, an environment not shared by others rarely nurtures faith and purpose. As adults, we are in this together. Learning and transformation are desired and expected by all, not just those we think we're ministering to or parenting.		

experiences they need to gain and what kind of support they need from friends, family, and other adults. You might even have them post a "WikiHow." We recommend that, in the context of your youth group, individuals reevaluate their "purpose *telos*" annually, encouraging reflection on what gives joy. Of course groups can always support a social media campaign where young people, their families, and leaders tweet and post images about #joyonpurpose.

Conclusion

One of the amazing things about joy is that it is vitalizing. Joy is a virtue unto itself, but it also goes somewhere—toward our *telos*. It's pointing us to a more profound way of being and living where purpose is the fuel for true joy. Joy gives us energy and motivation—it calls out reflection and so drives our purposes. Joy has an expanding effect that helps us to be more human and more holy as our purposes draw us toward one another. The more we pursue purpose, the more opportunity there is for joy. The more joy we experience, the more we are propelled to pursue our purpose. Pursuing a purpose is powerful. Please note that having a purpose is not the point. It is not only the content or aim of the purpose but also the pursuing or taking action that activates all the potential resources for joy. Pursuing purpose is a joy booster. When identified and followed thoughtfully, purpose prevents young people from defaulting to inspiring but abstract statements like glorifying God or loving God and loving others. A specific purpose enables youth to honor God in their everyday lives. Such a purpose equips young people to pursue something meaningful to themselves and the greater world. Since these purposes have more an ultimate *telos* that inspires our efforts and promotes joy, how might we think about "joy on purpose" not merely as an inspirational slogan but an ongoing declaration that gives traction to our everyday lives? Perhaps a modern-day prayer might be this: *Lord Jesus, may our everyday actions automatically tweet #joyonpurpose as we bless you, bless others, and are blessed ourselves. Amen.*

5

Worship

Dancing in the Joy of the Trinity

Fred P. Edie and Alaina Kleinbeck

As veteran youth workers, we have experienced more than the typical dose of youth worship. (Fred has the hearing loss to prove it!) Over the last decade, we have also participated in a very different pattern and style of joyful worship in a community that blends young people and adults together in all kinds of cultural worship styles following a pattern featuring word and sacrament. We'll say more about that worship below, but for now we want to share a story of worshipful anger transformed to joy.

A few years back, the first worship service in this (temporary) community included "Aaron," who was then a sixteen-year-old high school student formed to worship in a grand if slightly starchy liturgical church. Just across the aisle was "Pete," the same age and stage as Aaron but, unlike him, formed to worship in a "happy-clappy" Pentecostal free church. From the first downbeat of the opening song of praise, Pete *praised.* He danced and shouted and sang with all his heart. Aaron (he of the grand solemnity) was aghast at Pete's seeming disrespect, to

Joy breaks in, then, through worship, breaks out and spills over everything.

the point that he crossed the aisle and told him to shut up. Pete was baffled and dismayed.

The community continued to worship together over the next week. Each night featured a worship practice not often included in youth worship: there was public confession of sin, a gesture of pardon, and an invitation to share Christ's peace with one another. Through the week Aaron and Pete had discovered their common humanity. In addition the Spirit had been working on Aaron. One night at worship, when it came time for the community to confess sin and be reconciled, he crossed the aisle again, but this time he begged Pete's forgiveness for failing days before to recognize his joyous worshipful praise for what it was. Forgiveness granted (no small thing!); the two then hugged one another in great joy as they exchanged the peace of Christ.

This really happened. And while in this case things admittedly got off to a rough start, it illustrates our contention that Christian worship may become for young people a primary setting for receiving and practicing divine joy, the joy that ultimately undergirds lives of flourishing. Below, therefore, we try to describe in general terms what joyous worship rich in word and sacrament can look like when it is fully inclusive of young people and to offer some theological support for worship as a crucial delivery system for joy. In addition we highlight what kinds of attitudes, practices, and knowledge help form young people capable of receiving this amazing Spirit gift. We're aware that many theorists of adolescence describe teens as uniquely primed for joy.[1] Developmentally speaking, they are a party waiting to happen, and when invited, they bring joy to whatever they're up to. Yet we also believe Christian joy ultimately springs as a gift from worshipful encounters with the transcendent God who comes as near as our own hearts through the incarnation of the Son by the power of the Holy Spirit.

---

1 For example, see G. Stanley Hall, *Adolescence: Its Psychology and its Relations to Physiology, Anthropology, Sociology, Sex, Crime, Religion and Education* (New York: Appleton, 1915), 131.

Background

We fancy ourselves part of a new breed of youth ministry leaders, theologically savvy and serious about authentic youth discipleship. When it came time to develop our own ministry, therefore, we ruled out the tendencies of youth ministry to devolve into mere entertainment or fun. In place of Mad Libs, lock-ins, and trendy group games, we fashioned robust worship grounded in scripture and sacrament, missional outreach to the community, theological reflection on texts and contexts, mentoring for Christian leadership, and urgent discernment of baptismal vocations for ministry.[2] Even so, while we labored toward serious formation, our students steadfastly refused NOT to enjoy it. Passing Christ's peace in worship morphed into a nightly hug-fest; the closing hymn became a half-hour praise jam; Taizé melodies received new lyrics sometimes gently lampooning community life and its dear leaders; the Jazz Four, a "quartet" with five members, appeared to "shake up the scene, man, shake up the scene" at random moments of the day including at worship.

Until recently we regarded these and a great many similar outbursts of joy as little more than cherries on top of a most excellent sundae. At the invitation of the Yale Center for Faith and Culture and at the behest of the Templeton Fund, however, we seek to reassess our ministry, this time peering through the lens of Christian joy. Yes, joy, the gift of the Spirit to an Easter People who together with the risen Christ and the company of saints sing unending praise and thanksgiving to God for God's unfailing embrace. How did we forget that?

---

2 Duke Divinity School established the Duke Youth Academy for Christian Formation (DYA) in 2001. DYA is a temporary intentional Christian community composed of high school youth and adults that meets on Duke's campus every summer. It now includes a year-long online component as well. Along with approximately fifty theological schools across North America, Duke Divinity School received a generous grant from the Lilly Endowment as part of their High School Theology Initiatives program in order to establish DYA.

Our Context for Youth Worship and How We Create That Worship

Something like monastic life, our community begins each day with prayer then features morning theological study followed by afternoon practices focused on justice, creativity, and theological/vocational reflection. Every day culminates with evening worship.[3] We follow a Word and Table pattern, meaning that worship always includes proclamation of and response to the scriptures followed by Holy Communion (known to some as the Lord's Supper or Eucharist). The heart of our Word and Table worship is preceded by a period of gathering and concludes with sending forth.

Gathering is simple shorthand for the assembly's coming together. It can be informal, a welcome into the presence of the triune God followed by songs of praise, or elaborate, as with processing behind a cross while hymning an ancient chant.

In addition to reading from the scriptures and preaching, proclamation of the **Word** and responding to it can take many other forms—singing, drama, testimony, prayer, video, or dance. Youth participate together with adults in these practices of proclaiming and responding to the Word. For example, on a day in our community featuring teach-ins, stories, and witnesses to the personal, relational, and social meanings of reconciliation in Christ, youths and adults together planned worship around that theme. An invited guest preached powerfully on how Jesus overcomes racial, economic, and personal divisions. Then, following a pause to meditate on Christ's reconciling mission, worshippers were first shocked then delighted when worship leaders suddenly

---

3 As noted, our youth ministry context is somewhat unusual, a temporary community formed at a divinity school in the summers. Nevertheless we believe that our patterns of worship and practices of formation share a great deal of overlap with the formational practices of local congregations. We invite readers to repeatedly ask themselves: "What might this worship teaching, planning, practicing, and reflecting look like in my local community?"

crashed through paper mural "walls" hung throughout the chapel, all while dancing and chanting, "Christ is reconciler, woot, woot! Christ is reconciler, woot, woot!," an acclamation taken up by the entire assembly. The last wall to fall revealed the prepared Table of the Lord. More praise!

The **Table** may be fully participative, too. The community confesses its sin before God and neighbor out loud and in public, seeks to practice God's reconciliation through the sharing of Christ's peace with one another (aka the hug-fest), then sings the prayer of thanksgiving (says grace) over the gifts of bread and cup. Worshippers receive the consecrated elements at the front of the assembly from servers oozing hospitality. It is a space where they may also pray before the altar, receive laying of hands, or dip their fingers in the waters of the baptismal font.

Worship concludes with the benedictory exhortation to go forth to serve the Lord. Often this **sending forth** features worshippers processing behind the cross, dancing and singing their way out of the chapel accompanied by youth and adult musicians jamming on guitars, drums, horns, or even a string bass on wheels.

In addition to praising God through scripture and sacrament, this worship strives to acknowledge the pain and suffering borne by God's people and all of creation. In addition to confessing sin, worship may name the travails of youth and adults while beseeching God to intervene. In 2015, at the same time of the day DYA gathered in Durham, North Carolina, nine African American worshippers who had gathered in their own sanctuary in Charleston, South Carolina, were murdered by a racially motivated killer. DYA worship the next evening voiced to God the assembly's dismay, anger, fear, and grief. No one felt the least bit joyful. That the community voiced its sorrows and doubts in worship, however, nevertheless enacted them into the hope that God is working to overcome evil in spite of what worshippers were thinking or feeling that evening. Youths may learn, therefore, that worship does not require strapping on their Sunday smiles and pretending all is well. God meets us where we are in worship.

As readers can tell, this community stresses embodied worship. It also seeks to elicit youths' full participation both as members of a unified worshipping assembly and through the contributions of their particular gifts. They sing, they dance, they dramatically interpret, they pray ancient prayers of the church, they create new prayers, they shout, they keep silence, they play instruments, they assist at the table, they decorate the space. The word "liturgy" means "work of the people," and in our community youth and adults are fully invested in doing this work. Since worship repeats a readily discernible pattern—gathering, word, table, sending forth—worship planners quickly learn to innovate upon it through their own styles, creativity, and theological interpretations (as in the case of the wall-crashing response to the Word). It taps into youths' disposition to joy. Sensing that they are sharing in this work together, worshippers feel the energy; some days are electric. At the same time, worship strives to be honest about the gap between God's promises and young people's current lived experience.

None of this happens by chance. We equip young people to interpret the themes and texts of worship through biblical and theological study, then make space for those interpretations in worship itself (think again of breaking down the walls). Youths also require mentoring and practice in the performance of worship—rehearsing lines or steps or music, learning to *e-nun-ci-ate,* cultivating a comfortable public presence, and so on. Overall DYA endeavors to equip youths with skills and knowledge for understanding theologically the basic pattern and ingredients of worship and worship leadership, involving them in the creation and practice of worship while lauding their efforts, then inviting them to ponder its outcomes. Put simply, we prepare youths for worship and engage them in the work of worship, then reflect with them upon worship. We do all this because the alternative—sidelining youths from worship, excluding their contributions, keeping them clueless about what is going on, or ignoring the transformational power of Word and Sacrament upon their lives and substituting a stage show instead—amounts to a massive killing of joy, effectively denying them abundant life. To make this point a bit more

When we worship, we participate in the very joy of God.

positively, faith communities may readily adapt this combination of teaching, training, creativity, performance, and reflection on their own circumstances, thereby enhancing young people's participation in the community's most important joy-delivering practices.

Theological Considerations for Christian Worship

Authentic worshipful joy ought to be attributed to more than strong formation and effective planning. We haven't forgotten that joy ultimately comes as a gift from God. This section traces the theological relationship between God, God's creatures, the human work of worship, and joy. Our account suggests that not only are youths (and the rest of us) created for joyous worship of our loving Creator, but we are also invited to participate in the joy of God as we worship. In turn this divine joy fuels young peoples' flourishing.

Created for Joy and Praise

The Psalter provides a rich source for exploring the relationship between God, human beings, joy, and worship. Take this psalm, for example:

> Make a joyful noise to the LORD, all the earth.
> Worship the LORD with gladness;
> come into his presence with singing.
> Know that the LORD is God.
> It is he that made us, and we are his;
> we are his people, and the sheep of his pasture.
> Enter his gates with thanksgiving,
> and his courts with praise.
> Give thanks to him, bless his name.
> For the LORD is good;
> his steadfast love endures forever,
> and his faithfulness to all generations. (Ps. 100, NRSV)

Psalms like this one were chanted in the Jerusalem Temple, sung at the synagogue, and prayed communally every day across Israel. Jesus knew them by heart and not just because he was Jesus. They were ubiquitous, so universally practiced that they filled the religious imaginations and the hearts of those who sang them.

So what was the content of this heartfelt imagination? Psalm 100 sums it up beautifully: God made us. We belong to God. God's steadfast love endures forever. In other words the psalmists testify that life comes to us as a gift. All that we have and all that we are originate beyond ourselves, bestowed by an utterly gratuitous Creator. Awash in delight at the absolute givenness of existence, in the blessedness that fills each breath, and overcome by the sheer abundance of it all, the psalmists launch into prayers of praise. C. S. Lewis explains this propensity for praise: "We delight to praise that which we enjoy." Indeed "praise completes the enjoyment; it is its appointed consummation."[4] In other words joy turns to worship, and worship turns to joy.

At the same time, the Psalms demand that we acknowledge the barriers to joy for youths and for all followers of God. As the psalmists confess, personal suffering and social oppression often threaten to overwhelm their faith. Instead of joy they cry out in lament. And they don't mince words. Read aloud this psalm of lament:

> O Lord, do not rebuke me in your anger,
>   or discipline me in your wrath.
> Be gracious to me, O Lord, for I am languishing;
>   O Lord, heal me, for my bones are shaking with terror.
> My soul also is struck with terror,
>   while you, O Lord—how long?
> Turn, O Lord, save my life;
>   deliver me for the sake of your steadfast love.
> For in death there is no remembrance of you;
>   in Sheol who can give you praise? (Ps. 6:1–5, NRSV)

---

4 C. S. Lewis, *Reflections on the Psalms* (New York: Harcourt, Brace, 1958), 80.

Not much joy there, we admit. The psalmist even gets in a sarcastic dig at God: "Hey, Lord, how do you expect me to shout praises to you if I'm dead?" (v. 5).

That psalms of lament are found alongside psalms of joy in the Psalter means that worshipful lament keeps joy honest. Joy does not require ignoring the world's or our own brokenness or pretending it's all good when it is not. Instead lament expresses hope in God's promises in spite of troubles. As biblical scholar Ellen Davis suggests, while psalms of lament typically begin with "complaint addressed to God, they move, however fitfully, in the direction of praise."[5] The cries of desperation at the beginning of Psalm 6 turn to affirmation of God's protection at the conclusion. It's not exactly joy, but it's getting there.

Entering Jesus's Joyful Kingdom

As a son of Israel, Jesus prayed the psalms daily. He too practiced praise and rejoicing as a way of life. His imagination was filled with the Psalter's language and images. Unsurprisingly, therefore, joy is central to his teaching and ministry focused on the kingdom of God. Jesus taught kingdom joy through parables. In the parable of the prodigal son, for example, father and son rejoice together in the son's return home. Jesus also delivers joy through his ministry of healing. The blind man at Jericho whose sight Jesus restores rejoices at seeing the light (Luke 18:35–43). So too the collection of sinners and tax collectors. Once excluded from Israel's promise, they rejoice at Jesus's inclusion of them in the kingdom he inaugurates (Luke 19:1–10). Even we Gentiles are invited into the kingdom! Joy multiplies exponentially as God's promises to Israel are extended to the entire world.

To cultivate a relationship with Jesus is to share in this kingdom joy. Being worshipful means encountering Christ as living Word in the scriptures and participating in his death and resurrected life through the sacraments.

---

5 Ellen Davis, *Getting Involved with God: Rediscovering the Old Testament* (Lanham, MD: Rowman and Littlefield, 2001), 17.

Joining the Joy of the Trinity

Early theologians used scripture and their experiences in worship to formulate what we today call the doctrine of the Holy Trinity. They knew from Genesis 1 and from John 1 that Spirit and Son (the latter in the form of creative "Word") were present with God the "Father" at creation. They sensed this threefold presence when gathering for worship. In the effort to come to terms with this mystery, theologians described a relational unity, the "three-in-one-ness" we profess about God today.

The glue of this triune relational unity is divine love. Indeed one church father describes the Trinity as a loving "dance," a pas de trois of mutual joy and delight.[6] In this dance each triune member steps in loving synchrony with the others so perfectly as to accomplish unity. Their mutual love for one another makes them one. At the same time, divine love allows each member to leap and twirl consistently with its creative, redemptive, and sanctifying mission. Perfect love and therefore perfect union between members of the Trinity goes hand in hand with each triune person's freedom to attend to its unique divine role.

Mutual loving relations between the Trinity amounted to a "surplus of love," which set in motion the original act of creation.[7] All creation, therefore, becomes an expression of God's love. Trinitarian theology further explains what the Psalms mandate: that humans created out of this abundance of love exist to praise their Maker.

As second person of the Trinity, Jesus puts flesh and blood on God. Through his incarnation Jesus also redeems the material world. That is how Jesus becomes present to worshippers through otherwise ordinary signs, symbols, and words. Worshippers may taste, touch, see, and hear Jesus through sacraments, ritual performances, and even the gathered

---

6 John of Damascus (7th c.) was the first to speak this way of the Trinity. See Frederic Chase Jr., trans., *The Orthodox Faith* 1.14:11–18, found in *Saint John of Damascus, Writings* (Washington: Catholic University of America Press, 1970), 202.

7 Christoph Schonborn, *YOUCAT: Youth Catechism of the Catholic Church* (San Francisco: Ignatius, 2011), 14.

assembly itself. They share in his Word through scripture, prayer, testimony, and songs of praise. The means of graced relationship with Jesus are available everywhere in the space and time of Christian worship.

God is also present to the assembly as Holy Spirit. The Spirit is what transforms human offerings into holy sacrament and divine Word. Without the Spirit a sermon is mere words and sharing the peace of Christ amounts to "How ya' doin'?" Through the Spirit the assembly manifests the kingdom of God. Christians are transformed into the body of Christ. Peace and glory reign. Joy in the Spirit propels worshippers out of worship and sends them into the world for service.

In summary the love of each triune member is present and offered in worship. Worshippers may rejoice in God's love poured into creation (including themselves) for their redemption and re-creation in Jesus and for the Spirit's transformation of the assembly into an expression of God's Kingdom.

Yet liturgical theologian Kimberly Belcher, speaking in this case of sacramental worship, proposes that worship intends even more. "The Trinitarian God," she suggests, "through the missions of the incarnate Word and the Holy Spirit [in worship], invites and enables human persons *to participate* in the eternal happiness of the Godhead."[8] The joy expressed in worship is more than just a human response to God's love. It also entails worshippers sharing in the transcendent joy of the Trinity itself; it is manifested through their worshipful absorption into the life and mission of God. More than testimony, more than response to good news, more than imitation, worship *incorporates* worshippers into the Trinity's mission of creation, redemption, and sanctification. Worship sweeps the assembly into the Holy Trinity's transcendent dance of joy. This is awesome!

This transformation partly explains why worship is often described as a glimpse of heaven and Holy Communion as a foretaste of the heavenly feast. As a special zone of grace, sacramental worship of the Trinity

---

8 Kimberly Belcher, *Efficacious Engagement: Sacramental Participation in the Triune Mystery* (Collegeville, MN: Liturgical, 2011), 2.

transforms the assembly into a living, breathing revelation of God's kingdom. The assembly's worship reveals and performs the "really real," flourishing life as God intends it. Through word, song, symbol, and gesture, it enacts the transcendent kingdom reality of grace, peace, compassion, and joyful praise that powerfully counters the broken existence that seeks to snare youth and the rest of us.

Joy That Lasts

Youth workers, including us, have observed young people who totally "have church" (they really, *really* get into it) and, like King David, completely abandon themselves to the joy of the Lord . . . only to do stupid stuff an hour later. (David is also instructive on this point.) As to why joy seems not to last, there are any number of possible explanations—the possibility that joy is not really invited into worship in their communities in the first place, the fact that youth remain unable to sense the connections between their worship and their lives outside the sanctuary, the fact that the human body only ladles out oxytocin (the "happy" hormone) in short-lived doses or that some young people face joy busters upon leaving church and returning to home, to school, or even to the street leading to these destinations.

Viewing worship as a Christian practice of formation—as something Christians do together over time in the presence of God in the effort to become more God-like, in other words—offers a helpful perspective on making joy last. It encourages taking the long view on Christian joy. An analogy can help here. Suppose Alaina wants to take up the ukulele. Learning to play will require her to practice chord fingering positions and strumming patterns for weeks and months. Over time her practice will ingrain these complex actions as habits in her body. Soon enough she'll be plucking out the tune to "Shine on Harvest Moon" with great finesse. Notice what else happens. Playing the ukulele gradually characterizes Alaina. She is no longer just Alaina the fab youth worker; she becomes Alaina the fab youth worker and accomplished ukulele strummer. Playing the ukulele has become part of her identity.

The same dynamics are at work for the practice of Christian worship. Over time—we're most likely talking years—Christians who practice praise and delight at sharing in the joy of the Trinity can hope not only to take up joy for an hour or two on Sunday morning but also to live joyous lives. Persons who pattern their lives by singing "Joyful, Joyful, We Adore Thee" (including the hip-hop version) may, by grace, become characterized by their practice. They grow to resemble the One whom they adore. They become joyful creatures of a joyful God.

In this case we seek to describe joy as more than a feeling. We are casting it as a lasting disposition, an affection of the heart that colors all other interactions with the world. Joy of this kind may get its start as a feeling, but gradually it becomes an orienting posture toward life.

Forming youth into dispositional joy is more than pie-in-the-sky Pollyannaism; it is profoundly practical. Youth workers recognize how young people are at greater risk for violence, poverty, and other threats to flourishing than adults. Racial minority and LGBTQ children face even greater risks. We envision dispositional joy, therefore, including the kind young people are formed to practice and receive in worship, as a crucial antidote to these threats. This is more than the power of positive thinking at work. Through their mysterious participation in the life of the Trinity and their worshipful performance of the Kingdom (really real life as God intends it), youths are provided with a vital source of resilience. When available in sufficient reserves, joy in companionship with hope can make the difference between perceiving a challenge as just an obstacle to get around or an unclimbable wall. Dispositional joy serves as the embodied reminder that God is on a mission culminating in a kingdom of flourishing. Cultivating lasting joy through worship is critical to enabling young people to keep on keeping on through life's valleys.

Theologian Willie James Jennings puts this claim in even bolder terms. He suggests that joy becomes an "act of resistance" against forces of despair, which we take to include the power of sin, both personal and systemic.[9] According to Jennings, oppressed persons and communities who are aware of injustices inflicted upon them but practice joy anyway witness to their freedom from sinful principalities and powers. The Apostle Paul's professions of joy even while incarcerated exemplify what Jennings is describing (Phil. 1). Christian Joy witnesses to faith and hope in God in the midst of present oppression. Even more than resilience, joy constitutes an expression of liberation from sin.

To reprise just a bit, Christians believe that joy is part of the DNA of creatures to rejoice in their Creator through worship; joy is also offered as a divine gift to Christians especially as they worship through their (admittedly mysterious) participation in the joyous triune relationships of the Godhead. Keeping joy honest, the practice of lament invites Christians to cry out in worship over their suffering and the sufferings of others and, through confession, to acknowledge their own complicity in sin that leads to suffering—while yet obeying the divine imperative to make a joyful noise to the Lord. Joy that endures suffering may be described as a disposition (habit) of the heart, body, and mind causing Christians to rejoice in God's promise of the coming kingdom even when darkness threatens. Young people who participate in joyous worship build vital reserves of joy, enabling them to persevere through difficult circumstances.

Misdirected Love, False Worship, Fake Joy (and Their Antidotes)

Like all human beings, youth are created by God to exercise their passions (their loves) for worship. They are engineered for seeking transcendence (connection to a greater reality that consists of more than just themselves). That propensity to worship can take many forms, however.

9 "Theology of Joy: Willie James Jennings with Miraslov Volf," posted by Yale Center for Faith and Culture, 19 Sept. 2014, https://www.youtube.com/watch?v=1fKD4Msh3rE.

It can fasten on Lady Gaga as readily as the biblical word, on throwing down gang signs instead of gesturing Christ's peace, on engaging mystery through opioids in place of Three in One. Humans are worshipping creatures—they just don't always worship the real God.

Christian philosopher James K. A. Smith explains how the passion intended for creaturely praise of God gets coopted by lesser gods. Smith paints a portrait of all human beings (not just youth) as desiring (passionate) beings, as "lovers" more than thinkers.[10] He also describes how this loving passion is drawn toward particular ends. He suggests that we learn who or what to love by way of "cultural liturgies," public rituals or symbolic events that recruit our loves often without our noticing.[11] Smith describes sporting events (think Super Bowl plus pregame and the all-important halftime show), nationalistic spectacles (celebrating American Independence Day on the Washington Mall with fireworks, military jet flyovers, and patriotic music), and even shopping at the mall (or "temple," as Smith calls it) as examples of cultural liturgies. Similarly, Friday night high school football often constitutes a form of cultural liturgy targeted to recruit young loves. All of these liturgies (forms of worship) offer spine-tingling experiences of transcendence plus the joy of being part of something far bigger than one's self.

The problem, of course, is that some cultural liturgies invite the worship of false gods. Christians who participate in them risk unconscious conversion to varieties of nationalism, tribalism, and consumerism that, Trojan horse–like, sneak in and distort love's faithful intent. Their loves coopted, young people find themselves worshipping and rejoicing in the wrong gods.

Christian worship, therefore, needs to become what Smith calls a Christian "counter-liturgy."[12] Obviously we can't compete with fighter jets, but we ought to give everything we've got (and everything God

---

10 James K. A. Smith, *Desiring the Kingdom: Worship, Worldview, and Cultural Formation* (Grand Rapids, MI: Baker Academic, 2009), chap. 1.

11 Smith, *Desiring the Kingdom*, 19–27. See also chap. 2.

12 Smith, 88.

has given us) to praising the one true God revealed in Christ by the power of the Spirit. That is key to receiving the transcendent, transformative joy that only the triune God can give. We must invite youth to bring all the passion they can summon to their encounter with divine passion. We trust that our best efforts will be met by divine transcendence and by grace.

A counter-liturgy also must be sufficiently robust not only to reveal God's transcendent presence but also to awaken loving devotion to the one true God. Two-word praise choruses directed to some vague deity won't suffice. The need to focus on not only the presence but also the identity of God is one reason we advocate frequent practice of the liturgical meal. Participation in this rite enacts worshippers into the story of God as revealed in and through Jesus. Holy Communion performs worshippers into stories of God's creation; they are made into church as they gather around the table sharing common bread and cup; they renew their covenant rooted in the death and resurrection of Christ; they rediscover their calling to meet the world's hungers just as Christ meets theirs in the meal; and they taste of the kingdom where all may feast together with God. Rather than tiring of the repetition, we have witnessed with our own eyes how repeated participation in this meal makes God's threefold love present to youth with special intensity. One of its gifts is pure joy. Perhaps for this reason, DYA alums report that they develop a hunger (a passion? a love?) to return to this table and to eat the sustenance only it can offer. Once worshippers taste divine love bursting with the flavor of joy, lesser foods will no longer suffice. They seek out communities where this feast, a portal to loving transcendence, is shared again and again.

Conclusion

God's grace abounds for young people. It is available everywhere. Nevertheless corporate worship can become a special zone of grace where God's love is palpably present. When youths are invited to participate fully in the ancient treasures of Christian worship (Word and Sacrament) and given the freedom to shape and respond to their encounters with loving transcendence, joy breaks in and then *breaks out*. Worshipful joy leads to joyous living. Only the triune God present in and acting in the worshipping church can give this transformative gift. So this is our plea: equip the kids for this joyous work.

6

Hope

A Pathway to Adolescent Joy and Flourishing

Anne E. Streaty Wimberly and Sarah F. Farmer

A Starting Point: Hope Matters

What do ministry leaders and other adults know about hope and joy in teens' lives? Truthfully these young people can tell us much. In fact, listening to their voices reveals not simply their need to share but also a depth and poignancy in what they say. In our conversations with teens, one said, for example, "With all the violence that's happening everywhere we turn, I just have the question 'Will I live to see tomorrow?'" Another shared, "I've already learned that there will be challenges. . . . But I am capable. I am doing well, and I am determined to keep doing it." Still another told of "a big challenge to hope for youth today. The challenge is having something to believe in. The world today doesn't exactly have too many things a youth can have hope in or cling onto in hard times. I need hope. Hope is needed in the world. What do we do to get it?"[1] About joy a teen reflected, "That's a hard one. I mean, it's

1 Results of conversations with teens about their experiences and assigned meanings of hope appear in Anne E. Streaty Wimberly and Sarah Frances

not just one thing that comes from one thing. Anyway, to be honest, sometimes I have it, sometimes I don't."

Whatever their views about hope and its connection with joy, it is also clear that teens recognize their lives are unfolding in an ever-widening technological explosion and that they're involved in multiple forms of human interconnectedness. They are not unaware of political, interracial, and interreligious turmoil in an increasingly diverse and globally connected society; of changing family structures; and of varying life opportunities, often in tandem with tough concerns faced in schools, homes, and wider communities. They grasp the value of individual achievement and attaining material possessions that affirm esteemed social standing and well-being even in fragile economic times. From them come words such as "I believe in God, but church is no fun!" In short, meanings of hope and joy form amid these realities. Yet in truth human beings are born to hope—to anticipate or have expectations for a desired good that brings satisfaction and intersects with joy.

Courageous, joy-filled hope is life-giving to teens in these rapidly changing and challenging times.

This chapter centers on meanings of courageous, joy-filled hope that must be empowered and nurtured in the lives of teens in rapidly changing and challenging times. We begin with a discussion of hope as an active, dynamic, life-affirming quality in the lives of humans. Attention then turns to hope as expectations leading to human flourishing in the multidimensional sojourn of life as well as to impediments to hope and the nature of hopelessness. Theological meanings and attributes of the intersection of joy and hope precede a discussion of the role of agents of hope in youths' formation of courageous, joy-filled hope. We conclude with some pedagogical suggestions.

Farmer, *Raising Hope: 4 Paths to Courageous Living for Black Youth* (Nashville: Wesley's Foundry Books, 2017), 26–28.

Hope as an Active, Dynamic, Life-Affirming Quality

Hope is defined by Erik Erikson as "the earliest and the most indispensable virtue inherent in the state of being alive."[2] An undeclared quality of hope that reveals a stance of longing or expectation appears in an infant child's reach and cry for the caring contact of another and the nourishment of food.[3] Anticipatory hope is implied in a youngster's eager desire for birthdays and other celebration, vacations, and visits to or from someone special. Hope is also a concretely expressed attitude and conviction about an open and possible future by youths entering or graduating from high school as well as by others who seek a promising way forward in life in the form of a job, mate, or home. And it is present in the anguish of those who are longing for a way out of or around tragedy and loss.[4] In fact, a plea for the necessity of hope is found in the words of a song: "Keep hope alive! Don't let the dream die!"[5] Hope is an essential aspect of human life. Indeed life has a way of evoking in human beings unspoken and spoken feelings, thoughts, declarations, and questions about hope.

---

2 Erik H. Erikson, "Human Strength and the Cycle of Generations," *Insight and Responsibility* (New York: W. W. Norton, 1964), 118.

3 Donald Capps draws attention to multivalent properties of hope that include *waiting* for the presence or appearance of something external to actually appear; *anticipation* of satisfying one's longing for the presence of a desired object; *pining* or recalling a missed object and desiring the satisfaction that object could provide; and *hoping* that involves one's believing that a desired object is not simply available but will satisfy one's desire. See: Donald Capps, *Agents of Hope: A Pastoral Psychology* (Minneapolis: Fortress, 1995), 33–37.

4 References of these opening views appear in: Wimberly and Farmer, *Raising Hope*, 29–30. Capps also identifies hope as an "attitudinal disposition" or "the implicit conviction or tacit belief that the future is an open one, and that it holds possibility for us." He also indicates that hope is an inherent strength. It is that sustaining element in life in the face of wounded confidence and impaired trust. See: Capps, *Agents of Hope*, 28.

5 The words and tune to the song, "Keep Hope Alive," were composed by Donald Vails with an arrangement of the music by Nolan Williams appearing in *African American Heritage Hymnal* (Chicago: GIA Publications, Inc., 2001), #405.

Hope is also a dynamic, ongoing reality that crosses times, places, people, and circumstances. Jürgen Moltmann reminds us that the theme of hope is ongoing, because new experiences occurring across history force us to come to terms with it.[6] He emphasizes the unequivocal necessity of hope, for without it, we succumb to "an internal catastrophe."[7] A teenager put it this way: "You have to have the drive that keeps you going when all odds are against you. For me, that is hope."[8] Yet it is also the case, says Christopher Rate, that courage matters: "It is increasingly difficult to face an unpredictable future—sure to offer challenges with varying levels of risks, fears, and moral decisions—without being able to call on courage if needed."[9] However, real impediments to hope exist. We have heard repeatedly the stories of teens reflecting barriers to hope that are marked by stress, anxiety, and grief and punctuated with the questions "What do we do to get it?" or "What hope is there?" or the cry "I don't see it!" These responses point to the need to probe more deeply into what hope is, how it wanes or becomes absent, and what is needed to affirm, nourish, and revive it.

Cultural Historical Understandings of Hope

Meanings of hope take shape within particular cultural settings. Hope happens contextually. For example black predecessors, African-Americans in the historic past, offer an understanding of hope infused

6 See Wimberly and Farmer, *Raising Hope*, and Rollo May, *The Courage to Create* (New York: W. W. Norton, 1975, Reprinted 1994), 14–17.

7 Jürgen Moltmann, *The Experiment of Hope,* edited and translated with foreword by M. Douglas Meeks (Philadelphia: Fortress, 1975), 186.

8 This statement was among many views of hope shared by youth and included in Anne E. Streaty Wimberly, ed., *Keep It Real: Working with Today's Black Youth* (Nashville: Abingdon, 2005), 120.

9 Christopher R. Rate, "Defining the Features of Courage: A Search for Meaning," in *The Psychology of Courage: Modern Research on an Ancient Virtue*, ed. Cynthia L.S. Pury and Shane J. Lopez (Washington, DC: American Psychological Association, 2010), 63.

by courage that was active, dynamic, and life-affirming. For them it was neither docile nor life-negating. Indeed this understanding provides a helpful foundation for conversations with young people about courageous hope and activities that help them act in positive and life-affirming ways. Four images of the nature of hope infused with courage emerge from a black historical perspective. These images offer guidance for embracing four particular dispositional qualities that point to markers of courageous hope to be formed in young people: courageous hope as a choice, as an empowering attitude, as a faith-filled posture in life's wilderness, and as an ongoing creative sojourn.[10]

Courageous Hope as a Choice

At the center of courageous hope is one's view of oneself as an actor on one's own behalf. Courageous hope evolves from a person's knowing that they have a choice and can decide on an optimistic course of life while at the same time recognizing the barriers life presents.[11] Such a choice, then, presumes an existing view of hope that centers on the psychological attributes of optimism and positivity. Donald Capps refers to this kind of perspective within the self as an "attitudinal disposition" or attitude toward life that things will work out in the unfolding of time. Within this disposition lies the belief in a future that holds possibilities rather than despairing outcomes.[12] Further understanding of this view is set forth by Jane E. Gillham and her associates, who cite an explanatory style that makes possible persons' maintaining motivation and the ability to cope and continue on amid adversity.[13]

---

10 References of these four images appear in Wimberly and Farmer, *Raising Hope*, 58–68.

11 References of these four images appear in Wimberly and Farmer, *Raising Hope*, 58–68.

12 Donald Capps, *Agents of Hope: A Pastoral Psychology* (Minneapolis: Fortress Press, 1995), 14, 28.

13 Jane E. Gillham, Andrew J. Shatte, Karen J. Reivich, and Martin E.P. Seligman, "Optimism, Pessimism, and Explanatory Style," 53–75, in Edward C. Chang, ed.,

The courage to choose hope simply means claiming for oneself the view "I'm gonna make it," which is akin to having the psychological frame of mind that reflects the resilient self.[14] Of course we recognize that difficult, dehumanizing, and traumatic life events or experiences emanating from racism and other forms of abuse have the propensity to impede a sense of positivity and bring about a sense of pessimism. We also recognize that hope cannot be forced on anyone. People cannot be made to choose hope. The truth is that a person may succumb to fatalism, as Capps notes.[15] On this basis the role of leaders is to be agents of hope who find ways to inspire, instill, and support courageous hope in young people.

Courageous Hope as an Empowering Attitude

In addition to being chosen, courageous hope also has an empowering capacity in young people's lives to the extent that they are enabled to envision goals that hold the potential of contributing to a hopeful outcome and are accorded pathways to move toward those goals. Even amid obstacles this capacity makes possible an inner power that we have already named as human agency. It includes the mental energy or psychological verve to move toward an identified goal, however great or small, quickly attained, delayed, or even unseen. The empowering capacity of courageous hope has at the center hope-filled positivity, the push from within that is likened to the slogan of Barack Obama's 2008 presidential campaign: "Yes we can." But it also requires the embrace of several key empowerment perspectives that may be called "weapons" against pessimism, passivity, and actions that negate self-affirmation and human flourishing.

The empowering function of courageous hope has particular salience in young people's lives because, as it made possible black

---

Optimism & Pessimism: Implications for Theory, Research, and Practice (Washington, DC: American Psychological Association, 2001), 67.

14 See Capps, *Agents of Hope*, 14.

15 Capps, 24–25.

forebears' courage to prevail and persevere in life, it engenders in youths the belief that they have both the physical wherewithal and mental energy to move toward and achieve an identified goal. Hope functions as an empowering capacity in young people in ways that allow them to see, reach for, and accomplish positive goals, even amid obstacles. This view reflects Carl Richard Snyder's definition of hope as "the perceived capability to derive pathways to desired goals and motivate oneself via agency-thinking to use those pathways."[16] Empowering hope energizes what Dana Michelle Harley calls "self-talk," or the push from within to shout: "I can do this! I'm not going to be stopped!"[17]

Courageous Hope as a Faith-Filled Posture in Life's Wilderness

What also comes across from the perspectives of black forebears is the centrality of faith in their embrace and practice of courageous hope. Their perspectives underscore the necessity of knowing and relying on God and of engaging in spiritual disciplines such as prayer. Moreover a gift of forebears from the era of slavery forward is the recognition of life as wilderness in which to learn and claim the ability to live and keep on keeping on, with courage and hope in life and even in the face of death.[18]

A faith-filled posture in life's wilderness must not be missed in the sojourn of today's youth. In fact we contend that there is the necessity

---

16 Carl Richard Snyder, "Hope Theory: Rainbows in the Mind," *Psychological Inquiry* 13(4), 2002:249–75 (249). See also the perspectives of Snyder in: C. R. Snyder, "Hypothesis: There Is Hope," 3–24, and "Genesis: The Birth and Growth of Hope," 25–38, in C.R. Snyder, *Handbook of Hope: Theory, Measures and Applications* (New York: Academic Press, 2000).

17 Dana Michelle Harley, *Perceptions of Hope and Hopelessness Among Low-Income African American Adolescents,* PhD dissertation, Graduate School, The Ohio State University, 2011, 24. Available at: http://etd.ohiolink.edu/rws_etd/document/get/osu1313009132/inline.

18 The idea of wilderness as a classroom appears in Scott C. Hammond, *Lessons of the Lost: Finding Hope and Resilience in Work, Life, and the Wilderness* (Bloomington, IN: iUniverse, 2013).

of exploring a wilderness theology with young people by inviting them to openly and honestly name the struggles and painful and broken places of their lives, engaging them in lament before God, and involving them in spiritual practices such as communal worship, Bible study, praying, singing, liturgical arts, and service that provide openings for them to search for, hear, and find God, and discern God's actions in their lives in the wilderness.

The Bible is particularly rich in offering perspectives on the wilderness and stories of exemplars who journeyed in the wilderness and encountered God there. For example the story of Hagar, a servant, reveals the difficult wilderness experience of being impregnated by and bearing a child, Ishmael, son of her master, because of the failure of the master's wife to bear a child. Her abuse by the master's wife and subsequent abandonment in the desert made even more difficult her painful struggle. Yet in her period of exile, Hagar recognized God's existence in a spring of water and in God's voice of promise. In short it must not be forgotten that, just as the dimension of faith was pivotal for past generations, so also it holds significance in the lives of the current generation of youth. Indeed Philip Dunston and Anne Wimberly, in their discussion of the connection between hope and self-discovery, state that "there is no empowerment, growth, or transformation without recognition and appreciation for the transcendental force present in all life forms. Black youth need guidance, on how to effectively commune with and develop a relationship with God."[19]

Courageous Hope as an Ongoing Creative Sojourn

The perspectives of forebears also remind us that past realities of life do not disappear completely with time. Rather each generation is met with concerns that are similar if not the same as previous ones. On the one hand, recognition of the repetition of issues over time raises questions about the germaneness of hope for transformation or change. On

19 Philip Dunston and Anne E. Streaty Wimberly, "A Matter of Discovery," in Wimberly, ed., *Keep It Real*, 39.

the other hand, while the ongoing presence of life's travail threatens to overwhelm and stifle efforts to continue on the journey, creativity can become a remarkable and renewing pathway of meaning making, survival, and inspiration. The ongoing creative spirit is further affirmed in Emilie Townes's personal perspective: "Trying to understand racism and other forms of hatred has been one of the most formative things I've done in my life, and I have now come to realize that it will remain a challenge until I draw my last breath. I learned at an early age that I must learn how to survive the daily small and sometimes large indignities of racism by negotiating it with creativity, imagination, and sometimes humor while maintaining my integrity and sense of self."[20] Reference has already been made to music, dance, and other artistic expressions as central to black people's chosen expression of agency. These idioms have been key means by which a black people's eschatology emerged.

Hope, Life Direction, and Human Flourishing: Expectations and Impediments

The foregoing ethnic-cultural views of hope point to particular expectations or desired prospects in the multidimensional affairs and passage of life. Actually for all human beings, hope centers on an anticipated direction of life that moves toward holistic well-being and flourishing. To draw on the views of Miroslav Volf, at the heart of hope is human beings' seeking an experience of life that goes well, feels well, and is lived well, otherwise regarded as an experience of the good life.[21] This

---

20 Emilie M. Townes, "Teaching and the Imagination," *Religious Education,* 111(4), July–September 2016:366–79 (367).

21 Volf describes these dimensions in terms of life that goes well as a circumstantial dimension; life that feels well as an affective dimension; and life that is lived well as an agential dimension in: Miroslav Volf, "The Crown of the Good Life: An Hypothesis," in *Joy and Human Flourishing: Essays on Theology, Culture, and the Good Life,* eds. Miroslav Volf and Justin E. Crisp (Minneapolis: Fortress Press, 2015), 127–36.

anticipated direction contains thoughts and beliefs about a positive outcome in a particular facet or attribute of life and what is involved in reaching it (a cognitive attribute of hope), associated feelings (an affective attribute of hope), and actions needed to influence the outcome (behavioral attribute of hope). Hope, then, is about an overarching human process of being and becoming that centers on the finest vision and optimal expectation of young people as they encounter and move through the multidimensional affairs of life.

Multidimensional Aspects of Hope

The question may well be asked: What expectations are associated with the multidimensional affairs and passage of life to which hope is connected? We propose here that hope is linked to seven interrelated dimensions of life: relational well-being, physical well-being, psychological well-being, vocational well-being, spiritual well-being, leisure and creative well-being, and environmental well-being. We present hope in the form of the finest vision and optimal expectation of young people in these dimensions.[22]

---

22 The dimensions being presented here appear in conversations on hope with Black adolescents including examples appearing in: Wimberly, *Keep It Real,* 120–22. The multi-dimensional and interrelated character of well-being is also described in pastoral care literature, principally by Howard Clinebell. See: Howard Clinebell, *Anchoring Your Well-Being: A Guide for Congregational Leaders* (Nashville: Upper Room, 1997). The dimensions are further framed in: Anne E. Streaty Wimberly, "Congregational Care in the Lives of Black Older Adults," in Melvin A. Kimble and Susan H. McFadden, eds., *Aging Spirituality, and Religion,* Volume 2 (Minneapolis: Fortress Press, 2003), 105–6. It is well to add that several dimensions including those associated with identity, emotional, social, cognitive and physical development appear as developmental domains in the report of the American Psychological Association (APA) Task Force on Resilience and Strength in Black Children and Adolescents, "Resilience in African American Children and Adolescents: A Vision for Optimal Development" (Washington, DC: American Psychological Association, 2008), 25.

Hope and Relational Well-Being

Young people envision, expect, and seek positive connectedness with the past or their memories of life behind them, with other people, and with the environment. Moreover, for them relation-oriented hope is about their longing for mutual participation in social environments, including peer, family, religious, and communal networks that affirm their value and belonging as human beings. When a group of youth in the Youth Hope-Builders Academy (YHBA), a theological program for high school youth at the Interdenominational Theological Center (ITC) in Atlanta, were asked the question "What would you name as one big desire or hope you have of adults?" their answer was "We would want someone to tell us that they love us." When asked what was the one thing they would want most to happen in their congregation, they answered: "That they would involve us, let us do things, and not just sit around." This aspect of hope also focuses on youths' need and search for life-sustaining human resources in community, such as programs that help them and respond to their interests and needs.[23]

Hope for Physical Well-Being

Young people envision, expect, and seek wellness of the body. This dimension emerges from their pointed opinion that nobody wants to be sick. They want to be able to function physically, to live healthy lives, to contribute to the same for others, and to have the necessary resources available to assure this outcome. They want to be safe and out of harm's way. In a seemingly persistent climate of violence, there is among youth a tenacious holding onto hope that impediments to safety will depart. Their hope is couched in a yearning for life, not death; and this hope takes on an active stance in demonstrations that spell out their insistent optimism that their life matters.[24]

---

23 A view of relational well-being is found in Wimberly and Farmer, *Raising Hope,* 19–20.

24 See Wimberly and Farmer, *Raising Hope,* 40–41.

Hope for Psychological Well-Being

In our ministries particularly with black youth, we have discovered that these young people envision, expect, and seek wholeness of mind, personal acceptance, and the valuing of their identities as youth for themselves as well as others. Black youths increasingly place this aspect of hope in practice with Afro-inspired hairstyles and dress while still desiring an inner peace and positive affirmation of their appearance, color, physique, size, motives, language, and cultural artifacts in a culture that repudiates black ethnic norms. But the reality is that all teens desire a positive self-identity and not only a personal sense of value of their humanity but also their being valued and affirmed by others. Young people also seek the capacity to deal with harsh realities of life in life-affirming, life-giving ways in contrast to self- and other-negating and destructive approaches while, at the same time, needing guidance and models in carrying out these approaches.[25]

Hope and Economic and Vocational Well-Being

Young people envision, expect, and seek access to economic resources needed to sustain life and care for self and others for whom they are responsible materially. Moreover, this facet of hope extends to their desire for a sense of life accomplishment, a recognition that God gave them intelligence, gifts, and talents that they're supposed to be able to develop and use, that somebody is supposed to help them develop, and that should lead to and go beyond economic and material sufficiency.[26]

Hope and Spiritual Well-Being

Earlier we referred to youths who proclaim their belief in God but do not consider the church a place to connect. At the same time, there are youths who communicate a clear need and search for a spiritual anchor or experiences with something beyond themselves that could provide

---

25 See Wimberly and Farmer, *Raising Hope*, 41.

26 See Wimberly and Farmer, *Raising Hope*, 42.

purpose and hope amid the tough stuff of life. These youths are not shy in raising the questions "Is God for real?" and "Where is God when I need God?"[27] Spiritual well-being is about persons' experiencing God as a life-giving, meaningful force on whom they rely in pressing forward with hope along the journey of life come what may. Importantly we have heard this view in the stories and statements of youths who speak of hope as a belief or faith in God as they encounter both triumphs and trials of life. When teens in the YHBA were asked about their understanding of hope, they said, for example, that "hope is believing there is a higher power that you can turn to in times of need" and "hope is an awareness of a spiritual presence that can guide you." Their views reflect an understanding that the source of hope is God or a transcendent, life-giving, meaning-generating force beyond themselves that is necessary for life to count for something.[28]

Hope and Leisure and Creative Well-Being

Young people envision, expect, and seek opportunities and modes for self-expression and recreational endeavors that revitalize the self, reaffirm one's gifts, and open avenues for fulfilling hope in other areas of life. Visual and performing arts as well as sports are high among these creative efforts. However this form of hope as an active endeavor encompasses young people's appeal for cultural enrichment that is found beyond the bounds of their neighborhoods.[29]

Hope and Environmental Well-Being

Young people envision, expect, and seek places to live that are environmentally safe and that includes their role in advocating and caring for the surroundings in which they live and the wider material, social, and political environment that impacts the whole of their lives.

---

27 This aspect of hope in Black adolescents is very much akin to that found in other adults. See: Wimberly, "Congregational Care," 105.

28 See Wimberly, "Congregational Care," 42–43.

29 See Wimberly, "Congregational Care," 44.

Hope, Impediments to Hope, and the Nature of Hopelessness

The research of Dana Michelle Harley does not describe in detail each one of the aforementioned dimensions and their connection to hope; however, she confirms that hope is insinuated in youths' experiences of spirituality, having educational goals and the desire for life's basic needs, and possessing the mentality or psychological frame of mind that they're going to make it, which may also be referred to as verve or resilience.[30] More important, Harley's study of youths aged thirteen to seventeen includes findings of qualities that promote hopelessness, including external constraints, the behaviors of others or self that impinge upon life quality or life itself, and deleterious environmental conditions.[31] In other words there are instances in which particular expectations or desired prospects in the multidimensional affairs and passage of young people's lives are called into question or are stunted. The anticipated direction of life that moves toward personal and communal well-being and flourishing goes awry.

Hope for positive future direction and human flourishing become short-circuited where bullying prevails, ill-treatment in school and society occurs, and threats of injury, sickness, and even death exist. This eventuality becomes further exacerbated by the internalization of adverse views of the self and future outlook that begins far before adolescence. This latter situation of preadolescent experiences of impediments to hope are highlighted in the research of Susan Weinger, in which black children ages five through thirteen and living in poverty were found already to have low expectancy of a promising career path. In these instances "the children associated having money with being able to get a job, even if developmentally they weren't yet able to understand this

30 Harley, *Perceptions of Hope*, 24.
31 Harley, 111–28.

interconnection."[32] The children intuited the links between a probable thwarted future and living in poverty, low school achievement, inappropriate clothing, and the improper completion of job application forms. It was as though the child's background functioned "as an intractable 'scarlet letter' that would close the doors to job possibilities."[33] At the same time, however, the researcher found that these children's hope died reluctantly, as reflected in their statements: "She could be anything she wants just as long as she gets good grades in school"; "If he gets pride, he can. He can try to be anything."[34]

The findings of research undertaken by Lopez and his colleagues link levels of hope to health. They show that high levels of hope in young people lead to their care of self and to making healthy choices. Hope, in turn, leads to positive views, expectations, and actions for the future.[35] Conversely youths may imagine a positive life direction for themselves, but the reality of limited access to health care compounded by unemployment and lack of other positive life chances results in untreated physical and mental health problems that stymie their hope. Additionally overall health and well-being has continued to be linked with poverty, unemployment among teenagers, living in substandard housing, and disconnection from needed resources and/or relational support.[36]

---

32 Susan Weinger, "Children Living in Poverty: Their Perception of Career Opportunities," *Social Work Faculty Publications,* paper 5, Western Michigan University ScholarWorks at WMU, 1998, 324. Accessed on http://scholarworks.wmich.edu/socialwork_pubs/5

33 Weinger, "Children Living in Poverty," 324.

34 Weinger, "Children Living in Poverty," 325.

35 Shane Lopez, Sage Rose, Cecil Robinson, Susana C. Marques, and Jose Pais-Ribeiro, "Measuring and Promoting Hope in Schoolchildren," in *Handbook of Positive Psychology in Schools,* eds. Richard Gilman, E. Scott Huebner, and Michael J. Furlong (New York: Routledge, 2009), 40.

36 See: Alwyn T. Cohall and Hope E. Bannister, "The Health Status of Children and Adolescents," in *Health Issues in the Black Community,* Second Edition, eds. Ronald L. Braithwaite and Sandra E. Taylor (San Francisco: Jossey-Bass Publishers, 2001), 27-31; and Anne E. Streaty Wimberly, "The Role of Black Faith Communities in Fostering Health," in *Health Issues in the Black Community,* Second

Researcher Janice Joseph also makes the point that truncated hope or hopelessness has the effect of contributing to drug and alcohol use, gang involvement, teen parenthood, crime and delinquency, and early death.[37] Moreover research results make clear that interpersonal struggles and violence between young people and adults or peers, whether experienced directly or observed, have the effect of cutting short youths' hopeful thinking.[38]

The Nature of Hopelessness

The portent or actual experience of hopelessness happens when the vision of, expectation of, and search for any of the above dimensions of hope are thwarted, repeatedly interrupted, or denied. Much has already been said about this very real and concrete circumstance of black youth. Yet it must not be assumed that hopelessness necessarily or always occurs spontaneously. Young people move into hopelessness in stages.

The first stage may be called hope questioning. In this stage youth ask the pointed question, "What is the use of hoping?" They don't experience hoped for changes or outcomes in their situation or chances. They question if God really answers prayers and conclude, "Right now, I don't see it." This stage is really a time of lament; if acknowledged with the help of caring support and direction from others, hope is restored.

A second stage may be called hope contingency. This stage is reflected in a reluctance to relinquish hope. Hope is maintained on the basis of potential yet uncertain outcomes. We note the embrace of this stage in the research of Weinger, who found that children as young as five held onto a fragment of hope of fulfilling their aspirations even in

---

Edition, eds. Ronald L. Braithwaite and Sandra E. Taylor (San Francisco: Jossey-Bass Publishers, 2001), 133.

37 Janice Joseph, *Black Youth, Delinquency, and Juvenile Justice* (Westport, CT: Praeger, 1995), 168–69.

38 Joseph, *Black Youth*, 42.

the face "of society's prejudicial assaults" if they were able to be a certain way or have a particular attitude.[39]

A third stage may be referred to as hope stagnation. In this stage, one or more dimensions of hope wanes, but utter hopelessness has not yet occurred. When asked how they are feeling about a particular situation in their lives and what they are looking forward to, young people may share statements rather than questions: "I don't know"; "I can't figure it out right now"; "I have to think about it." The danger in this stage is the movement of the young person into depression and reticence to talk with anyone.

The fourth stage is captured in what may be called activated hopelessness. This is a stage of utter hopelessness in which there may be pronounced depression or, as Janice Joseph demonstrated, drug and alcohol use, gang involvement, teen parenthood, crime and delinquency, black on black violence, and early death.[40]

Each stage toward hopelessness represents a movement away from meaning, purpose, and a valued sense of self. When young people cannot make sense of their circumstances and feelings, they are more likely to surrender to hopelessness. Where there is hopelessness, joy cannot abound. At the same time, young people who have the internal and external resources to contend with the many questions and feelings that emerge during these stages can overcome hopelessness. When young people have joy, they are more likely to have hope.

The Intersection of Joy and Hope: Theological Meanings and Attributes

But what is joy? Joy is a person's taste or experience of God and the good gifts that God offers. As people sense or perceive internally and externally this nature of God, they become enlivened, built up, and

39 Weinger, "Children Living in Poverty," 325.

40 Joseph, *Black Youth*, 168–69.

nourished by God, and their hope is enriched. Romans 15:13 illustrates this biblical theology of joy: "May the God of hope fill you with all joy and peace as you trust in him, so that you may overflow with hope by the power of the Holy Spirit" (NIV). In this passage the writer connects hope with joy. Hope flows from the God of hope, filling those who trust in God with joy and peace. A person's experience of joy, then, is rooted in placing their confidence in a reliable God who has the capacity to walk with them in the midst of life's circumstances while at the same time imbuing them with what is needed to transcend those very circumstances. But how does this apply to young people in circumstances that inflict pain on their being? As part of God's family, young people are among those who can transcend life's circumstances and be filled with joy and peace when they have a taste of the God of hope. God as giver of hope provides the grounds of joyful existence by which they can trust in the future while enduring the present.

A biblical theological view of joy is experientially captured in the testimonies of young people. In one instance a young participant in the Black Joy Project asserted that joy is holding to the assurance proclaimed in Psalm 23: "The Lord is my Shepherd, I shall not want; As I walk through the valley of death, I fear no evil; for thou art with me." For this person both joy and hope derive from God as the protector who enables the resistance to the troubles of the world and the temptation to stop pressing forward.[41]

It is impossible to experience joy void of hope.

It is important to note that the presence and power of hope does not always appear as a uniquely separate expression. Hope is a distinctive feature of joy. While it might be possible to experience hope without an outward expression of joy, we contend that it

41 This religious basis for a hopeful way of moving forward is captured in the voice of a young person in: Cody Charles, "Black Joy, We Deserve It," February 17, 2017. Accessed on: https://medium.com/reclaiming-anger/black-joy-we-deserve-it-1ab8dc7569b1

is impossible to experience joy void of hope. Hope is a prerequisite of joy, and joy is a sustainer of hope. Hope makes joy possible. Where there is hope, joy often bursts forth in ways that affirm a close connection between the two. We have found, for example, that songs, sermons, and prayers reveal at least four attributes and meanings of the intersection of joy and hope: joy as an evocative trigger and sustainer of hope; hope as an expressive prelude to joy; joyful expression as outcome of claimed hope and joy; joy and hope as equal dispositions and works of God.

Joy as an Evocative Trigger and Sustainer of Joy

Where is joy found? Kirk Franklin's contemporary gospel song "God's Great Joy" testifies to the evocative nature of joy made possible by God's presence deep in the human soul.

> Joy, joy, God's great joy.
> Joy, joy, deep in my soul.[42]

The song conveys the message that this nature of joy evokes within the self a vital resistance to hopelessness. Joy abides within the very essence of the self. It gives strength and power to continue with hope in life even when food that nourishes the physical body is in short demand. Joy is deemed a "sweet, beautiful, soul-saving" gift of an able God that provides hope for the present and anticipation of life with God after mortal life. From this perspective joy is an eschatological reality deeply felt in the present and expected in the future. Joy replenishes the soul and provides a greater depth of hope in the face of insurmountable odds.

Hope as an Expressive Prelude to Joy

While movement away from hope leads to hopelessness, the decision to hold on to hope, rooted in God, moves one toward joy. In a prayer

---

42 Kirk Franklin, "God's Great Joy," as sung by the Georgia Mass Choir, accessed on http://allgospellyrics.com/?sec+listing&lyricid+12908.

of Richard Allen, who lived in the late eighteenth and early nineteenth centuries, hope is claimed as a way of life based on trust in a suffering God. He addresses God by declaring that in the throes of danger, "I will hope in thee who art almighty power, and therefore able to relieve me; who are infinite goodness and therefore ready and willing to assist me."[43] For Allen the suffering God in whom he trusts knows about human suffering and is a model of hope, thereby making possible his assertion that "I undoubtedly know my Redeemer lives and shall raise me up at the last day."[44]

Allen continues by connecting hope in God to joy in God. For him the sadness of hope in God amid affliction embraces the surety that "tears shall one day be turned into joy and that joy none should take from me" (paraphrase of Ps. 30:5).[45] The intersection of hope that is a prelude to joy is not passive. Hope that turns to joy requires active and steadfast engagement in enacting God's hope for the world. Thus Allen prayed: "Blessed hope! Be thou my chief delight in life, and then I shall be steadfast and immovable, always abounding in the work of the Lord."[46] Overall Allen's prayer indicates the important view that hope expresses itself in a joy that imbues strength for one's own journey while at the same time embodying God's joy in the world.

Joyful Expression as an Outcome of Claimed Hope and Joy

One's ability to rejoice is a direct result of an inner disposition of the heart. In Tramaine Hawkins's contemporary gospel song "I Never Lost My Praise," the key message is one of praising God, which is an act of rejoicing. Joyful praise is evoked by an inwardly claimed hope and joy.

---

43 James Melvin Washington, ed. *Conversations with God: Two Centuries of Prayer by African Americans* (New York: Haper Collins Publishers, 1994), 10.

44 Washington, *Conversations with God*, 10.

45 Washington, 10.

46 Washington, 10.

Joy and Hope as Equal Dispositions and Works of God

The contemporary gospel song "As Far as You Can See" reveals hope and joy as attributes of God. They are equal dispositions and works of God, given to us by faith in God. They are attributes for which we can petition God. Thus the song reiterates the biblical message that "Eyes have not seen, ears have not heard . . . what God has in store for those who truly love him (1 Cor. 2:9)—simply ask him and believe. God is our joy in sorrow, our hope for tomorrow. God will give you as far you can see; all you have to do is look ahead—keep the faith."

Hope and joy are also justly claimed in "I Never Lost My Praise." The testimony is that even amid life's crisis, losses, disappointments, and seasons of pain, struggle, and wayward focus,

> I never lost my hope,
> I never lost my joy.

This reality is also tied to never losing faith in God. Moreover, because of this claimed experience, "I never lost my praise." Both hope and joy are declared as unshakable truths of life accessed in relationship with God even in the throes of unbearable hardship; this claimed and concretely experienced truth of both hope and joy is reason for praising God. Despite the difficult things that happened, the songwriter declares over and over again, "I never lost my praise." This declaration of unwavering praise is another way of saying that one never lost sight of the good. Joy-filled hope flourishes when one can keep the good in sight.

Courageous and Joy-Filled Hope: The Role of Agents of Hope

Our position is that it is both possible and necessary to nurture courageous, joy-filled hope in young people. By nurturing hope youth workers enhance the possibility that youths might experience joy. Indeed youth workers must use approaches that oppose and prevent activities and circumstances that lead to youths' entering stages of hopelessness. Pathways and means of achieving them are needed to stimulate courageous and joy-filled hope and rekindle destroyed hope. This is the role of agents of hope. In every instance the underlying view is that there is an eternal hopefulness on which Christian faith stands and pathways through which courageous and joy-filled hope are activated. The intent of pedagogies of hope to which we turn in the final section is the necessary task of agents of hope. The starting point is the agents' belief in God's promises, the faithful nearness and activity of God, and God's empowerment of youths and all of us to embrace and activate the courage to hope that makes possible a vision of life's possibilities and the ability to act on it.[47] But more important, this belief is intended to be passed on to youth.

Why courage? Agents of hope must be aware of the plain truth that it's difficult, if not impossible, to face and move beyond life's mayhem and its associated dangers and anxiety without summoning courage, which may also be known as an audacious faith or just plain guts. But they must also be attentive to some caveats. Courage is not the opposite of despair. It is not construed as stubbornness; nor is it about thoughtlessly roughing one's way forward in order to prove one's "bigness" or need to compensate for perceived inadequacies. Rather it is what Rollo May calls "the capacity to move ahead in spite of despair."[48]

---

47 This theological framework is set forth in a Black pedagogy of hope that uses a historical biographical method that engages the role of the adult griot/guide as a key agent of hope who tells the stories of forebears, engages participants first as listeners, then in conversation that is to evoke mirroring through artistic expression. The pedagogical model is found in Anne E. Streaty Wimberly, "A Black Christian Pedagogy of Hope: Religious Education in Black Perspective," in *Religious Education in the Third Millennium*, ed. James Michael Lee (Birmingham: Religious Education Press, 2000), 158–77.

48 May, *The Courage to Create*, 12–13. Additional features of courage are set forth in Christopher Rate, "Defining the Features of Courage: A Search for Meaning," in *The Psychology of Courage: Modern Research on an Ancient Virtue*, Cynthia L.S. Pury and Shane J. Lopez, eds. (Washington, DC: American Psychological Association, 2010).

The task of agents of hope is one of promoting youths' claiming their God-given agency and the wherewithal inside themselves that propels them forward in ways that prevent their giving up and embracing apathy and hopelessness. As agents of hope, we are after young people's enactment of the attitude that they must keep on keeping on in spite of whatever the challenge or situation of mayhem is. Moreover the intent is for them to choose to resist the impact of internal and external impediments to hope and, in fact, to consider what God is calling them to be and do to confront and repudiate these impediments. In a real way, it entails guiding teens to consider critically the nature of false hopes offered by activities in the world that take them nowhere and to bring into view the kind of joy that is articulated, for example, in an African American spiritual: "This joy I have, the world didn't give it and the world can't take it away." In short, the courageous and joy-filled hope we are after in the lives of young people privileges their agency as a source of hope while claiming God as the ultimate source of hope and joy.

Agents of Hope as Conduits of Courage and Joy: Pedagogical Suggestions

Agents of hope help to create pathways to joy. These pathways represent experiences that serve as channels for young people's multidimensional well-being and environments for joy.[49] Pedagogically the role of these agents in contributing to young people's courageous, joy-filled hope happens through hearing the stories of teens and providing guidance that fosters this hope. As with hope, leaders' attention to joy evolves from recognition that there is much adolescents want and need to tell about their lives. Joy becomes an outgrowth of hope as young people experience the welcome and caring presence of adults

49 References of these pedagogical pathways appear in Wimberly and Farmer, *Raising Hope*, 93–94.

and, in this presence, form a deep knowing that their lives are given by God—that they are valued, affirmed, and nurtured and have a purpose given by God. Within caring relationships, courageous, joy-filled hope emerges from their surety of God's love, which does not come from simply saying to them, "There's reason to be hopeful and joyful. So have hope and be joyful!" Rather the conditions for hope and joy begin to surface when caring others hear and invite young people's stories both of struggle and lament and of triumph and celebration. In this way agents of hope become the incarnational presence of Christ who sit with, listen to, walk with, share with, support, and encourage youth and engage them in rituals of blessings, communion with God, and service.

As conduits of courageous, joy-filled hope, the role of agents of hope extends to that of praying for and finding ways to take action in the church to assure young people's rightful participation in the public sphere and to assure their well-being. In our age of interpersonal discord, a public theological stance occurs when a congregation offers conflict transformation initiatives or experiential activities intended to engage youths in talking, role-playing, and listening actively to the things that matter to them as means of learning alternative paths by which to understand and act on new responses to conflict.[50] Courageous, joy-filled hope is nurtured when congregations engage young people in

- Spiritual enrichment opportunities that seek to awaken one's soul and promote spiritual growth. In an earlier section, we suggested inviting youth to openly and honestly name the painful places, struggles, and broken places of their lives that characterize a wilderness; engaging them in lament before God; and involving them in spiritual practices such as communal worship, Bible

50 See "Help Increase the Peace (HIPP) Program—PEACE in Action," accessed on: http://www.promotingpeace.org/2006/2/liss.html; and Ed Mahon, "Teens Give Peace a Chance: Four Week Program Helps Chester-Area Youth Find Healthy Ways of Resolving Personal Conflicts," Posted July 2008. Accessed on: http://articles.philly.com/2008-07-20/news/25245691_1_peace-camp-chester-area-peace-program

study, praying, singing, liturgical arts, and endeavors that provide openings for them to search for, hear, and find God and discern God's actions in their lives in the wilderness. We add to these youth-led worship, discipleship studies, labyrinths, retreats, and nature walks.[51] Ultimately these opportunities are to promote what Howard Thurman calls "a discovery of the soul, when God makes known [God's] presence" to young people so they discern their identity in God and their purpose in the world and experience courageous, hope-filled joy that the world cannot give.[52]

- Cultural enrichment opportunities that "provide valuable life skills by enhancing youths' awareness of diverse cultural practices," including "increasing awareness of cultural, intellectual, social, and artistic achievement of one's own culture as well as other cultures."[53]
- Community service opportunities that enhance youths' formation of hope and joy occurring deep in the heart by caring for others through, for example, supplies for needy students, "mission trips, service in hospitals, nursing homes, shelters for homeless people, and soup kitchens, and neighborhood clean-ups."[54]
- Overall health and well-being opportunities carried out by congregations that include, for example, adopting a school and promoting it as a safe zone; providing mentors for youth and supplies for needy students; supporting and celebrating teachers; sponsoring forums for youth and parents; and advocating for neighborhood or church-sponsored health clinics to promote physical and mental well-being. These actions contribute to a hope-bearing future for young people.

---

51 Wimberly and Farmer, *Raising Hope*, 209.

52 Howard Thurman, *Deep Is the Hunger* (Richmond, IN: Friends United Press, Reprint from Harper and Row, Inc., 1951), 160.

53 Thurman, *Deep Is the Hunger*, 209.

54 Thurman, 214.

These pedagogical suggestions actually reflect a pastoral theological perspective that, to build on Mary Clark Moschella's view, shows courageous, joy-filled hope as action. In this perspective "hope might be considered a form of anticipatory joy. Experiences of hope have a future-oriented focus that can support our capacity to imagine new and better worlds."[55] The aim is for young people to arrive at the point of saying, "I get it! I know that God knows me and God has placed God's hands on me!" When agents of hope also become conduits of joy, young people are placed in a position to claim that joy is "confidence in the midst of struggle and hope in the midst of pain. It's pep in my step that keeps me energized just enough to keep going."[56]

---

55 Mary Clark Moschella, *Caring for Joy: Narrative, Theology, and Practice* (Boston: Brill, 2016), 225

56 See Charles, "Black Joy," accessed on https://www.instagram.com/theblackjoy project/.

7

Testimony

The Joy of Adolescent Witness

Amanda Hontz Drury

At twelve years old, I was convinced I was in the throes of religious persecution. My adolescent self was shocked to hear my seventh-grade science teacher speak of creation and evolution in the same class lecture as if both were valid ways of understanding the origins of our universe. What troubled me even more, however, was that one of my own friends didn't believe in a literal seven-day creation story. This friend—I'll call him Ryan—made it clear he ascribed to the Big Bang Theory, and I left the class certain this was a personal war on my faith.

My twelve-year-old self knew precisely what to do. I knew what the proper Christian response was. I knew this was a test, and I was being called to challenge my friend to a lunchtime debate where I could publicly testify that I was not ashamed of the Gospel of Jesus Christ. I was going to stand up for my Lord and Savior lest he be crucified all over again. I would share my faith and end the persecution of my fellow creationists.

And so, in front of my small lunchtime table, I extended the debate invitation to Ryan, who promptly told me no. He wasn't interested in a debate; he just wanted to eat lunch and play cards like we normally did. Nevertheless I knew this was my chance to speak truth into Ryan's life. He might not be up for the debate, but I certainly was. Yes, I was nervous about this debate, especially since my opponent hadn't exactly agreed to participate; but I knew I had to be ready in season and out of season. I knew I needed to be prepared to explain the hope I had in Christ. I knew I would be blessed when I was persecuted and that even if Ryan rejected me, it wasn't really me he was rejecting, but the Lord.

I was eager to tell my youth pastor about my upcoming debate. (I gave myself a week to prepare.) He loaded me up with books on apologetics. My small group prayed for me. And after a week I was ready to jump into that fiery furnace, filled with lions, armed with nothing but five smooth stones and a sling.

The day of the debate arrived. Ryan, myself, and two unsuspecting friends sat at the table together as I mustered up the courage to initiate what I knew was going to be a life-altering conversation. I looked Ryan straight in the eye and asked him if he was ready to engage in a debate concerning the origins of life. "Not really," he said. I was speechless. I was expecting something—anything that would cue my speech. A challenge. A question. Anything. Instead, he said, "I don't really want to talk about it," and then he dealt out the cards for us to start our euchre game.

I had an internal moment of panic. What about my testimony? What would I tell my youth pastor? How would I explain this to my small group? My spirits settled as I came to the conclusion that surely, at the very least, I had "planted a seed."

I didn't have a lot of friends in middle school.

As I reflect on this story, I feel shame, embarrassment, resentment, and a mixture of sadness and anger that perhaps my difficult adolescence didn't need to be quite so difficult. I think the practice of testifying is crucial to faith formation, but it sure made my life difficult. The Word of God was sharper than a double-edged sword, and I was being called to throw myself upon it.

My embarrassment with this story is tempered with compassion. I can appreciate my twelve-year-old self's display of courage as well as my genuine concern for my friends. Mostly, however, I have compassion for my younger self, who put so much pressure on herself to save the world. Somehow at my young age, I had come to see myself as some kind of defense lawyer for the divine, speaking up for this silent, misunderstood Messiah. God needed me to defend his honor. The Savior needed saving. I was the Obi-Wan Kenobi to God's Princess Leia. I could hear him calling to me: "Help me, Mandy. You are my only hope."

Not all of my conversations, however, were as cringeworthy as the one mentioned above. Many of the God conversations I had growing up were life-giving. Some of the most spiritually formative conversations of my first twenty years of life took place with my mother, my youth pastor, and the young man who would later become my husband. All of that is to say that most of my adolescent experiences of talking about God fall into one of two buckets: conversations about God that enhanced joy and conversations about God that inhibited joy.

Creating opportunities and space for teenagers to testify offers them a means of joy.

Ultimately this topic of conversations about God belongs in the more theologically robust category of "testimony," or, if you'd prefer, "witness." Both "testimony" and "witness" come from the same Greek word "mart," from which we get our term "martyr." Before "martyr" took on the meaning we know today, it was simply a term for one who speaks of God. With this understanding one could argue that the deacon Stephen was a martyr even before he was killed in Acts 7. My operating definition for the word "testimony" is simple: a testimony is a story we tell in which God is one of the characters.

Despite my embarrassing adolescent testimonies, I believe a case can be made that the practice of testifying is nevertheless indispensable to the adolescent experience of joy; and when we neglect to create opportunities and space for teenagers to testify, we are robbing them of a means of joy. Of course, not all conversations about God result in joy. There are those conversations about God that seem to suck the life right out of us. So what does it look like to cultivate joy through the practice of testimony? Three ways in which we cultivate this joy are (1) giving our teenagers eyes to see where and how God may be present in their own lives, (2) providing the space and opportunity for teenagers to testify, and (3) recognizing the testimonies shared in a way that offers honor and respect.[1]

The Joy of the Event: Helping Adolescents See God

> Then Jacob awoke from his sleep and said, "Surely the LORD is in this place, and I did not know it." (Gen. 28:16, ESV)

I was in college when my now husband convinced me to watch the movie *The Sixth Sense*. It was one of those films that has a startling reveal at the end that makes you want to rewatch it as soon as it's finished. There is a kind of delight that emerges when you realize the story you were experiencing has another interpretation that sheds a completely different light on the narrative. And so you revisit the story and find new significance to the plot line you had originally followed.

Life can only be understood backward; but it must be lived forward.—Søren Kierkegaard

We interpret things differently when we have new information. Consider Mary's encounter with the empty tomb early Easter morning. We can speak of an empty tomb with a glint in our eye knowing she is about to see the resurrected Jesus; but to Mary the empty tomb is initially terrifying. According to the Gospel of Mark, even when the angel appears and tells her that

1 My past research on the practice of testimony has revolved around a Theory of Articulation whereby we work out and reinforce our faith as we speak it aloud in the presence of others. When we testify to an experience, we are not merely telling a story about the past, we are actually constructing the present as well. Amanda Hontz Drury, *Saying Is Believing: The Necessity of Testimony in Adolescent Spiritual Development* (Downers Grove, IL: InterVarsity Press, 2015).

Jesus has risen from the dead, she and her companion are still terrified. They flee the tomb, "for terror and amazement had seized them; and they said nothing to anyone, for they were afraid" (Mark 16:8, NRSV). If we piece together the rest of the story, we are left with a woman whose terror likely turned to joy as the implications of the angel's words were made clear. With time we might say the tomb transformed from a place of despair to a place of hope and promise.

Perhaps one of the roles of the youth worker is to help a teenager reinterpret their experiences, looking for where God may have been present. We are, perhaps, the Eli to their Samuel, instructing the young that the voices they are hearing just might be the voice of God calling them to something deeper. Perhaps one of the greatest gifts we could give our teenagers are lenses in which they might see where God is discernably at work.

Oftentimes if a church does invite their youth to attempt to discern the movements of God, it's following a mission trip or during a youth camp experience—those highly concentrated times when we might be particularly mindful of the Holy Spirit. If a church does create space for testimony to occur, it's often after events of this sort: "I went on a retreat and here's what happened . . ." We have a big experience, and then we come back home and talk about it. While I'm grateful for these kinds of sanctioned spaces to allow for testimony, my fear is that if these are the only times we are giving teenagers space to testify, we are implicitly sending the signal that God only shows up at the big events as opposed to just a normal Tuesday in the middle of February. We should be inviting our teenagers into a kind of "perpetual advent" whereby we live life with the hopeful expectation of God's presence.[2]

Seventeen-year-old Madie[3] began living in a perpetual advent soon after her youth group began a time of regular testimonies. Every Sunday morning seniors in high school would stand in front of their peers

2 Drury, *Saying Is Believing*, 166.

3 Names and identifying details have been changed to protect the privacy of individuals.

and share their spiritual stories. Madie shared with me how surprised she was by the kind of teenagers sharing their stories. She had assumed it would be the outgoing kids—the ones that gravitated toward the spotlight. What she noticed, however, was that the people who were sharing were the kids "that didn't really stand out in our youth group."[4] This was inspiring to Madie, because, as she said, "I'm pretty shy. I'm kind of in the background, too." Madie reasoned: if they can do it, maybe I can as well. She told me she was planning on sharing part of her story the following spring. When I asked what she was going to talk about, she responded, "I don't know, but I've got my eyes open to see where God shows up."[5] Somewhere along the way, someone had given Madie the eyes to see.

Interestingly enough, the more we see, the more we see. Four years ago my institution began a summer Ignatian Examen program with a group of thirty high schoolers. Every night for two weeks we used the Examen to process our days, attempting to identify those places where it seemed as if God's presence was keenly felt as well as those places where it was difficult to sense the presence of the Lord. Drawing from Mark E. Thibodeaux's book *Reimagining the Ignatian Examen*,[6] we spent every evening asking questions like "Who wore God's face today?" and "When were we clinging? When were we avoiding? When were things just right?"

By the time we got halfway through the program, teenagers began making comments like "I don't know why, but it just seems like I'm noticing God more in my day." It wasn't that God seemed to be intervening in any new kind of way; rather their perspectives were shifting. When teenagers were able to identify where God may have been present in the past, they became more aware of where God seemed to be

4 Madie, interview by Amanda Drury, digital recording. Holland, Michigan, November 19, 2011.

5 Madie interview, Drury.

6 Mark E. Thibodeaux, *Reimagining the Ignatian Examen: Fresh Ways to Pray from Your Day* (Chicago: Loyola, 2015).

moving in the present. Along with this shift in perspective came a kind of joy that they were not alone. This was not just the case when things were going well; that same presence was often testified to during painful moments of the day as well. For many of these teenagers, the main thing they needed in order to be mindful of the presence of God was an explicit invitation to do so within life-giving communities.

Warning

Of course, any time we move into the territory of pointing out where we think God may be present, we find ourselves on tricky theological ground. How can we claim something is of God? Not long ago my three-year-old woke me up in the middle of the night because he couldn't find his beloved monkey. I groggily shuffled to his room and began rummaging around for the small stuffed animal. As the time ticked on, I found myself getting a bit desperate. Finding this monkey seemed to be the only path back to my warm bed. Paul was becoming agitated as well. I said one of those desperate prayers that seem silly in the daylight but profoundly necessary where toddlers and sleep are concerned: "God, help us to find this monkey," I said out loud. "No!" came Paul's startling response. "I don't want God to find my monkey. I want YOU to find my monkey." He was clearly bothered that I would outsource such an important job. When Paul finally reached under a blanket and triumphantly pulled out the monkey, we were relieved. "Thank you, God, for finding the monkey," I murmured without much thought. "No!" yelled Paul again. "God didn't find my monkey! I found my monkey!"

The toddler has a point.

When we start talking about testifying to the divine, we've entered dangerous territory. In the case of the missing monkey, some might question bringing God into the conversation. Is this how God works—finding monkeys and car keys like our personal valet? Those of us hoping to cultivate joy through the practice of testimony would be wise to temper our language with words like "I wonder," "maybe," or "perhaps."

Such circumspect language contains within it an implicit humility that offers up a story to the church for validation or challenge.

This kind of language of humility might also temper the fear of speaking of something that is unspeakable. Public speaking is daunting enough, and the thought of speaking about the divine is perhaps even more intimidating. It is impossible to testify truthfully of the divine. Even the testimony that God is good is untrue in that the goodness I speak of pales in comparison to the true goodness of God. Our words are inadequate, and so we are failing before we've even begun to speak. "He is at one and the same time knowable and unknowable to us," writes Swiss theologian Karl Barth. "At every point, therefore, we have to be silent, but we have also to speak."[7] Our words may be inadequate, but our words are blessed.

The Joy of Articulation: Finding the Space to Speak

> I have seen and I testify that this is God's Chosen One. (John 1:34, NIV)

> You will be my witnesses in Jerusalem, and in all Judea and Samaria, and to the ends of the earth. (Acts 1:8, NIV)

Testifying requires humility. Testifying also requires words. It's not enough to simply notice where the Holy Spirit may be moving. The act of testifying to these stories is also a necessary component of the adolescent experience of joy. In fact we are inhibiting joy when we do not allow space for adolescents to speak their experiences and beliefs aloud. There's an old Franciscan saying: "Preach the Gospel at all times. If necessary, use words."[8] We Christians tend to like this saying because

---

7 Karl Barth, *Church Dogmatics* II/1.322, (Edinburgh: T&T Clark, 1957), 341–50.

8 Commonly attributed to St. Francis of Assisi. While this seems to be a loose translation, the substance can be found in his Rule of 1221, chapter XII, on how

it keeps us actively engaged in the world. We get to physically, tangibly show people our love of God. We are not those hypocrites who simply talk the faith without living out the faith. We also like this saying because it lets us off the hook. It leaves us with the impression that if we just act like a people of faith, then we don't have to actually talk about our faith.

But words matter. One of the major findings of Christian Smith and Melinda Denton's seminal work *Soul Searching* is that teenagers are largely inarticulate when it comes to faith and their beliefs.[9] They are active participants at their local churches, but when they are asked to speak of their faith, they are speechless. Various sociological studies suggest that when someone has a hard time talking about something, that person often has a hard time believing that thing is true. If we can't talk about our faith, we will have a hard time taking our faith seriously. When we talk about our faith, we become more faithful people. Joy flourishes not only when teenagers see the presence of God, but also when they speak to what they see.

When *Soul Searching* was published, youth workers scrambled to revamp basic doctrine curriculum, the logic being that if teenagers don't know what they believe, we should tell them. This well-intended response, however, may not have been that effective. Consider the average seventh grader. Every day this teenager picks up between ten and fifteen new words. Few of these words, however, are picked up through formal instruction; most are acquired through more organic methods. New words are learned in conversation, and unfamiliar words can be teased out in context. This understanding is broadly known as latent

---

the Franciscans should practice their preaching: "No brother should preach contrary to the form and regulations of the holy Church nor unless he has been permitted by his minister . . . All the Friars . . . should preach by their deeds."

9 Christian Smith and Melinda Lundquist Denton, *Soul Searching: The Religious and Spiritual Lives of American Teenagers* (Oxford: Oxford University Press, 2005), 131.

semantic analysis (LSA).[10] The abridged thesis of LSA is that the majority of language that we acquire doesn't come through formal, intentional instruction but is picked up through everyday life experiences. The core principle of LSA is that individuals are capable of figuring out words and their concepts in the context of more informal settings.

Psychologist Jerome Bruner laid the groundwork for LSA with his work on how infants acquire language. Bruner observed numerous mothers reading stories to their toddlers. He found that the toddlers who had mothers who paused for them to participate in the story tended to learn words faster than those who were simply passive recipients of the story. A simple cue like "The cow says—" followed by a pause seemed instrumental in the acquisition of language.[11] Where do we pause in the church? Where are we creating space for teenagers to reflect on where they might be seeing the Holy Spirit? Perhaps the greatest sermon we will ever give is a well-crafted, thoughtful, engaging question that elicits testimony.

Too often we are asking teenagers to simply be passive recipients of our words, and so rather than creating space for teenagers to speak about God, we fill that space ourselves. This makes sense. Anyone who has spent time teaching has probably had the experience of asking a question and being met with deafening silence. And in a room full of teenagers, the sound of those crickets seems to be amplified. But if teenagers are not invited to talk about God at church, if they are not given space to try out their language on religious matters, then where will conversations like this take place? You expect the topic of health to come up when you're in a doctor's office. When you walk into a restaurant, it's expected you will order food. And if you show up at a book

---

10 Thomas K. Landauer and Susan T. Dumais, "A Solution to Plato's Problem: The Latent Semantic Analysis Theory of Acquisition, Induction, and Representation of Knowledge," *Psychological Review* 104:2 (1997): 211–40. For further reading see Thomas K. Landauer, *Handbook of Latent Semantic Analysis* (Mahwah, NJ: Lawrence Erlbaum Associates, 2007).

11 Anat Ninio and Jerome Bruner, "The Achievement and Antecedents of Labelling," *Journal of Child Language* 5, no. 1 (1978).

club, there's a good chance that at some point the conversation will get around to the actual book. You don't walk into a shoe store with the intention of talking about the stock market. And yet testifying or even articulating one's faith in general seems to be something that's done apologetically if at all. Perhaps we give space to talk, but the conversations are on everything but faith.

I often hear the sentiment, "Even if my teenagers were aware of the presence of God, they are not the kinds of kids who could actually talk about it." In their extensive interviews, Smith and Denton surmised that their direct questions about faith seemed to the be first time teenagers were even asked to articulate their beliefs: "Our impression as interviewers," they wrote,

> was that many teenagers could not articulate matters of faith because they have not been effectively educated in and provided opportunities to practice talking about their faith. Indeed, it was our distinct sense that for many of the teens we interviewed, our interview was the first time that any adult had ever asked them what they believed and how it mattered in their lives.[12]

When I travelled the country researching youth groups that incorporated testimony into their ministries, I was struck by a similarity: with rare exception none of the teenagers were volunteering to speak. Instead their stories were often invited by leaders in the church. The stories were drawn out from the teens, oftentimes with an adult talking them through it in advance to alleviate fears. And it can be frightening—those same testifying teenagers would tell you that's the point.

I rode my first roller coaster at an amusement park with my youth group. I was terrified. There was a long wait for the ride, and every minute increased my terror. The designers of the ride staged a dreary car-accident scene complete with a spraying fire hydrant to keep us occupied as we walked slowly through the line. I remember telling God

---

12 Smith and Denton, *Soul Searching*, 133.

that if he just allowed me to make it through unscathed, I would promise to never ride another roller coaster again. I knew I could step out of the line at any time, but I didn't want to be the only one to bow out. By the time I reached the front of the line, I was in tears. Nevertheless I climbed aboard, triple-checked my harness, and shot through the sky, suspended from above, looping and twisting with excessive speed.

I loved it. Afterward I immediately got back in line to repeat the experience, forgetting all about my vow to the Lord. The rest of the day was spent looking upward and walking toward the tallest structures I could see. I didn't use my map; I simply followed the tall towers of twisting metal and the sounds of terror.

Public speaking is terrifying. Public speaking about God, perhaps even more so. Interestingly enough it was the image of a roller coaster that one teenager gave when asked about her experience with testimony. It was terrifying, Meredith said, yet there was also something exhilarating about it. According to Meredith, part of the exhilaration was largely due to the corresponding fear:

> I think that you experience joy most when you're pushed just barely outside of your comfort zone, because you want to be comfortable but sometimes when you are comfortable you don't get to experience it fully. Like when you're on a roller coaster you're not comfortable but you're just outside of it and you know you won't be hurt but it's just enough of not comfortable that it makes you be joyful.

Meredith essentially described Lev Vygotsky's zone of proximal development (ZPD). The ZPD consists of three concentric circles. The smallest circle represents those things one can do by themselves. The outside ring represents those things that the individual cannot do. The middle ring represents what the individual can do when guided by another. Teenagers might think they are incapable of speaking about God, but with the guidance of a thoughtful youth worker, they may be surprised by what they are capable of. We might not have teenagers

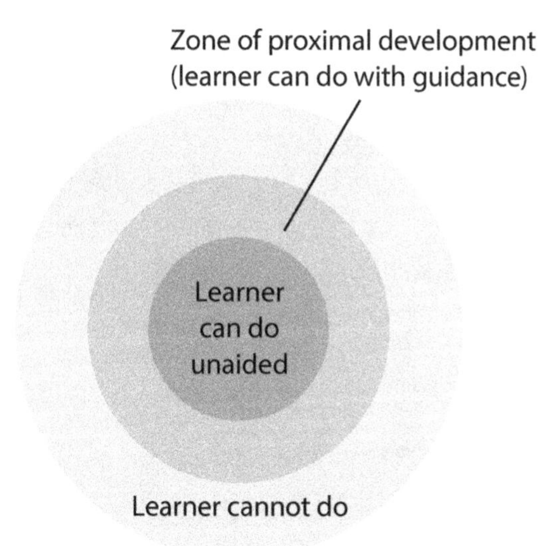

who can easily testify by themselves, but perhaps they can with supportive coaches along the way.[13]

Of course, some testimonies are easier to give than others. If we look for those places where teenagers are already talking, we might see ways in which we might help our teenagers lean in to testimony. If a youth group regularly participates in a weekly update of "highs and lows," what would it look like to tweak that practice slightly to incorporate testimony? Perhaps instead of asking "What was the best part of your week?" we ask, "Where did it seem like God might have shown up this week?" or "Where did it seem like God was absent this week?" Those places where teenagers are already talking could in fact be a kind of ZPD that Vygotsky wrote about.

Jerome Bruner built upon Vygotsky's theory to introduce the concept of instructional scaffolding within educational theory. Just as raising a scaffold can aid in the construction of a building, so too, Bruner

---

13 "Understanding Language and Learning: The Zone of Proximal Development" Open University, accessed May 20, 2018, http://www.open.edu/openlearn/languages/understanding-language-and-learning/content-section-6.

says, we create scaffolds for others who are in the process of building their identities in relationship to the world they inhabit. "As a teacher, you do not wait for readiness to happen," Bruner writes. "You foster or 'scaffold' it by deepening the child's powers at the stage where you find him or her now."[14] What would it look like for us to provide scaffolding in order to push our teenagers just beyond their comfort level? What if we could help them access these joy-filled, intimacy-creating conversations?

Warning

Constructing scaffolding to assist teenagers in testifying doesn't automatically lead to joy. Testimony can lead to joy, but, as discussed earlier, it can also inhibit joy. Some of my interviews on testimony took place at a large evangelical church in the Midwest. A number of the teenagers interviewed reported how much they enjoyed their weekly discipleship groups where they talked about God. Hannah explained: "It's my favorite time of the week, to have that time not even necessarily where we spend a lot of time talking/reflecting about God but just talking about life in general and just seeing God play out through that."[15] Hannah can clearly articulate the joy she finds in her weekly small group. Unfortunately for Hannah, this doesn't count as testimony.

Regardless of the language we use (testimony, God-talk, a story about God, etc.), these teenagers hear one thing: convert non-Christians. From the start it quickly became clear that when we said "God-talk," the teenagers were hearing "evangelical sales pitch." When we said "conversation," they were thinking "conversion." In fact, what we might consider the more natural and organic God conversations that emerged within small groups often seemed to be dismissed. Talking about God in small groups is fine, but the gold standard is converting

---

14 Jerome Bruner, *The Culture of Education* (Cambridge, MA: Harvard University Press, 1997), 120.

15 Hannah, in person interview by Matthew Beck, Travis Bannon, and Anderson Kursonis, Marion, Indiana, November 2015.

the stranger or the atheist at school. Those are the conversations that really count. The primary hindrance to joy was not what they were saying about God; the hindrance was what they thought they should be saying about God.

By far the biggest hindrance to joy in terms of testimony came in the form of guilt teens felt that they were withholding the ultimate antidote for the world. Jesus is their Savior and healer, and they have a responsibility to administer the drug before the world succumbs to the disease. It seemed as if God was a giant EpiPen, and our responsibility was to inject the dying around us. And not just the dying, but to approach person after person, asking, "Are you allergic to peanuts? Do you have an EpiPen?" After all, what kind of monster keeps an EpiPen hidden in their pocket when the world is dying of a peanut allergy?

Even when they think the conversation goes well, the joy these teenagers described was somewhat distorted. James describes the joy he feels after talking about God: "I can look back at the scenario and think, okay, I got through that hard instance and I was able to share my faith with someone even though it was hard. So, I am overjoyed because I can do what God asked me—asks us to do as Christians."[16] In other words he didn't feel joy until the conversation was over and he realized he had done it. This kind of extrinsic joy is not sustainable. The teenager who plays soccer and hates every minute of it but finds joy only after the game ("Phew, glad that's over") will probably not be playing soccer for long.

For many of the articulate teenagers interviewed, there was a scaffold in place giving them the guidance and confidence to testify, but at the top of that scaffold was a shiny gold star, and if their words weren't quite good enough, they failed. Where adolescents seemed to encounter their greatest hindrance of joy was when they testified in order to reach a particular end. Perhaps Bruner's image of the scaffold is problematic in this setting. Perhaps rather than a vertical ladder to traverse,

---

16 James, in person interview by Matthew Beck, Travis Bannon, and Anderson Kursonis, Marion, Indiana, November 2015.

we are better off seeing testimony as a kind of Möbius strip that we climb on and through and around. There is no goal in climbing—just the joy of play and sharing space.

The Joy of Recognition: Receiving and Honoring Testimony

> Samuel lay until morning; then he opened the doors of the house of the LORD. And Samuel was afraid to tell the vision to Eli. But Eli called Samuel and said, "Samuel, my son." And he said, "Here I am." And Eli said, "What was it that he told you? Do not hide it from me." (1 Sam. 3:15–17, ESV)

Sixteen-year-old Justin's camp experience didn't end when he stepped off of the youth group bus. One of the best parts about youth camp was not camp itself. While he reported a fun and meaningful week with his youth group, what really caught his attention was the experience of talking about camp soon after with a friend. Within a few weeks of returning home, Justin ran into a friend who had recently come back from another church camp. The friends got to talking and shared their experiences with one another. Justin explained why this conversation was so meaningful to him:

> It was just the feeling that I'm not alone and that somebody else felt the same way that I did. Me and this person are a lot alike and they went to a different camp, but when we came back and talked about it we were like, "We had similar experiences!" And it was really neat to hear that we were feeling the same feelings about things. . . . I felt like it was God pointing out to me that I'm not the only one out there that feels certain ways.[17]

---

17 Justin, in person interview by Matthew Beck, Travis Bannon, and Anderson Kursonis, Marion, Indiana, November 2015.

When we receive the testimony of teenagers, we are taking seriously a priesthood of believers that does not discriminate by age. For some there is a temptation to meet a teenager's testimony with condescension. Sometimes we patronize what God intends to be prophetic. If there is one thing we learn from Samuel and Mary in Scripture, it's that teenagers can be trustworthy narrators of their own experiences, and we're all better off when we pay careful attention to what they say.

But what if the teenager says something absolutely crazy? What if the words don't make sense, or are somehow dangerous or misleading? How do we recognize words we are not quite sure we accept? On more than one occasion, I've been in a small group of middle-school girls who, when asked where it seemed like God had shown up that week, make comments like, "I saw God this week when we won the volleyball game." Was this God's doing? Was this win a God-ordained moment? Is this an image of God we want to lift up—one where God lets you win games? The task then becomes to respond to this teenager in a way that recognizes her words while encouraging her into something deeper. And so in this particular case, I might congratulate the teenager on the win and then pose the question "I wonder how God may have been present for the team who lost?"

Recognition does not require agreement. We can hear and receive words we question. A testimony is given, and it now hovers before the small group, waiting for us to engage. We've all had that experience of things we say going unrecognized. Dr. Gregory Ellison describes words that "plop."[18] These are the words that we say that spew from our mouths and hover briefly before falling to the ground, unrecognized. Receiving testimony is the opposite. Receiving testimony means instead of allowing words to plop to the ground, we receive them and allow them to confirm, challenge, or transform our understandings of God's being and action.

---

18 Gregory Ellison, *Fearless Dialogues* (Louisville: Westminster John Knox Press, 2017), 67–68. Ellison draws on the works of Jane Vella for this concept.

Warning

Sometimes recognizing a testimony has unintended consequences. Some of the teenagers interviewed admitted they felt jealous when a friend shared about a place in their life where it seemed like God showed up. The word most used to describe God by these teenagers was "friend." While the concept of friendship is generally thought to be a positive one, we would be remiss to not consider the role and function of teenage friendships. The recently coined word "frenemy" describes the adolescent friendship culture well. Within these friendships is also the propensity toward jealousy should their friend Jesus spend more time with another person.

One high school student described it this way: "I have a problem with listening to God. I don't do a very good job of it. I kinda wish I could hear from Him. So when somebody else says that they heard from God, I feel kinda like, ah man, why didn't I hear from God too? Why wouldn't God speak to me?" This same teenager admitted this kind of jealousy was not something she was necessarily proud of: "I know that it's not really a good way to think about it, but when you're comparing your spiritual lives, I'm like, I go to church more than them, or I'm in the Word more than they are, or I try so much harder than they do, and I still haven't heard from God. So why have they been called by God or spoken to by Him and I haven't?"

For those of us who often use familial terms to describe God, we would be wise to include those descriptors that transcend human relationships. Yes, God might be described as a friend, but God is also light, and we cannot hurt a light's feelings. By drawing on images of this sort, we are able to model for our teenagers a God who transcends the human relationships we experience with one another.

Conclusion

Youth workers are invited to play a role in a teenager's unfolding story, helping them see the presence of God, inviting them to speak to that experience, and acknowledging and honoring the words they say. This practice of testimony is indispensable to the adolescent experience of joy within the church, and when we neglect to create the space and encourage the practice, we are robbing these teenagers of a means of joy. While there are certainly warning signs along the way, ultimately we worship a God who not only is actively moving within the world, but who also allows us to testify to this work. The joy that comes with testimony is not limited to adolescents alone. When we are able to shepherd teenagers into joy through the practice of testimony, we experience joy ourselves in witnessing this practice emerge within a young person. We are invited into the joy of seeing a young person grow in fluency in a language they perhaps knew long ago but have since forgotten. And it is here where we can stand alongside the Apostle John and testify ourselves: "I have no greater joy than this, to hear that my children are walking in the truth" (3 John 1:4 NRSV).

8

Agency

The Joy of Activism

Almeda M. Wright and Nyle Fort

While researching joy in and across African American life, religion, culture, and history, we began to wrestle with the historical dimensions of black joy and how cultural memory helps youth and young adults (and even adults) embrace lives of joy and flourishing, but we also began to think about the components or characteristics of this historical black joy. In that research we summarized that black joy (or joy in African American culture and history) was multidimensional.

Black joy is searched and yearned for. People want to see, envision, and experience joy in the midst of and beyond life's trials and tribulations. Black joy is expressed, embodied, and encountered. Joy is not simply expressed orally or verbally. It is expressed, embodied, and encountered in music, dance, smiles, shouts, hugs, food, and laughter shared between loved ones and strangers and as the result of religious, celebratory, and critical life experiences. Black joy is cultivated and chosen. In spite of all that rails against joy, people make a conscious decision to enter into what they envision and expect to be a joy-promising and joy-infusing experience, often with and invited by God. Black joy is resistance and justice. Joy is a way of being and triumphing or having the last word in the face of wounding, life-negating, and life-taking systems, structures, and societies that say black people are not worthy of living, let alone enjoying life. Black joy is intergenerational, communal, eco-connected, and transcendent. Joy has vertical and horizontal dimensions. Joy does not happen in isolation. It is not a one-directional experience. It happens horizontally in relation to and in mutual exchanges across generations, in communities, and with the natural world. It happens vertically in relation to God in response to God's invitation to lean, trust, call on God, and step out on God's word.

> **Youth need agency to choose and more fully experience joy.**

Building on this multidimensional nature of black joy, in this chapter we focus more carefully on the ways that joy is often chosen and cultivated and how we might invite youth and young adults to experience joy for themselves or to see joy as an option in spite of all that life throws at them. One of the important dimensions of choosing joy is agency. In fact, agency is an allied or parallel skill that youth and young adults need in order to choose and more fully experience joy.

What Is Agency?

Why is agency important to adolescent flourishing and to empowering youth to choose and experience joy? Like joy, agency is another concept that defies easy definition and articulation. Without rehearsing many of the debates regarding agency in the social sciences, we note that most often agency is viewed as simply a belief in one's self-regulative capability to attain goals,[1] or as the "capacity of individuals to

1 Barry J. Zimmerman and Timothy Cleary, "Adolescents' Development of Personal Agency: The Role Of Self-Efficacy Beliefs And Self-Regulatory Skill" in *Self Efficacy Beliefs of Adolescents* (Greenwich, CT: Information Age Publishing, 2006), 47.

act independently and to make their own free choices."[2] Agency often is described in individual and personal terms—deriving from our theorizing about a singular agent or actor. However there is also collective and social agency. In particular many social scientists spend years wrestling with the social dimensions of agency and attempting to determine to what extent social structures, including things such as class, sex/gender, and race, affect one's agency or ability to act independently. In part this debate can be summarized as a question of agency vs. structure.[3]

Looking specifically at ethnic minority youths and young adults and their communities, it is important to recognize several potential pitfalls in discussions of agency. Often when we discuss structures and systems, we downplay or overlook the agency of black and brown youths and young adults in the face of immense social structures and systems. While it is important to note fully the power of oppressive structures and the impact of years of oppression on individuals and communities, means of cultivating agency must also be discussed in order for minority youths to flourish. Without a genuine belief in their ability to act and make choices even in the face of structures and systems that are rigged against their success, minority youth and young adults cannot even enter discussions of thriving. In other words, it is important for us to recognize that all youths and young adults have agency—the ability to make decisions that affect their life outcomes—even in the harshest and most oppressive situations.

We cannot downplay their agency, and we must remember the instructions of earlier liberation educators and organizers such as Septima Clark and Paulo Freire, who emphasized the necessity of believing in and trusting people to be agents and actors in their own liberation

2 "Agency" in *Stanford Encyclopedia of Philosophy,* Stanford University, accessed June 18, 2018, https://plato.stanford.edu/entries/agency/. See also Nicki Lisa Cole, "How Sociologists Define Human Agency," ThoughtCo., accessed June 18, 2018, https://www.thoughtco.com/agency-definition-3026036.

3 "Agency," Stanford.

and success.[4] Part of Freire's discussion of the process of humanization (or overturning dehumanization) was that people must see themselves and others as capable of creating change in their own lives. Agency resists attempts at both dehumanization and rendering others powerless (or making people feel as if they are powerless). Similarly Clark's success in training an entire generation of disenfranchised black southerners to read and write so that they could register to vote rests in her inherent belief that they were capable not only of basic literacy but also of full participation in their communities and in the government. She trusted them to be full citizens and agents of social transformation.

This belief in people has to be expanded to youths and young adults, so that we never overlook the capacities of youths to fully participate in their lives and contribute to their communities and world right now. Several religious educators and youth workers have noted the ways that in the United States we have (in the words of David White) domesticated adolescents—pushing them to the sidelines of adult life.[5] And while we don't want youths to have to take on undue and unfair adult responsibilities too soon, we need to recognize their capacities. Likewise we must recognize the differences that youths from ethnic minority communities experience in terms of responsibilities and assumption of adult roles.

Poetry by ethnic minority young women writers shares the collective experiences of many nondominant youths and young adults. These poems describe the responsibilities that minority youths have had to take on even as middle schoolers and teens. The words of Nova Venerable, a young poet featured in the documentary *Louder than a Bomb*,[6]

4 See Paolo Freire, *Pedagogy of the Oppressed* (New York: Continuum, 2003) and Katherine Charron, *Freedom's Teacher* (Chapel Hill: The University of North Carolina Press, 2009) for a fuller discussion of Freire and Clark's strategies and emphasis on love and trust of people in education and social change.

5 See David White, *Practicing Discernment with Youth* (Cleveland, OH: Pilgrim, 2005).

6 *Louder than a Bomb*, dir. Greg Jacobs and Jon Siskel. Siskel/Jacobs Productions, 2011.

as she describes her care of her brother, Cody, epitomize the ways many minority adolescents do not have the privilege to simply wait to grow up. Her poem points to the ways that agency and responsibility look different for many youths.

> Nova writes:
> My youngest brother was born with my grandfather's nose
> round like spools of thread,
> my father's eyes and my mother's genes.
> . . .
> But I can't help but wonder
> Can his brain still hold the times I meshed his food up when he was 8 or changed his diapers at 7.
> Will he miss me when I am not there to run my fingers through his hair like Pink Oil when he wakes up from ear tube surgeries or seizures.
> Will he remember how he slept in my bed every night after mama left, and
> I held him like an extra pillow.
> Or when my arms were his restraints when daddy said put him in middle without seatbelt so he would be the first to die in car accident.
> Can he know how he found a mother in big sister?
> . . .
> I hope that he won't grow accustomed to not pronouncing my name when I go away to college,
> and I pray I pray that his seizures won't kill him before his diabetes does.[7]

Her words force us to wrestle with what agency, joy, and flourishing look like for Nova and many others like her. In many ways she is the epitome of agency. She reminds adults and her peers through her

7 Nova Venerable, LTAB 2013. https://www.youtube.com/watch?v=3kpt1rCtPEQ (accessed April 30, 2018).

creative art that these are her experiences and that she has been making choices about how to care for her brother for years, in spite of the adults around her. She demonstrates agency in choosing not only to live this but also to share parts of her life in her art—speaking to and with other youths to offer the larger society reminders of the health disparities in many communities, as well as reminding religious people that often our platitudes about God don't make sense in light of the lived realities of people all around us. Nova reminds us of the role of agency and making choices that might appear resistant to the stereotypes of young adults while describing how she faces head on the reality that she is being expected to be a parent to her brother long before her more privileged counterparts might have even a part-time job or a student government position.

As concerned adults we must be aware of these differences and be intentional about cultivating the agency of youth and young adults across the spectrum in the United States. Katherine Turpin and Anne Carter Walker, in their book *Nurturing Different Dreams*,[8] remind us that agency for youths, particularly minority or nondominant youths, looks different and can often take on an oppositional or resistance stance/character. Agency is connected to identity, one's sense of who one is and will become (as well as who people, society, etc., expects one to be). Agency is also intricately connected to resisting attempts to prescribe or limit this sense of who and what a person can do and be. Walker and Turpin give examples of students who already have to contribute to their families economically and through childcare and chores, resisting the middle-class narrative that adolescence is simply a time of preparation for the future, where students pass through classes without fully considering what contributions they could make to their lives now. Instead some students resist and protest these expectations, with positive and negative results—but in any case, they demonstrate their agency in the matter. Turpin and Walker write

8 Katherine Turpin and Anne Carter Walker, *Nurturing Different Dreams: Youth Ministry across Lines of Difference* (Eugene: Pickwick, 2014).

> Youth agency, whether developed in authorized or unauthorized forms, serves a key function in helping young people grow into their full sense of vocation. Attending to the multiple sites of agency development among non-dominant youth requires movement beyond typical understandings of entitlement to consider practices of resistance and collective agency in new ways. Often that agency enlivens to fulfill dreams that may be distinctive from those of their adult mentors.[9]

So, what does this all mean for us? How do we help youth cultivate various forms of agency? And in particular, where should we look to take seriously the variety of agency that youths and young adults have and demonstrate right now?

Black Youth Agency as Activism

Where are black youths and young adults experiencing or exhibiting agency and joy? One of the most frequent manifestations of agency among youths and young adults is work in their communities. In particular we focus on their collective agency in resisting attempts to domesticate them and to make them spectators in their own lives. Over the past few years, we have observed increasing numbers of students resisting this passive image of adolescence by participating in acts of resistance and civil disobedience. One example took place in a Chicago high school a few years back. The mayor of Chicago visited an esteemed high school, where he usually gets a warm reception and where the students represent success stories of urban youth with a 100 percent graduation rate and college acceptance rate.[10] Instead of standing to recite the school's creed, the students started chanting, "Sixteen

---

9 Turpin and Walker, *Nurturing Different Dreams*, 54.

10 "Students Chant '16 Shots!' As Emanuel Visits Urban Prep," CBS Chicago, December 16, 2015, accessed June 22, 2016, http://chicago.cbslocal.com/2015/12/16/students-chant-16-shots-as-emanuel-visits-urban-prep/.

shots! Sixteen shots! Sixteen shots!" It became a rallying cry and a well-timed exhibition of their collective agency.

But why? Why would these "good" kids decide to chant against the mayor instead of standing to recite the school's creed? They were protesting the fatal police shooting of seventeen-year-old Laquan McDonald and calling for the mayor's resignation for his delaying and possible cover-up of the information that led to the indictment of Officer Jason Van Dyke. These well-behaved and respectable students made a conscious choice to participate in a legacy of civil disobedience in order to bring attention to injustices around them. In truth the frustrations and outright rage at systems and structures that continue to oppress minorities and youth in the United States offer many snapshots of the role of agency in adolescence and demonstrate where and how youth participate in their larger communities—making decisions and choices that not only affect their individual lives and future trajectories but also have the potential to impact the larger society for good.

The last seven to ten years have experienced an uptick in youth activism and political engagement—notably the resurgence of a type of activism across socioeconomic classes and an increased interest in community organizing—with an emphasis on the unique role of social media. Protests such as Occupy Wall Street, #BlackLivesMatter, and most recently March for Our Lives are becoming key historical markers and movements for recent generations of young people.

Activism and Faith

However, as a Christian practical theologian, my (Almeda) work also forces me not only to wrestle with what is going in society in general but also to look specifically at how and where we see examples of youth agency in Christian communities and how faith connects or does not connect with questions of agency and adolescent flourishing. Therefore I went looking for examples of youths and young adults exemplifying agency as activism and how this activism and agency was inspired by or inspiring their faith. Part of this research entailed exploring exemplars of black Christian youth activism, even though young people do not understand their social and political agency primarily as Christian. Inclusion of the narratives of young Christian activists counters some of the dominant narratives about youth agency and spirituality and offers important models to other youths of the interconnection and integration of faith and activism.

As I looked at the array of youth activism, the landscape included individuals and groups who were directly involved in starting movements and others who later took them up and began to protest, write about, and reflect on the current injustices facing people of color locally and around the globe.[11] Within these groups are also strong African American Christians who have vocally participated in and reflected upon the ways that activism is strengthening and often challenging their faith and practices. For example Jonathan Butler, a graduate student, participated in a hunger strike at the University of Missouri in order to demand change on that campus. Jonathan took seriously what he was embarking upon and recounted to me how he had to draw on his faith, pray, and call his mentors and pastors, because he knew that he could die fighting for what he believed in.[12] Another example is Bree Newsome, who is best-known for scaling the flagpole in South Carolina to remove the Confederate flag days after nine people were massacred in Emanuel African Methodist Episcopal Church. Newsome's work stood out because of the ways that she publicly quoted psalms and prayers as she protested, offering youth and adults another model of black public faith and witness.

---

11 The list of people who are now part of the Black Lives Matter movement and the many organizations that have been created as a direct spin-off (and at times in opposition to the ways that the original creators wanted their work used) are innumerable. Part of the generativity of the hashtag has a great deal to do with the ways that social media is changing how they protest and share information. It also allows for a different type of activism and movement, one which does not depend on a singular charismatic (and often male) leader.

12 See Dana Ford, "Jonathan Butler: Man behind the Missouri Hunger Strike," CNN, November 10, 2015, accessed June 23, 2016.

This landscape of black Christian activism also includes young seminarians and students on campuses across the country who sponsored marches, "die-ins," and protests against national injustices and campus racism (such as the names of buildings that reflect parts of their schools' offensive and unacknowledged history). These groups also coalesced around issues such as racial profiling and harassment by campus police and sexual abuse on campus. In other words, there are a wealth of exemplars of black youth activism and protest just from the past few years.

One example stands out in particular for his integration of faith and activism. Nyle Fort serves as an exemplar of young adult agency and Christian activism. His narrative helps us to better theorize about joy, agency, faith, and resistance in the United States.

Nyle's Story

Two months after I graduated from seminary, white police officer Darren Wilson shot and killed eighteen-year-old Michael Brown in Ferguson, Missouri. It was 2014. The country was about to be rocked by arguably the most dramatic people's movement since the 1960s. I had planned on spending the following year applying to PhD programs. I'm the first in my family to go to college, so the opportunity to get a doctoral degree is a big deal for my family and me. But I had to ask myself: what would it mean for me to get a PhD while people who look like me are being gunned down in the streets by those sworn to protect and serve? And what does it mean for me, a person of faith, to study religion in an ivory tower while black people are being sacrificed on the altar of white supremacy every day? I wasn't okay with pursuing an American dream while so many live an American nightmare. So I got on a bus and went to Ferguson not only to protest police brutality but to do what I believe is God's will: to speak truth to power and fight for freedom and justice.

Michael Brown was no anomaly. It's important to understand that Mike Brown's murder was not a case of bad apples but the strange fruit of a tree rooted in white supremacy. Just weeks before Brown's murder, Eric Garner was choked to death by NYPD officer Daniel Pantaleo for allegedly selling "loosies." Garner spoke for so many black Americans when he gasped, eleven times, "I can't breathe." This epidemic of racialized state violence has a long history in this country, from slavery and lynching to Jim Crow and mass incarceration. James Cone wrote in his book *The Cross and the Lynching Tree*, "Every time a white mob lynched a black person, they lynched Jesus."[13] The state-sponsored execution of Jesus can be directly linked, both theologically and politically, to the execution of black people in America. The question, for me, was simple: What is the church's response to the deaths of Amadou Diallo, Shantel Davis, Michael Brown, Eric Garner, Renisha McBride, Trayvon Martin, Sean Bell, just to name a few? For many churches the responses were, at best, prayer and, at worst, silence.

On the bus ride back from Ferguson, that silence haunted me. I needed to do something. More than prayer. More than a moment of silence. But I struggled to name a church where I could articulate my rage, my righteous indignation in the face of racial injustice. I began to think of Cone, of that rich tradition of black liberation theology, and of growing up in the church. I remembered the many Seven Last Words services I'd been to and how, in my eyes, Good Friday—not Easter Sunday—always felt like the highlight of the black church calendar. (For those who may not know: Seven Last Words services are services organized on Good Friday where preachers exegete and preach the last words of Jesus according to scripture.) As I sat on the bus an idea came to me to remix the traditional Seven Last Words service and, instead of preaching the last words of Jesus, preach the last words of black people killed by police. We called the service "Strange Fruit Speaks."

"I want to go home." These were the last words of Renisha McBride. She was nineteen years old and looking for help after a car accident when she knocked on Theodore Wafer's door. She never got help. She got a bullet to the head. "Mom, I want to go to college." These were the

13 James Cone, *The Cross and the Lynching Tree* (Maryknoll, NY: Orbis, 2011), 158.

last words of Amadou Diallo. He was twenty-three years old, shot forty-one times because he fit the "general" description. "I love you." These were the last words of Sean Bell. Shot fifty times by the NYPD after leaving his bachelor party. He wore the same suit to his funeral that he was going to wear to his wedding.

We held the first service at Shiloh Baptist Church in Trenton, New Jersey. I preached the last words of Jordan Davis.[14] Jordan was seventeen years old. He and his friends drove to a local gas station to buy gum and cigarettes. As they sat in the car listening to music, forty-seven-year-old Michael Dunn became irritated after they refused to turn their music down. He then reached inside his glove compartment for a handgun and shot Jordan to death. Jordan's last words to his friends were "F*** that, n***, turn that s*** up!"

If we were to take a poll asking the American church as a whole, "Whose side are you on, my friend?" the answer would not be Jordan Davis. It would be, at best, silence and, at worst, Michael Dunn. What do I mean? I mean that the church, more often than not, has a Michael Dunn ministry rather than a Jordan Davis message. How often does the church, like Michael Dunn, silence the voices and stereotype the culture of black youth because our music is too loud, our pants too low, and our language too real? How often does the church, like Michael Dunn, murder the futures of black girls and boys who do not fit into the definitions of what white dominant society deems as holy, acceptable, and good? The hard truth today is that every time a black youth is not welcomed by the church—because of the way we look, because of the way we talk, because of the way we dress—we are perpetuating the same pattern that took Jordan Davis's life. We are murdering our babies and doing so in the name of Jesus.

What does this have to do with joy? In black life, joy and suffering are inseparable. That means we cannot talk about joy seriously without

---

14 See Leigh Owens, "Michael Dunn Claims Shotgun Was Wielded Prompting His Shooting of Jordan Davis," *Huffington Post*, November 28, 2012, https://www.huffpost.com/entry/michael-dunn-claims-shotgon-wielded-_n_2207287.

talking about the death-dealing conditions that impede on the possibility of black joy and black life. Otherwise we miss the miracle of Jordan Davis's last words. That staring in the face of death, he insisted on turning that shit up. How we remember those crucified in our midst, how we mourn and memorialize them through song and dance and storytelling, is a kind of celebration. It is a refusal to let death have the last word.

What Can We Learn from Nyle and Many Others Like Him?

After encountering youth and young adults who are integrating strong passions for justice, taking action in the world around them, and looking for ways to integrate this with their faith life, myriad probing questions emerge. How did Nyle (or Jordan) get here? What shaped them? Who are they reading, watching, listening to? Where did they go to school? What injustices shaped their experience? Who taught them that they could or should act and have agency? Nyle shares answers to many of these questions, and he goes further in his self-reflection to help youth workers create strategies for nurturing this type of faith and agency in youth and young adults. Therefore, in the final section of this chapter, we attempt to wrestle with the question of how youth workers can cultivate agency in youths and young adults. While this research has not illuminated all of the things that we might do, it helps unearth several crucial points to get us started.

Learn from History.

Black youth activism, and activism in general, did not emerge in the past ten years. Young people of African descent have been protesting injustice, participating in civil disobedience, and working to enhance their quality of life in every moment in American history. Black youth activism has many historical antecedents. In other research I discuss the trends towards cultural amnesia (or an ahistorical nature) in which young people, in particular, do not fully connect with or claim the precursors of particular traditions and events.[15] However, it is our work as youth leaders and concerned adults, in addition to exploring and offering models of contemporary black youth and Christian activism, to place this contemporary activism into conversation with the larger history of movements for change and the tradition of Christian social witness.

Part of the narrative that often goes overlooked in the discussions of activism in general is the consistent presence of radical young leaders, activists, and organizers. Children, teens, and college students were on the front lines of the mid-twentieth-century civil rights work. Yet before the civil rights movement, children and youth participated in and led the first mass African American march in 1917.[16] The march through the streets of New York City was organized to protest the mistreatment of blacks during a race riot in East St. Louis, Illinois, and to protest lynching and "lawless treatment of Blacks nationwide."[17] According to newspaper reports, there were eight hundred children, some as young as six years old, participating in this silent protest.[18] This event speaks greatly

---

15 John Fea, *Why Study History? Reflecting on the Importance of the Past* (Grand Rapids, MI: Baker Academic, 2013), 173.

16 James Barron, "A History of Making Protest Messages Heard, Silently," *City Room* (blog), June 15, 2012, accessed June 23, 2016. http://cityroom.blogs.nytimes.com/2012/06/15/a-history-of-making-messages-heard-silently/?_r=1; "The First Massive African American Protest in U.S. History Was Led by Children Marching Against Lynching In The Silent Protest Parade," *Black Then* (blog), May 12, 2015, accessed June 23, 2016. https://Blackthen.com/first-massive-african-american-protest-in-u-s-history-was-led-by-children-marching-against-lynching-in-the-silent-protest-parade/.

17 Barron; "The First Massive African American."

18 The National Humanities Center has published primary source materials online which show a memorandum with several banners and slogans to be carried during the silent march. They include the ones listed above and many others with religious connotations and direct biblical quotes. *NAACP Silent Protest Parade, Flyer & Memo, July 1917*, PDF, (Research Triangle Park, NC: National Humanities Center, 2014); See also Barron, "A History of Making Protest."

to the significant and long history of youth activism in African American struggles for freedom and just treatment.

The significance of telling the longer history of activism among young African Americans lies in part in the need to speak to the broader society of the ongoing import and value of the critical reflection and practices of young people. However it also reminds young African Americans of what others like them have accomplished and how they can expand upon the foundations and actions created by others. The stories of contemporary activists combined with this larger history are invitations to explore how youth will contribute to creating change in their historical moment.

Learn from and with Youth and Young Adult Agents of Change.

One of the joys of my job is that I get to hang out with young people. Researching and writing about youth activism and spirituality requires that I get into the fray of their action and activity, that I learn where youths are and go there. Part of our work as youth workers and leaders is to also go where youth are. Far too often we ask or demand that youth come to us—for an hour on Sunday, for class, and so forth—and we fail to see them in the places and realities where they are. We have also failed to ask them where they would like to be, where they are going, or what is most pressing in their needs that they are attending to now.

Our work is to learn from and with youth and young adult agents of change such that we are no longer surprised when teens at Parkland are articulate and have clear visions for the future, but expect that to be the case because we have already seen them in action and know that they have opinions about what is going on in the world around them before, in, and after a crisis. Closely related to our need to learn with and from youth is the recognition that we must constantly remind ourselves that youths have so much to teach us and that they are already capable of contributing to their families, schools, and communities.

Learn to Listen.

One of the major pedagogical and research tools that emerged in my many years of researching youths and young adults is the power of listening. It sounds obvious, but one of the gifts that adults must give to youth and young adults is the power of a listening ear—one that does not come with a preestablished agenda or set of expectations for how a youth or young adult will respond but with a genuine sense that what they have to say and whatever they share is important.

Part of our calling as youth workers is to mirror back to youth the choices and capacities that they have, while pushing them to participate fully in their lives and communities. Essential to this work is developing the discernment to know when to speak and when to listen. Adolescents, particularly minority youth, spend too much time struggling with voice and voicelessness. This is not to say that adolescents are not speaking, but too often when they speak what they say is dismissed or considered invalid.[19] It is our job to listen even when others do not and even when youth feel that what they have to say is not important. I am constantly reminded of Nell Morton's powerful concept of "hearing people into speech,"[20] and that is part of the work we have to do—to help youth see and remember their own agency.

Learn to Embrace Joy.

Finally our discussions of agency and joy have pointed to the many ways that youths and adults need to learn to embrace joy. In particular it is important to help youth embrace joy as an essential part of who they are and not simply a sidebar to their identity and agency. Nyle reminds us that joy and agency are often found in places we do not

19 See Almeda M. Wright, "The Power of Testimony: Spiritual Formation and Ministry with Youth" in *Children, Youth and Spirituality in a Troubling World,* eds. Mary Elizabeth Moore and Almeda Wright, (St. Louis: Chalice Press, 2008), 182-195.

20 Nelle Morton, *The Journey Is Home,* (Boston: Beacon Press, 1985), 54.

expect to see them, such as in the face of death and in a desire to choose joy and freedom even in a world that polices the joy and joyfulness of young black people. Experiences such as these remind us of the importance of helping youth, particularly minority youth, to embrace joy and not to be afraid of it or think that it is something that is beyond their grasp.

Joy cannot be taken away no matter what.

Within Christian communities we often fail to help youth understand what it means for them to affirm the joy that is placed inside of them by God. This is a joy that cannot be taken away even by the most insidious of life circumstances, but that does not mean that youths do not need help and reminders to embrace this part of their life and spirituality. They need constant reminders that they were created for joy, for flourishing, and for love, to be strong, creative, and so much more.

9

Forgiveness and Joy

MIROSLAV VOLF

I write and speak about many topics: about God and God's relation to the world, about Christ and the Holy Spirit, about Christian life, about joy and suffering, about flourishing life, about Christian hope; about religion and politics, religion and economics, religion and identity, religion and violence; about interfaith relations. I also write and speak about forgiveness. No other topic that I engage as a writer and speaker comes close to generating as much consistent interest as does forgiveness. In my experience, limited as it is, forgiveness is as alive a topic today as it ever was, as pressing in Brazil, China, Croatia, and Australia as it is in the United States.

In this text I draw on the three-year study "Joy and the Good Life" at the Yale Center for Faith and Culture (funded by the John Templeton Foundation) and on the ideas in my writings on forgiveness, reconciliation, and memory, including *Exclusion and Embrace: A Theological Exploration of Identity, Otherness, and Reconciliation*, rev. ed. (Nashville: Abingdon, 2019); *Flourishing: Why We Need Religion in a Globalized World* (New Haven: Yale University Press, 2016); *The End of Memory: Remembering Rightly in a Violent World* (Grand Rapids, MI: Eerdmans, 2006); and *Free of Charge: Giving and Forgiving in a Culture Stripped of Grace* (Grand Rapids, MI: Zondervan, 2005).

Our interest in forgiveness stems from a need like that of removing a stone from our shoe. It is about relieving the pain of having wronged someone or of having been wronged by someone. Not surprisingly, then, forgiveness has its joys. "Happy are those whose transgression is forgiven, whose sin is covered," sings King David, according to Psalm 32:1 (NRSV). The Apostle Paul referred to these very words when, in Romans, he noted that "David speaks" of "the blessedness" of those whose iniquities are forgiven and to whom God therefore "reckons righteousness apart from works" (Rom. 4:6 NRSV). "Happiness" and "blessedness" in David's and Paul's sense are not exactly the same as joy, but joy is an integral part of them. The NRSV translators of the Hebrew Bible thought so; they titled Psalm 32 "The Joy of Forgiveness."

We rejoice and we forgive differently at different life stages.

My theme in this essay is forgiveness and the kind of joy that is peculiar to forgiveness. What is forgiveness, and why does it matter so much? What is joy, and how is it experienced (or not) in forgiveness? When I write here about forgiveness and joy, I have in mind primarily personal forgiveness and personal joy. There is group forgiveness, when one social group forgives another, and there is also political forgiveness, when people forgive agents of a state. Similarly there is communal joy—when whole communities celebrate and in celebrating create something like a space of joy. I leave these social and political kinds of forgiveness and these communal and "territorial" kinds of joy aside in this text. My interest is in more personal forgiveness and joy.

The book in which this essay appears is about forgiveness and joy in adolescence. We rejoice and we forgive differently at different life stages. Compare the joy of a child with the joy of a person at the sunset of their life—both genuine, both beautiful, and each different. The first is immediate, like the sound of many bells ringing all at once, and unencumbered by memories and hopes; the second is subdued and rich, with traces of sorrow and fear that linger in it and give it depth, like the bouquet of a good and aged wine. The forgiveness of a child and the forgiveness of an elderly person are different in similar ways. Somebody else, better qualified than I, would need to write about the specific character of forgiveness and joy in a life that is no longer that of a child but isn't yet that of an adult. This essay, even though it appears in a book about adolescent joy, is about what is common in forgiveness and joy as most of us experience them, including adolescents.

Even after I have limited my topic to transgenerational human and personal forgiveness and joy, it remains vast. My text, on the other hand, is short. What I offer is a brief sketch.

Forgiveness

Why Forgiveness Matters

To see why forgiveness matters, we need to identify situations in which forgiveness is needed. It is the frequent occurrence of one individual wronging another individual. (It is possible also to wrong oneself and to forgive oneself, but self-forgiveness, though both crucial and difficult, is a special case of forgiveness, deserving distinct treatment.) Crucial to the sense of the need for forgiveness is the fact that a wrongdoing isn't just an event that happens and is then over, swallowed by time. As a rule it continues to live in the memories of both parties, especially the victim.[1]

First, wrongdoing qualifies the continued relation of the wronged person to him- or herself as well as to the perpetrator, whether that relation happens in mutual exchanges in real life or only in imagination. Second, wrongdoing can make it hard for victims to live with themselves, as they may be plagued by a sense of shame and resentment. For both of these reasons, wrongdoing often makes it impossible for the victim and perpetrator to live together. Victims cry for some sort of punishment, and perpetrators seek to justify themselves and sometimes even

---

1 Increasingly it also shapes the public perception of the parties involved, as it often lives not just in their memories but in electronic databases of social media and surveillance networks.

counter-accuse victims. Both stances reinforce enmity: the perpetrator sees the victim's cry for punishment as aggression, and the victim takes the perpetrator's self-justifications as a threat of new violations.

Forgiveness is designed to start building a bridge between victim and perpetrator. As I will explain shortly, for the bridge to be completed, more than forgiveness, such as apology, restitution, and trust-building, will be needed. What makes the need for forgiveness pressing is, first, the simple "metaphysical" fact that, once committed, a wrong cannot be undone; we cannot change the direction of the arrow of time. Though the passage of time may heal some wounds, it doesn't rectify any wrongdoings. Second, payback is not a workable alternative to forgiveness. It is intended to even the score, but it almost always starts a cycle of wrongdoing: what a victim considers just retribution, a perpetrator often considers excessive vengeance; what a perpetrator may agree to as proper restitution, a victim dismisses as an insulting flight from responsibility.

From a Christian perspective, forgiveness is a moral obligation; it is always the right thing to do (though there are wrong ways of doing it, and some of them are related to the readiness for forgiveness). In cases when both victim and perpetrator can each go their own way, they may not experience forgiveness as pressing. Often, though, separation is either not possible or is too costly, and sometimes neither party wants it: they are siblings, spouses, business partners, or members of the same club, for example, and each has a stake in continuing the relationship. In such circumstances forgiveness is not just morally required; it is also the only workable option.

What Forgiveness Is and Isn't

Forgiveness isn't the name of the work a victim may need to do to overcome resentment the wrongdoing may have caused. Such therapeutic work may be necessary so that a person can cast off the freight of the troubling past and walk into the future unburdened. But that therapeutic work is not forgiveness, though forgiveness will likely *help* in overcoming resentment. Inversely, too, overcoming at least a degree of resentment may be necessary for the process of forgiveness to begin. Overcoming resentment and forgiveness are both important and related, but they are not identical.

Second, forgiveness isn't just shrugging the wrongdoing off, implicitly declaring that it doesn't really matter. True, some minor transgressions deserve no more than disregard. Sometimes that's what we do with wrongs we suffer. But to disregard is not to forgive; it is to recognize that in the lives of humans minor transgressions occur all the time and to decide that a given transgression isn't significant enough to merit forgiveness. Certain kinds of minor transgressions are systemic—what we call today microaggressions—and they therefore require not so much apology and forgiveness as change in cultural perception and culturally acceptable patterns of behavior. Only when microaggressions are deliberate and culpable do they require forgiveness.

Properly understood, forgiveness happens *between* a victim and a perpetrator, not just in the interiority of the victim, just as the wrongdoing that calls for forgiveness has happened between them even as it was done to the victim. (Overcoming resentment and disregard are both processes internal to the victim.) Forgiveness happens between victim and perpetrator even when the perpetrator doesn't want to be forgiven or isn't around to be forgiven. Forgiveness has the structure of a gift: somebody gives something to somebody else. I never just forgive; I always forgive *someone*. If that other person is not present in flesh, they will be present in my imagination as the intended recipient of the gift of forgiveness. And if an actual perpetrator facing the victim refuses the gift of forgiveness, the refusal, just as the gift itself, will have happened between the two of them.

The gift of forgiveness has two key elements. The first is *naming* the wrongdoing that was done *as wrong*. Even when I simply say to you, "I forgive you," I imply that you have somehow wronged me; it makes sense for me to use that phrase only when I know that you know—or when I think that you ought to know—that you have wronged me in a specific way. But most often I say, "I forgive you for . . ." and then name the wrong, because I want to be sure that we agree on the matter. I cannot just forgive; I must forgive *something*, some case of wrongdoing. The second element of forgiveness is not counting the wrong against the one who committed it (as when the psalmist writes: "Blessed are those whose iniquities are forgiven, and whose sins are covered; blessed is the one against whom the Lord will not reckon sin" [Ps. 32:1–2; Rom. 4:6–8] NRSV). This not counting of the wrongdoing is the gift that forgiveness is, the heart of forgiveness: In forgiving I declare myself ready—though not necessarily fully able—not to hold against the wrongdoer the wrong they have committed.

Not counting or holding wrongdoing against the wrongdoer is not the same as treating the wrongdoer as if they had not committed the wrong. It is easy to see the difference if one considers the relation between forgiveness and punishment. If I treat the wrongdoer as if they have not committed the wrong, I cannot legitimately punish them. It is different if I don't count the wrong against them. Forgiveness is then, of course, incompatible with retribution; if I don't count the wrong a person has committed against them, I cannot pay them back for having committed it. But forgiveness as not counting against is compatible with other goals of punishment—the rehabilitation and incarceration of wrongdoers, for instance. When I seek to rehabilitate the wrongdoer, I treat them as a wrongdoer but as a wrongdoer forgiven.

Goals of Forgiveness

I already noted what is *not* the main goal of forgiveness: it is not to help the victim overcome resentment. The overcoming of resentment is one possible consequence of forgiveness; it can therefore be one of its subsidiary goals. When we give a gift to others, we do so mainly for their sake—if the gift is a genuine gift—even if it is true that we ourselves benefit from having given them a gift. The same is true of forgiveness: we forgive mainly for the sake of the wrongdoer and as a step toward restoring the relationship damaged by wrongdoing. Overcoming resentment that we experience as a result is a welcome additional benefit of forgiveness. In the sermon "Two Kinds of Righteousness" (1519), Martin Luther expressed the gift character of forgiveness better than anyone I know. Those who follow Christ, he wrote,

> grieve more over the sin of their offenders than over the loss or offense to themselves. And they do this that they may recall those offenders from their sin rather than avenge the wrongs they themselves have suffered. Therefore, they put off the form of their own righteousness and put on the form of those others, praying for their persecutors, blessing those who curse, doing good to the evil-doers, preparing to pay the penalty and make satisfaction for their very enemies that they may be saved.

He concludes the passage, "This is the Gospel and the example of Christ."[2]

Once the perpetrators are restored to the good from which they had fallen in committing the wrong, the possibility of reconciliation is opened. *Possibility*, I write, because forgiveness takes care of the burden of the past, preventing the dead hand of transgression from reaching into the future. For reconciliation to happen and life together to result, trust needs to be restored and commitment to the relationship renewed. Forgiveness doesn't restore trust or renew commitment, but it prepares the way for restoration and renewal of commitment.

Forgiveness, Repentance, Restitution

Forgiveness is a gift, and most gifts need to be received for them to be properly given. That's the case with forgiveness as well. When a victim gives a gift of forgiveness to a perpetrator, the perpetrator needs to receive it by repenting. What does it mean to repent, to apologize? It means to *say* to the person we have wronged that we are sorry—sorry not that we have been caught, sorry not merely that the other person

2 Martin Luther, in *Luther's Works*, vol. 31, ed. Harold J. Grimm (Philadelphia: Fortress, 1957), 306.

has been wronged, but sorry also that we committed the wrong; and sorry not so much for our guilt and shame as for the suffering we have caused. We pull down the veil of silence behind which we often hide wrongdoing, and we bring the moral stain of our misdeed into light.

If it is to be rightly done, apology must be sincere. In the Christian sacrament of confession, for instance, *contrition of the heart* must accompany confession of the mouth. To repent we must mean what we say; our mouth cannot tell a lie about the state of our heart. Finally, in saying and meaning that we are sorry, we commit ourselves to act otherwise in the future. We state to the victim and the wider public that the wrongdoing isn't a true expression of who we aspire to be and therefore how we intend to act in the future but a culpable aberration in our moral history we are determined not to repeat.

For the apology as a whole not to be a sham—and for it to prepare the way for reconciliation—wrongdoers must make a good-faith effort to remove as much as is reasonably possible of the damage their wrong has caused. They show the genuineness of their repentance by reparation. True, sincere apology already removes some of the damage: in disavowing the deed, the wrongdoer removes from the victim the harm of having disrespected them. As a rule, however, a wrong involves more than mere disrespect; some further damage occurs—to the person, family, community, or the possessions of the victim. That damage ought to be repaired as well, to the extent that this is possible. Without willingness to repair that damage, the wrongdoer's apology remains hollow, mere words and empty sentiments, hovering over a damaged relationship rather than altering it and inviting a suspicion that the purpose of the apology was not to acknowledge the wrongdoing but to repair the wrongdoer's reputation on the cheap and to allow them to continue benefiting from wrongdoing.

Why Forgiveness Is Hard

While I was working on *Free of Charge*, a book about giving and forgiving, a woman wrote me a letter. "Let him burn in hell forever!" she wrote.

"Him" was Josip Broz, or Marshal Tito, the authoritarian ruler of socialist Yugoslavia. The woman who wrote was from Croatia, and in the political turmoil following World War II, she had lost everything she and her family possessed. They had suffered the fate of many of Tito's "enemies of the people" (and the terrible fate that even some of Tito's sympathizers, like my father, suffered as well). When she wrote to me, she had just seen a TV special on my work, done by the PBS program *Religion and Ethics Newsweekly.* In it, reconciliation and forgiveness—the main themes of my book *Exclusion and Embrace*—had featured prominently. She liked none of what she had seen and heard me say. Not forgiveness but vengeance was what she was after, even fifty years after the crime. Tito had ruined her life; she had had to rebuild it from scratch in the New World; Tito's life ought to be ruined, she felt—irredeemably and forever.

It is not hard to empathize with her. The wrongs she suffered continued to live in memory and in its effects on her life, and the victim found herself longing for revenge. Foregoing revenge or any form of payback is the hard work a forgiver is required to do. But it seems unfair for the one upon whom wrongdoing was inflicted to have to do the labor of repairing the damage. They first suffer the injustice of the violation, and then they suffer the injustice of forgiveness and repair.

It may be that forgiveness is the strategy of the weak, and those thinking in the trail of Friedrich Nietzsche like to say this. But the strategy also requires power and is empowering. For in forgiving I am not surrendering or submitting. I exercise moral agency and thereby reaffirm myself as more than a mere victim: I am an agent who, despite having suffered wrong, acts with moral integrity and moral excellence, whereas the wrongdoer has morally debased themselves. In the act of forgiveness, the wrongdoer appears publicly—or at least in the interchange between the two—as what they are, a condemnable wrongdoer. The victim, on the other hand, is not merely acknowledged as having been wronged and as being magnanimous; forgiveness is a power act to release from condemnation the one who deserves punishment. That's why in many cases it seems easier to forgive than to repent.

Why We Should Forgive

Those who think that forgiveness is primarily about managing victims' resentment believe that we should forgive because forgiving is good for us. By forgiving we give ourselves a gift of freedom; by withholding forgiveness we sink into the bog of bitterness, rage, and malice. Though it is true that resentment is bad for us psychologically, according to the Christian faith we forgive for a more noble reason. In forgiving we enact our true humanity; resentment, and its stronger sibling, hate, is a "sickness of the soul," as Etty Hillesum, a young Jewish woman living in Amsterdam under Nazi occupation, wrote.[3]

But why is forgiveness an enactment of our true humanity? The Christian answer is this: human beings are the image of the God of unconditional love. That is a statement of fact about God and humans, articulated and affirmed in faith and hope. We cannot just observe the world and draw this conclusion; we confess this to be true. God is love, and out of love God created the world. God's aim in creating the world was to make the world God's and humans' home in one. A key element in the world's becoming God's home is for human beings, all our diversity notwithstanding, to come to echo God's character in becoming both givers and recipients of unconditional love.

Unconditional love does not get us to forgiveness by itself, though. The ultimate object of Christian hope is that when the world truly becomes God's home, unconditional love will be universally enacted in a world without wrongdoing. The world to come will be a world without forgiveness. The world in which forgiveness is needed is this present world, a world in which wrongdoing, sometimes of the most egregious kind, is a daily occurrence. When unconditional love encounters wrongdoing, forgiveness is born—not just forgiveness, of course, but the entire movement of returning wrongdoers to the good from which they had fallen and transforming broken relationships into

---

3 Etty Hillesum, *An Interrupted Life and Letters from Westbrook*, trans. Arnold J. Pomerans (New York: Holt, 1996), 11.

exchanges of gifts freely given and gladly received. But forgiveness is an indispensable part of that movement. Forgiveness is a fruit of unconditional love turned toward the wrongdoer, an aspect of the practice of true humanity in a world of sin.[4]

Why No Forgiveness Is Perfect

The need for forgiveness arises in a world in which wrongdoing happens. The world's imperfection makes forgiveness necessary. But the world's imperfection also makes forgiveness *necessarily imperfect*—or at least this is what Christians, especially those who follow in the footsteps of Martin Luther, will tend to think.

The imperfections of forgiveness all stem from a combination of finitude, fragility, and self-centeredness that qualifies being human in the present age of the world. To forgive perfectly, we would need to know and agree on the exact nature of wrongdoing, for instance, but as finite beings we cannot know exactly and are highly unlikely to truly agree. To forgive perfectly, we would need to be free from the worry that a forgiven perpetrator would repeat the wrongdoing, against us or against someone else, but unless we are blindly naive about human self-centeredness and propensity to evil, the worry will persist. To forgive perfectly, we would need to impart the gift of forgiveness without a sense of moral superiority and without humiliating the forgiven wrongdoer and keeping them in our debt, but that would be to expect too much from most victims, all fragile humans wounded by wrongdoing.

Those who insist on forgiving perfectly will never forgive; those who expect to receive perfect forgiveness will never be forgiven. Those who insist on perfect repentance or wait for perfect restitution will always remain disappointed and will likely withdraw the gift of forgiveness from those who want to receive it with impure hands. As Christians we ought to strive to improve the ways we forgive and receive forgiveness but not let the imperfection of our forgiveness and our reception

4 See Volf, *Exclusion and Embrace*, 356–67.

of it deter us from forgiving. All human acts of forgiveness in the course of history are an echo of God's reconciling of human beings with God and with one another through the death of Christ on the cross. They are best understood as anticipation of the final Day of Judgment, which will also be the Day of Reconciliation,[5] when God will complete the work of reconciliation and all humans will be brought into harmony with one another and with God.

Forgiveness and Its Joy

What Joy Is and Isn't

Forgiveness is complicated, but joy should be simple, we may be tempted to think. Joy is three little girls running through sprinklers on a sweltering summer day and squealing with delight. Joy is those same girls picking half a bucket of crab apples, setting up a stand on the curb of a street, charging two cents per apple, and having a driver, who hasn't forgotten what it means to be a child, stop and purchase two crab apples for a dollar. Joy is their uncle observing these scenes with a twinkle and a smile of quiet delight and exclaiming to their aunt, "Isn't this splendid?"

If you pick apart these experiences of joy—and the experience of analyzing these experiences as well, provided you enjoy certain kinds of intellectual puzzles—you can identify some key elements of joy. First, joy involves a positive feeling, often expressed bodily in laughter, clapping of hands, or dancing. Second, joy is feeling good about something good. Though it is possible to just feel good, we never just rejoice; we always rejoice *over* something: when we find a valuable lost coin or when our lost child returns home (see Luke 15). Third, we rejoice over good things that happen either to us or to those for whom we care.

---

5 On the idea of eschatological reconciliation, see Miroslav Volf, "The Final Reconciliation: Reflections on a Social Dimension of the Eschatological Transition," *Modern Theology* 16 (2000): 91–113.

More precisely we rejoice over things we deem to be good, for we will rejoice over something that in fact is bad, even evil, if we believe that it is good. (If a fish could experience joy, it would rejoice seeing and biting a worm hanging from a hook, but it wouldn't take it long to realize that its joy, though genuine, was misplaced.)[6] Fourth, we tend to like better rejoicing with others than alone; when we feel joy, we like to call a friend or a relative and say, explicitly or implicitly, "Rejoice with me!" (Luke 15:6 NRSV). Finally, for the most part, we rejoice when we experience the good things coming to us as gratuitous and surprising rather than as a matter of course, for instance, when we fall in love or when we fear that we have done badly on a test but get a good grade.

It would seem that forgiveness would be a prime occasion for rejoicing, at least for the wrongdoer. A wronged person gives the wrongdoer the gift of not counting their wrongdoing against them. A gift has been given, a gift that removes the stain from the wrongdoer's character and opens a way to a restored relationship. Forgiveness should elicit joy. Yet often the predominant emotions associated with forgiveness are negative.

Forgiveness and Negative Emotions

Forgiveness is always imperfect, I wrote earlier. There are many ways in which forgiveness is not just imperfect but gets morally twisted and becomes injurious, a wrong of sorts in its own right. Some negative emotions accompany and follow most forgiving, but they abound when forgiveness goes wrong. Positive emotions, including joy, are often present as well, as we would expect; the better the forgiveness, the more joy will accompany it. But that's forgiveness done right. Let's examine first the emotional tonality of forgiveness gone wrong.

To forgive and to receive forgiveness is to remember, and if we remember well a wrong suffered and committed, we may remember not just the fact of it but also the emotions that accompanied it. A victim

6 The second and third features of joy are consequences of joy being an emotion that involves judgment rather than a mere affective reaction to a stimulus.

might remember their own pain, shame, and anger as well as the perpetrator's pride, sense of power over them, and self-satisfied gloating. A perpetrator may remember those same triumphant emotions that the victim had recognized in them; but they may also remember shame and self-loathing that followed the wrong. The memory of emotions experienced during the violation and in its aftermath will hover over the process of forgiveness, because we cannot forgive a wrong without remembering it. Little joy is likely to be found among these emotions, unless we count schadenfreude as joy.

Negative emotions swirl around other dimensions of forgiving as well. Consider, first, emotions associated with the receiving end of forgiveness, with repentance. In forgiving, the forgiver separates the wrongful deed from the doer, removes the perpetrator's stain. That is an exceptional gift that should elicit joy. But the very act of forgiving names and highlights the contrasting moral standings of the two parties. The perpetrator is guilty, and the victim is innocent, and innocent precisely to the degree that forgiveness is appropriate. In granting forgiveness, the victim may show contempt for the perpetrator and flaunt their moral superiority, injecting their gift with the poison of derisive and aggressive innocence. In response, the perpetrator will likely feel abased by having been an object of such insufferably self-righteous forgiveness. In fact, the more genuine the repentance, "the more deeply [he] feels his wrong and in that way also his defeat, the more he must feel repelled" from the one who forgives, wrote Søren Kierkegaard in *Works of Love*.[7] Kierkegaard wrote these words about the reaction to forgiveness done well, to the forgiver who "lovingly deals" the wrongdoer the "merciful blow" of forgiveness. How much more do they apply to forgiveness done wrongly! Forgiveness may be a gift that makes the wrongdoer retreat in shame rather than dance with joy.

In repenting, the wrongdoer acknowledges and condemns the wrong they have committed and underscores that the deed was not

7 Søren Kierkegaard, *Works of Love*, trans. Howard V. Hong and Edna H. Hong (Princeton: Princeton University Press, 1995), 339.

a true expression of the kind of human being they aspire to be. If forgiveness precedes apology, in repenting the wrongdoer affirms in their own right their separation from the deed that the forgiving enacts. Guilt, shame, and remorse are emotions appropriate to repentance. As we will see, joy will be present as well, but in a way, guilt, shame, and remorse are conditions of that joy.

Negative emotions will slither into forgiveness through the memory of wrongdoing and through the way the gift of forgiveness is both given and received. They can also infest forgiveness through uncertainty about its results, uncertainty being fundamental to forgiveness as a free act of grace. Repenting and forgiving both involve risk. Apologizing, the perpetrator is unsure whether the apology will remove shame and guilt or publicly display and therefore enhance them. The victim, on the other hand, may fear that the apology may not come or that it may be false: the perpetrator is repenting not so much to acknowledge the wrong but to evade the responsibility; their apology is a fresh wrong rather than a repair of the original one. The process of forgiveness often generates fear in both victim and perpetrator. And fear keeps joy at bay.

Joy of Forgiveness

With many negative emotions churning in such close proximity to forgiveness and accompanying its very exercise, is there any room for joy? If we are after pure joy, we won't find it in forgiveness; in fact we won't find it anywhere this side of the transition into the world to come. Except in the moments of a self-forgetting and world-forgetting ecstasy, no self-aware joy will be pure. Since all forgiveness is imperfect as well, as I have noted earlier, and is, moreover, tied to wrongdoing, negative emotion will complicate all joy brought about by forgiveness. But it would be a mistake to let negative emotion occlude the brightness of the joy of forgiveness. Let's revisit victim, perpetrator, and their future made possible by forgiveness, focusing this time on forgiveness done right rather than forgiveness gone wrong. We will find joy in each of these moments of forgiveness. In fact I propose that the presence of genuine joy is one of the signs of forgiveness done right.

Consider, first, a repentant perpetrator receiving the gift of forgiveness. The dominant emotion will be remorse, sorrow for the injury he or she caused, and sorrow for having betrayed God's law of love and therefore also his or her own humanity. But this will be a "bright sorrow," to borrow the phrase from Alexander Schmemann.[8] He used the phrase to describe joy more generally, because joy ought always also to "honor" the pain of the world. But the image of bright sorrow does not sufficiently honor joy's joyfulness; perhaps it is better to call all joy, more clumsily, "sorrowful brightness."

But the phrase "bright sorrow" describes well the kind of joy that accompanies genuine repentance. Joy, subtle and quiet, is an integral part of repentance and not just a result of genuine repentance. For repentance is not a mere neutral zone between evil and good through which those who have committed wrong must pass in order to return to the good. In repenting I am differentiating myself from my wrongdoing; I am embracing the good in renouncing my wrongdoing. That act is therefore properly an object of joy. Jesus implies as much when, in the stories of the lost sheep and lost coin (Luke 15:1–10), he speaks of the joy in Heaven not simply over the sinner who has repented, but, more precisely, over a "repenting sinner" (vv. 7 and 10). As God rejoices over the act of repentance, so should humans, both forgiving victims and repentant perpetrators. Though the emotion attending repentance is mainly sorrow—"godly grief" is the phrase the Apostle Paul uses in 2 Corinthians 7:9–11—true repentance already includes in itself joy. And leads to joy, of course, the joy of freedom from condemnation and guilt.

Consider, second, the victim imparting the gift of forgiveness rightly. In forgiving I relinquish the counting of the offense against the offender and the claim to a payback; I give something up to which I have a right. Forgiveness is therefore sacrifice. Can I rejoice in a sacrifice, and if so, in

8 *The Journals of Father Alexander Schmemann 1973–1983*, trans. Juliana Schmemann (Crestwood, NY: St. Vladimir's Seminary Press, 2000), 137.

what kind? Yes, I can and I should—when sacrificing would enact my humanity and when failing to sacrifice would diminish my humanity. When I stay with my rightful resentment and insist on payback, I diminish myself. When, out of love, I forgive the wrongdoer without condoning the wrong and when I seek to return them to the good from which they had fallen, I enact my humanity. For I act then a bit like the God who makes the "sun rise on the evil and on the good, and sends rain on the righteous and on the unrighteous" (Matt. 5:45 NRSV). Obeying the law of love, which is the law of my humanity, I can rejoice. In fact if I do not rejoice in obeying the law of love—if I don't serve "the LORD [my] God joyfully and with gladness of heart" (Deut. 28:47 NRSV)—I haven't returned yet fully to myself as a creature made in God's image.

God's rain and God's sun are not withheld from the evil and the unrighteous until they have mended their ways; they are not given to the good and righteous only as long as they remain good and righteous. God does not give to pay for service rendered or to manipulate into rendering God service. It is similar with good forgiveness (taking into account the fact that as forgivers we are not holy gods but sinful humans). Givers of forgiveness do not elevate themselves above the receivers as morally superior, and they do not seek to control the receivers by forgiving. Those who forgive well rejoice not in their superior moral excellence but in the beauty of giving and in the good they are generating. That's why those who know how to receive forgiveness well are able to rejoice in the gift.

Finally forgiveness well given enacts and reaffirms the forgivers' comfort with themselves as God's image; similarly forgiveness well received brings the repentant back home to themselves as God's image. Both return to their common home, and both rejoice together.

The story of the prodigal son (Luke 15:11–32) illustrates the process well. In leaving home the younger son intended to "un-son" himself, "un-father" the father, "un-brother" his older brother, and "un-home" the home for all of them. His journey home starts with him "coming to himself" (v. 17), realizing who he was and what he had failed to live up to. In receiving the son back, the father, too, came to himself, though in a different way: the inner split of having stayed at home while at the same time following with longing the son into the far country was finally overcome. The two of them rejoiced together, and, organizing a feast in the reconstituted home, shared their joy with others. And what of the older brother?

Forgiveness, Dues-Paying Morality, and Joy

From the perspective of the older brother, the common joy of his brother's repentance and his father's forgiveness was false, because the father's forgiveness was false. That's why he excluded himself from the celebration and therefore also from having a common home with the other two. His objection to forgiveness seems to have been principled. Forgiveness was a vice and not a virtue. It disrupted the proper order of things according to which one reaps what one sows and one pays the debt one has incurred. One celebrates when duties are faithfully and excellently discharged and when successes come as a result. One does not celebrate blowing half an inheritance in dissolute living and returning home looking like a scarecrow. He was angry at the irresponsible young man who squandered and at the sentimental old fool who forgave. For those who believe that it is morally wrong not to count the wrongdoing against the one who committed it, there is no joy and mustn't be any joy in forgiveness and repentance.

Prior to forgiveness is unconditional love. Those who rejoice in such love will rejoice in forgiveness done well.

10

Creativity

The Joy of Imagining the Possible

Stephanie Paulsell and Vanessa Zoltan

It's an interesting time to be talking about adolescents and joy, because adolescents have been leading the way in expressing a deep dissatisfaction with how things are going in the United States. They took their lament to the streets after Trayvon Martin's killer was set free. They lay down on highways and church steps and the sidewalks of their cities wearing masks that said "I can't breathe" after Eric Garner was killed. They marched for weeks in Ferguson, Missouri, after the shooting of Michael Brown and started a movement for black lives that continues to challenge our status quo. Survivors of a high school massacre in Florida and young people who have grown up in neighborhoods plagued by gun violence stand together to say that it is not acceptable that our country cares more about easy access to assault rifles than it does about the slaughter of our children. Anyone who heard Parkland High School senior Emma Gonzalez's powerful speech two days after the shooting knows what it sounds like when someone has had it. All of these kids, from Ferguson to Florida to Chicago, have had it with the violence directed at them and with adult complacency in the face of it.

Powerful forces have a vested interest in silencing these young, deeply dissatisfied voices. And one of the ways they do so is to encourage the shaming of these young people if they show any capacity for joy. "Why all the laughter?" some ask, when they see the Parkland kids cracking jokes on social media. "I thought you were mourning your friends." "How offensive," some said when Beyoncé released her video "Formation," in which a young boy dances joyfully between a line of police officers in riot gear and a wall that has been painted with the words "Stop shooting us." Our culture often seems comfortable with young people's expressions of dissatisfaction with the way things are only if they are performed off camera, in silence and in tears. When they post smiling photos of themselves with their arms wrapped around each other or videos of themselves singing along to the *Hamilton* soundtrack as they travel to Tallahassee to lobby their legislators—well, that's different. Why all the joy if they're supposed to be so sad?

It's worth asking if our institutions, including our churches, really do want adolescents to experience joy. Because joy will not create compliant young people. Joy is excessive; it spills over from one part of life to another. It makes us feel that we can do more—and be more—than we once thought we could do and be. Joy opens us up. Joy reaches us in the deepest parts of ourselves. Joy is a potentially transformative force. It has the power to change us.

Joy is linked to dissatisfaction with the way things are, because it results from imagining the way things can be.

Joy, however, is not synonymous with happiness. And certainly it is not the same thing as satisfaction. In the Bible joy seems often to be connected with dissatisfaction; the word "joy" often follows the words "and yet" or "but." In the Psalms true joy emerges from experiences of dissatisfaction. Psalm 13:2 (NRSV) opens with "How long must I bear pain in my soul, and have sorrow in my heart all day long?" It ends with "But . . . my heart shall rejoice in your salvation." In Psalm 30 we hear that "weeping may linger for the night, but joy comes with the morning." My enemies are plotting against me, Psalm 71 says, "but I will hope continually, and will praise you yet more and more." That kind of radical hope in the face of pain and injustice seems to be a crucial part of joy for the psalmist. It makes of joy, as Willie Jennings has said, an "act of resistance against the forces of despair."[1] It is an act of resistance and an act of resilience. The psalmist whose pain and sorrow did not keep him from making a joyful noise and the teenagers who hid in a closest while a shooter rampaged outside the door but who are still capable of laughing with their friends until it hurts are all saying: I have not been destroyed. I am still capable of joy.

Joy is often closely associated with dissatisfaction with the way things are, because it is born from the creative work of imagining the way things might be. "People feel joy, as opposed to mere pleasure," the social critic Ivan Illich has written, "to the extent that their activities are creative."[2] Creativity and imagination are capacities that have the potential to generate a deep and sustaining joy—for adolescents and for us all.

God's Creativity and Ours

The novelist Virginia Woolf once described the world as a work of art[3] of which we ourselves are a part. The author of the opening of the book of Genesis seems to have believed that, too. God is the artist in this gorgeous hymn to creation, speaking the world into being, defining the edges of earth and sky, creating a home for life in all its forms.

Because the first chapter of Genesis has been so thoroughly co-opted in cultural debates about science and religion, it's easy to forget that it was not written as an argument against Charles Darwin's theory of natural selection. This account of creation was written during a particular

1 Willie Jennings, "Joy That Gathers." *Yale Center for Faith and Culture*, Yale Divinity School, Aug. 2014, faith.yale.edu/sites/default/files/jennings_-_joy_that_gathers.pdf.

2 Ivan Illich, *Tools for Conviviality* (Glasgow: Fontana, 1975), 34.

3 Virginia Woolf, *Moments of Being*, ed. Jeanne Schulkind (San Diego: Harcourt, 1985), 72.

historical moment, composed by an artist during a time of hopelessness and despair for a people who had been conquered and exiled.

What might the exiled people of Israel have heard in the verses of Genesis 1? Perhaps they would have heard that things could be otherwise. Perhaps they would have heard that change is possible, that something wholly new can happen. Chaos can be transformed into a habitable work of art, beloved by God and proclaimed to be good. As the scholar Walter Brueggemann has noted, the God of the first chapter of Genesis does not say "There must be light" but rather "Let there be light."[4] God does not decree creation like an authoritarian ruler signing executive orders. God sets unpredictable, creative possibility loose in the world: let there be light, let there be fish in the sea, let us make human beings in our own image.

This, of course, is one of the most arresting sentences in the Genesis litany of creation for anyone who hears it—for the people of Israel in exile, for us in twenty-first-century America. God made human beings in God's own image. Even in exile, even in sorrow, there is something about us that mirrors God back to God.

What is that something that marks our creation in God's image? It is more than we can know or explain, for sure. But if we are made in the image of the God who made the world, perhaps one answer can be found in the creative impulse that is so much a part of our humanity. To be made in God's image is to have within us the capacity for creativity. And so when we are making something—whether it's a poem, a service of worship, a meal, or a movement for justice—we participate in God's own creativity.

If human creativity is a sign of our creation in God's image, then it is surely found at the heart of the life of faith. So often, when religion is discussed in our culture, it's portrayed solely as a set of beliefs to be accepted or rejected rather than imaginative, creative work. But what is any faith if not something assembled from disparate elements—from

---

4 Walter Brueggemann, *Genesis* (Atlanta: John Knox Press, 1982).

scriptures, images, relationships, experiences—into something that is saturated with meaning?

In the Gospels Jesus shows us how this works by inviting us to exercise our religious imagination. He does this, as he does so much of his teaching, by telling stories and painting pictures with words:

- The kingdom of Heaven, he says, is like a mustard seed that starts out small and grows into a tree so large that birds build their nests in its branches;
- The kingdom of Heaven is like the yeast a woman stirs into flour so that she can make bread;
- The kingdom of Heaven is like treasure hidden in a field or like a single, perfect pearl hidden in plain sight among other pearls;
- The kingdom of Heaven is a like a net that brings up from the sea every kind of fish.

There's a lot to learn from these parables. We learn that the kingdom of Heaven does its secret work in hidden places. That it can be found in the ordinary stuff of life. That once it is added, it cannot be subtracted. That it begins as something so small we can barely see it but grows large enough to be lived in or transforms into something nourishing enough to sustain our lives.

But perhaps the most important thing we learn from the stories Jesus tells is that there is no one correct answer to the question of what the kingdom of Heaven is like. That question has multiple answers, maybe even infinite ones.

By offering us a few of his, Jesus opens a space within which we might create our own stories, our own parables. He invites us to look around, to see where the seeds of the kingdom of Heaven might be waiting:

- Maybe the kingdom of Heaven is like a book that a young person comes across by accident in the library and whose life is changed by what she reads in it;

- Maybe the kingdom of Heaven is like a film whose vision of what the world might be is so powerful that it inspires the kids who see it to start working on their own world;
- Maybe the kingdom of Heaven is like a shared meal that dissolves, for a moment, the distances between us;
- Maybe the kingdom of Heaven is like a single act of resistance to cruelty that grows into a movement for change;
- Maybe the kingdom of Heaven is like a hymn sung by a conquered people far from home about a God who delights in creating something new, a hymn about the creativity of God from which they draw hope.

Believing is often lifted up as the main way we express our faith. But imagining is just as important as believing. Indeed believing depends on our ability to imagine—to imagine a God we cannot see or to feel the claim on us, in this time and place, of ancient words whose meanings are not always clear.

With his parables Jesus reminds us that imagination is an irreplaceable dimension of the life of faith, a practice of the freedom of the glory of the children of God. His parables don't offer a definition of God's kingdom. They don't answer the question of what the kingdom of God is. They answer the question of what the kingdom of God is like: a seed, a pearl, a net, yeast, a hidden treasure. In his cascade of images, Jesus teaches us to cultivate what the theologian David Tracy once called an analogical imagination.[5] He invites us to think with things we can see and touch about things we can only imagine.

If imagination is at the heart of the theological work of faith, it is also at the heart of the ethical choices to which Jesus calls us. During the last brutal months of the First World War, Virginia Woolf wrote in her diary that the willingness to kill must be a failure of the imagination—an

---

5 David Tracy, *The Analogical Imagination: Christian Theology and the Culture of Pluralism* (Chicago: Herder & Herder, 1998).

inability to imagine another person's life and what it might become.[6] The imaginative work at the heart of the life of faith challenges us to cultivate our capacity to imagine lives other than our own—and to care about them enough to take them into account as we make choices about how we will live. If we can't imagine what the lives of others are like, if we can't feel reverence for the worlds they contain within them, if all we can do is project our own fears and desires onto them, then we become dangerous to them. To lack imagination is to lack mercy. The young survivors of gun violence we've been hearing from know this.

In the Gospel of Matthew, after Jesus has told his parables about what the kingdom of Heaven is like, he offers his followers a last teaching for the day. "Every scribe who has been trained for the kingdom of heaven," he says, "is like a master of a house, who brings out of his treasure what is new and what is old" (Mt. 13:52 ESV). This is how Jesus himself created. He took what was new (the ordinary experiences of the people around him) and what was old (the ancient wisdom that he inherited and reinterpreted), and he made something out of that combination that awakened the creativity and imagination of his hearers and continues to awaken ours.

This is the practice we want to commend: to focus on sources of joy in young people's lives and use the wisdom of ancient practices to help them go deeper, together, in community.

Going Deeper in Community

Our young people are already engaged in spiritual practices of imagination and creativity. But it's rare that our culture tells them that. What our culture tells them is not that they are creators but that they are consumers. But young people who are seeing the film *Black Panther* multiple times or watching Beyoncé's *Lemonade* and listening to the album over

6 Ann Oliver Bell, ed., *The Diary of Virginia Woolf, Vol. 1: 1915–1919* (Boston: Mariner Books, 1979), 186.

and over, or who are on their fourth or fifth reading of the Harry Potter books or *A Wrinkle in Time*, are not just consuming. They are thinking. They are wondering. And through their love of and devotion to these films, songs, books and videos, they are engaged in a spiritual practice. As Casper ter Kuile of the How We Gather project[7] has taught, one of the things we can do as teachers, youth leaders, and mentors is to help our young people recognize and have confidence in the spiritual practices they are already doing.

Take, for example, the popular podcast *Harry Potter and the Sacred Text*.[8] The hosts, Vanessa Zoltan and Casper ter Kuile, are working their way through all seven books in the Harry Potter series, one chapter at a time, discussing each chapter in the light of themes such as friendship, betrayal, privilege, and faith. Then they choose a portion of the text to read closely using an ancient spiritual reading practice such as *lectio divina* or *Pardes*. Lastly they each offer a blessing for one of the characters. This podcast has a faithful, enthusiastic audience, most of whom grew up with the Harry Potter books. They are mostly millennials, but there are also many younger listeners in middle school and high school. Sometimes the kids are introduced to the podcast through their English teachers, who want them to hear what it sounds like when two thoughtful people bring real questions to a book and talk about them together. But most of the time, young people find the podcast on iTunes as they look for podcasts related to their great love, the Harry Potter novels. *Harry Potter and the Sacred Text* has been downloaded, as of this writing, 12.5 million times.

One of the things that I think has surprised those who work on the podcast is how active and engaged their listeners are. They are constantly receiving email and voice mails from listeners who sometimes write to thank them, sometimes to disagree with something Zoltan or ter Kuile has said about the chapter under discussion, and sometimes to

---

7 Casper ter Kuile, How We Gather, www.howwegather.org.

8 Casper ter Kuile and Vanessa Zoltan, *Harry Potter and the Sacred Text*, www.harrypottersacredtext.com.

offer their own ideas about the text. Sometimes they tell the hosts difficult truths about their lives: they were abused as children, some write, and reading about Harry Potter navigating his own childhood abuse helped them survive. Some write that because of their experience of abuse, it hurts when the hosts talk about forgiveness. Because of their own experiences, the Harry Potter books were sacred to them long before they found the podcast. Responding pastorally to this far-flung community has been one of the unexpected challenges of this work.

Recently the podcast received an email from a teenager in tenth grade. The subject line read: "From a high schooler: Dear Casper, Vanessa, Ariana, and everyone who contributes to Harry Potter and the Sacred Text. My name is Sophie and I LOVE your podcast!"[9] This youth wrote about stumbling onto the podcast on the internet, listening to the first episode, and getting hooked. She went on to say that she had recently read all the Harry Potter books and had fallen in love with them. "I would read [the books] whenever I could," she wrote, "and on weekends, I barely did anything else. By the end of December, I finished the series and I was so in love with the story and the whole wizarding world. I cried a few times after I finished. I was so desperate for something to keep the momentum going because the feeling of having nothing else was so overwhelming."

Youth ministers, parents, and teachers are familiar with this kind of overwhelming devotion. It might not be Harry Potter that gets their kids excited, but there's something they love and cannot get enough of.

In her email Sophie wrote that she was so glad to find the podcast because it's making her "see things differently" from when she read the books through the first time. She listens to one episode a night trying to catch up, reading the chapter and taking notes on the theme Zoltan and ter Kuile have chosen. At the end of the letter, she wrote: "What I hate more than anything is waking up in the morning, but now I'm

---

9 Actual names and identifying details have been changed to protect the privacy of individuals.

happy to wake up because I know that it means I get to listen to an episode on the bus and take notes about what you both have to say!"

This is the kind of joy that we hope our young people will experience. We want them to have something that makes them excited to get up in the morning or that keeps them up late at night. To love something so much that it calls to them while they're still in their beds, hating to get up because they're tired, depressed, or overwhelmed by the demands of their lives. "I slept but my heart was awake" (Song of Songs 5:2 NIV), one of the lovers in the Song of Songs says about the way her love for her beloved keeps her always listening for his voice. Joy keeps our hearts awake, even when we're sleeping. That is the kind of joy that gives meaning to our days and has the power to shape our lives.

Kids sometimes get criticized for this kind of joy. They're told that they love what they love a little too much, and could they please stop talking constantly about Harry Potter or the Black Panther or Beyoncé. Sometimes kids are criticized for their reading or viewing or listening because the adults around them consider their books, movies, and music escapist and would rather they focus on something more serious. But as the great science fiction writer Ursula K. Le Guin once wondered, why do we criticize people for wanting to escape? For "nobody . . . escapes to jail," she wrote. "The direction of escape is toward freedom."[10]

The writer Annie Dillard describes in her autobiography the way she followed books toward freedom and depth as a child. What she was looking for in books, she wrote, "was imagination. It was depth, depth of thought and feeling; some sort of extreme of subject matter; some nearness to death; some call to courage. I myself was getting wild; I wanted wildness, originality, genius, rapture, hope. . . . Those of us who read carried around with us like martyrs a secret knowledge, a secret joy, and a secret hope . . . that there is a life worth living . . . [which] could

10 Ursula K. Le Guin, *No Time to Spare: Thinking About What Matters* (Boston: Houghton Mifflin Harcourt, 2017), 83.

be found and joined, like the Resistance. I kept this exhilarating faith alive in myself."[11]

Our kids are often carrying around that kind of exhilarating faith in the possibilities of their lives that is awakened in them by what they read, watch, and listen to. What if their church said to them: you know that feeling you have when you are watching Wakanda unfurl on the screen, or when you're reading about Harry Potter finding out that he is not a forgotten orphan but a longed-for wizard, or when you're watching Beyoncé knit together poetry and music and dance into a wholly new work of art? What if we said to them that feeling is a reflection of your creation in the image of God? And church is a place to explore, in community, the things that you love and that make you feel creative and alive. It's a place to find ways of responding with your own stories, your own poetry, your own music and images, your own lives. What if we said that the books, films, and music that are lighting up your imagination are sacred because they connect you to the most sacred part of yourself—your creativity, your imagination, your reflection of God's image.

Sacred texts are so full of meaning that they spill over and invite us to exercise our own creativity, the way Jesus invited those around him, and still invites us, to hear his parables and to compose our own out of the stuff of our lives. Sacred texts are worthy of being read closely, prayerfully, contemplatively, in community. They stand up well to careful scrutiny. They are rich in meaning that keeps unfolding and unfolding. Sacred texts are generative—they create more texts, more commentary, more hymns and prayers, more music, more books and films, more and more ideas about how to live. And sacred texts are made sacred by a community that thinks with them, prays with them, hopes with them, finds joy in them.

How can we help our kids engage the sacred texts they are already reading, watching, and listening to? How can we help them recognize what they are doing as a spiritual practice?

---

11 Annie Dillard, *An American Childhood* (New York: HarperPerennial, 1987), 183.

First we'll need to recognize that ourselves. Whatever is inspiring creativity in our young people, whatever is giving them joy, is worth the attention of their community of faith. We will need our young people to guide us—to show us the books, films, and music that are full of meaning for them, the ones that are leading them deeper and deeper into their most urgent questions and their fiercest hopes.

Second, we'll need to assure our kids that all of who they are—including what they love and are inspired by—is welcome in church. Every community will have its own unique ways of supporting its young people's engagement with the sacred and learning from them in the process. A church that is good at Bible study can bring its ways of reading to the texts in which young people find joy. A church that cares about social justice can join its young people in their demonstrations of resistance. A church that cultivates spiritual practices can think with its young people about the spiritually formative power of stories and images and actions and make space for them to respond to that power in community—through discussion, through artmaking, through organizing. Bible study, social justice, spirituality—faith communities have a lot of shareable wisdom about these practices. By offering them at the threshold of where our young people's lives meet the life of our churches, we will not only offer them a fresh welcome but we will also learn from our young people more about our own sacred texts and our sacred responsibilities.

Harry Potter and the Sacred Text offers an example of what can be done by experimenting with bringing ancient religious reading practices to bear on the Harry Potter books. Approaching those books through Jewish and Christian reading practices—*lectio divina*, *Pardes*, *havruta*, the creation of florilegia, and sacred imagination—Vanessa Zoltan and her colleagues have invited young people who already love the Harry Potter books to go deeper, to use those books to think about their lives and the life of the world. Using the practice of sacred imagination, they try to place themselves inside a scene from the story, smell its smells and take in its sights, and, most important, to empathize with one of the characters, to try to see the world through their eyes, to practice walking in their shoes, and to think ethically and spiritually about the choices that character makes. They have encouraged their listeners to create florilegia—collections of their favorite sentences from the text. This medieval practice of writing down fragments of one's reading in a collection creates a new text in which seemingly unrelated fragments begin to speak to each other and new meanings begin to emerge. With *havruta*, they encourage their listeners to find a partner with whom to question the text. Through *lectio divina* and *Pardes*, they invite their listeners to consider the multiple layers of meaning that can be excavated even from a single sentence and to learn from that close reading something meaningful about how to live.

We all need opportunities to experience the joy of seeking meaning together in community, young people and older people alike. And we need opportunities to respond to the meaning we find, opportunities that are experimental and generative, that open us to the joy of creative engagement with the world. Creativity and imagination are our inheritance as children of a God who is always creating and forever inviting us—as Jesus does in the parables—to join in. With their passionate devotion to the things they love, our young people remind us that exercising the creativity that is at the heart of the life of faith generates the kind of joy that wakes us up in the morning, gives us the strength to resist what must be resisted, and inspires new visions of what the world might become.

We need opportunities to experience the joy of seeking meaning together in community.

11

Belonging

Paul's Notion of Autarkēs

Michal Beth Dinkler

I worked in youth ministry part-time all through college and then full-time for a few years after college. I worked with a high school youth group at a large church in Northern California, in the heart of Silicon Valley. One of the greatest privileges of my life was leading a weekly small group of girls—in our ministry we called them STRIVE groups. STRIVE groups had an open-door policy; anyone and everyone was welcome at any time. Some girls came and went, but there was a core group who stayed the same. This group of girls and I started meeting their freshman year in high school, and we met every single week through their high school graduation.

We went through a lot together over those four years: the normal stresses of high school, of course—body image, their latest romantic crush, frustrations with friends, their parents' rules. We served others together: feeding the homeless in Los Angeles, caring for children with disabilities in the Dominican Republic, building houses in Mexican villages. And I got to be there for the milestones: the sports tryouts, driver's tests, the SATs, applying to college. I took pictures before every school dance. That STRIVE group and I also went through some really hard times together: deaths and divorce, a father's abuse, bulimia, and bullying. One of the girls was hospitalized with a life-threatening illness and barely survived.

Through it all, through all our striving, and in truth in spite of ourselves, we became a real community—the kind of community where those teenage girls could come and be their true, authentic, messy selves and know they belonged and were loved, no matter what.

We became the kind of community that transforms lives.

I don't take any of that for granted. After a few years, the girls told me that before they met me, one of them had said, "Her name's Michal Beth. She's probably ugly." Another girl confessed that for nearly a year, she had only attended STRIVE group because her mother paid her to do so. I said, "Oh, great, so you're hanging out with me for money?"—to which she responded, "Well, not now. Now I hang out with you for free!"

That's the goal, right? We want them to hang out with us for free. But it's not easy, because in many ways, today's youth are not free. Most parents won't pay their kids to go to a church youth group. Some parents, perhaps, would prefer they stayed away. High school students have to go to practice, or rehearsal, or a job. They have to get into a top university, ideally with a scholarship. The animating idea behind all of this parental striving is that if their children succeed at such things, they will find happiness in life. Parents want their children to grow up and be content.

We find a passage in the Apostle Paul's letter to the church in Philippi that might well serve as a kind of manifesto for parents today. At the end of the letter, in Philippians 4:11–13 NIV, Paul thanks the recipients for supporting him, and then he says: "I am not saying this because I am in need, for I have learned to be content whatever the circumstances. I know what it is to be in need, and I know what it is to have plenty. I have learned the secret of being content in any and every situation, whether well fed or hungry, whether living in plenty or in want. I can do all this through him who gives me strength."

One English dictionary defines "content" as being "in a state of peaceful happiness." That sounds about right when it comes to parenting, doesn't it? Who wouldn't want their kids to be in a state of peaceful happiness in any and all circumstances?

Still, if I'm honest, for a long time, I didn't like this passage. It didn't seem fair or realistic to me. Constant, peaceful happiness is impossible. And we don't have to look far for the evidence of that. As humans we're vulnerable. Brené Brown, a sociologist who researches vulnerability,[1] has asked thousands of people the question, What is vulnerability to you? Vulnerability, people told her, is

- presenting my product to the world and getting no response;
- waiting for the biopsy to come back;
- getting pregnant after two miscarriages;
- signing up my wife for hospice care;
- sending my third-grader off to school with his violin excited to try out for first chair and knowing he's not going to get it.

But it's not just suffering and pain. Joy can make us vulnerable, too. People told Brown that vulnerability is

- driving my newborn baby home from the hospital;
- saying "I love you" first;
- taking art lessons again after decades;
- my wedding day;
- celebrating the life of my grandmother who recently passed away.

Those are the uncontrollable moments when we come face to face with the precarity and fragility of life. Perhaps it's easier to be content in moments of joyful vulnerability. But what about the more difficult times? I want to say to Paul, "Really? We're supposed to be in a state of peaceful happiness in any and all circumstances?"

Several years ago I faced the fragility of my own life when I went whitewater rafting on the Nile River. You should know I am not an adventurous person by nature. I like my books and my couch, in my

---

1 Brené Brown, *The Power of Vulnerability: Teachings on Authenticity, Connection, and Courage*, audiobook narrated by Brené Brown, Sounds True, 2013.

house, by my fire. But one summer I was teaching at a seminary near the source of the Nile in Uganda, and my husband convinced me to go.

"It's a once-in-a-lifetime thing," he said. Right, I thought, because it will end my lifetime. But I decided to do it. I was terrified because the Nile has some of the world's roughest waters, including Class 5 rapids, which are the highest level you're allowed to navigate commercially.

When we arrived, I felt vindicated in my fear for two reasons: one was that I learned the Ugandans had labeled the rapids with disconcerting names like "Jaws," or the really infamous one, called simply "The Bad Place"; the second was that I noticed villagers lining up on a cliff above the river. When I asked one of them why they were lining up, he responded, "We like to watch white people pay to do stupid things." (Frankly I thought that was an apt description.)

Spoiler alert: I survived. I didn't drown that day, but our boat did flip over and dump us out more than once. Every single time a wave would hoist us up, and, suspended in midair, I'd stare down at the water churning violently beneath me—and in a split second I'd be launched headfirst and helpless into a pit of froth and foam. Down . . . down . . . my lungs, burning . . . a thought would hit me: this is how I am going to die. And every time I'd pop back up, gasping for air and eager to climb back onto the boat to safety.

To be heavy-handed about it, this strikes me as such a marvelous analogy for life. After all, life sometimes feels like you're hanging suspended, frozen in that eternal second of uncertainty, when you don't know if the raft to which you've been clinging so desperately will level out and save you or if you'll be dumped out into the violence and chaos below. Brown's examples of vulnerability I shared feel like "suspended life raft" moments—when life threatens to throw us over into the Bad Place and contentment just seems impossible. I'm sure we all could add to the list:

- We could add my friend who had to tell her teenaged son not to wear the hoodie he got for his birthday because it's not safe for African Americans to wear hoodies in white neighborhoods.

- We could add gun violence. A few weeks ago, my six-year-old son was upset because my husband and I were going out. I said, "Buddy, you know grown-ups always come back." And he looked up at me, eyes wide and serious, and said, "Not if someone shoots you."
- We could add the parents whose children are taken from them at the US border because they don't have the correct legal documents to enter the country.

Are we supposed to tell these folks that the Bible says to be content in all circumstances? If so, I have a problem with that. Sometimes contentment feels not just impossible or unwelcome but offensive, even obscene.

All of this means that the parental goal of helping children achieve happiness is like trying to will the rapids to stop being rapids. It's impossible.

When we tell young people that happiness should be their goal, we're setting them up to fail from the start. And when they keep encountering heartache, they'll feel like they've failed. Maybe they'll feel like we lied to them. And they'd be right.

Happiness is not the goal, but joy is. So we need to know and be able to explain the difference.

The problem with that passage in Philippians is that "content" is not a great English translation of the Greek original. The word Paul uses—*autarkēs*—is rare in the New Testament. *Autarkēs* means "self-sufficient" or "independent." Thus Paul says in verses 4:11–12, "Not that I am referring to being in need. I have learned to be self-sufficient with whatever I have." A popular word right now in parenting and educational literature is "grit." Most parents will admit that constant contentment is unattainable, but independence, self-sufficiency, and grit sound like worthy goals for our children.

Contemporary American culture seriously values competence. Calling someone needy is not a compliment. Our culture tells us that if we need help, there's something wrong with us. We're weak. And even deeper, underlying all that, we're told that if we're weak, we're less valuable. Is Paul saying we should aim not for neediness but for self-sufficiency in any and all circumstances? This picture of Paul works for us: Paul as American superhero.

But there's a problem with that, too. We all know this. Total self-sufficiency is a myth. Life is far more like the raft, tossed high above the whitewater rapids of the Nile. Reality is hard and unfair, and we are limited. We can't do life alone.

Joy is a deep inner sense of delight and well-being.

Telling young people that not needing others should be their goal also sets them up to fail. When we tell them to be omni-competent, we're giving them the wrong job description. We're telling them it's their job to control the rapids or, at the very least, to ensure that their raft won't capsize. And then when it does flip (because it inevitably will), as they tumble out into the waves and think they're about to drown, they'll also be thinking that they're failures. Or that we lied to them. And they'd be right about us.

But notice this: self-sufficiency wasn't actually Paul's reality. Remember that just before 4:11, Paul thanks the Philippians for their help, which implies that he needed their help in the first place. He's also writing to them from prison. He's clearly not self-sufficient. Paul's needy.

So if it's not peaceful happiness, and it's not independence, then what does Paul mean when he says, "I have learned to be *autarkēs* . . . in any and all circumstances"?

Paul adopts this word *autarkēs* from Greek philosophy. In Stoicism *autarkeia* was a high virtue. To be self-sufficient meant just what it sounds like: you, in yourself, are sufficient. Enough. The Stoics taught that being *autarkēs* means that one is unaffected by outward circumstances. Being *autarkēs* means that you have the internal resources to handle anything, because you know that who you are is not defined by whether you're admired or despised, in prison or in the penthouse. If you're *autarkēs*, then all the posturing, comparisons, and judgments that you see every day are pointless. Hierarchies collapse, our culture's messages about worth fall away, and you're free simply to be.

Paul uses the Stoic word *autarkēs*. But the really crucial part of the passage in Philippians is 4:13, where he adds a twist that turns the concept on its head: he says he is *autarkēs* through the one who gives him strength (literally, strengthener). The Stoics taught that self-sufficiency results from rigorously training the self to detach from emotion and relationship. (We still use the adjective "stoic" in that way.) In contrast, Paul says he has learned the "secret" that self-sufficiency comes not from oneself but from the God who is the strengthener.

Let's dig into this.

An Anatomy of *Autarkeia*

According to Paul, being *autarkēs*—sufficient in one's self—comes not from detaching from reality or relationships but from facing reality in relationship with the Spirit who is love. In other words, we don't tell ourselves to be happy no matter what or isolate ourselves from others in self-protection disguised as bravery. Instead we face reality head-on, because strength and sufficiency are God-given.

This is what gives Paul the strength to go on. He knows that he's most likely going to be killed, just like the one he follows was killed. But he also knows he's free in the midst of those circumstances, because he's *autarkēs*. He knows that the price of following Jesus is high. But the reward is real freedom—the freedom to be fully ourselves and know that we're fully loved.

Maya Angelou said, "You are only free when you realize you belong no place—you belong every place—no place at all. The price is high. The reward is great."[2] Paul might say that it's when we recognize that we belong to God that we belong everywhere and nowhere, all at once.

We often think of belonging as fitting in, and we often teach our children to fit in by following rules, both spoken and unspoken. True

---

2 Maria Popova, "Maya Angelou on Freedom: A 1973 Conversation with Bill Moyers," *Brain Pickings*, accessed 21 November, 2018, www.brainpickings.org/2013/06/14/maya-angelou-bill-moyers-1973/.

belonging, however, isn't about either of those things. True belonging sometimes means having the courage not to fit in—the courage to stand alone. That kind of belonging is freedom. It isn't about circumstances at all. It's unconditional.

What if we look to Paul's life as an example of what that kind of freedom looks like? Paul started out as Saul. Saul was a rule follower. He fit in quite well with his people. He belonged. Then he met Jesus, and according to the book of Acts, there was a plot to kill him (9:23–25). After escaping that, he was later stoned and left for dead (14:8–22); a violent mob acted out against him (19:23–34); he was attacked by Jews and then arrested by Romans (chaps. 21–23).

The irony, of course, is that Jesus's self-proclaimed mission was to bring freedom to the captives, and yet Paul's life was punctuated by imprisonment, rejection, and persecution. But this irony is instructive. Paul was a prisoner literally. He was marginalized and judged by those in power. He was no longer following their rules and no longer fit in. But on a deeper level, Paul was free already. That's what made him brave.

The price is high. But the reward is great.

The reward is the freedom that being *autarkēs* can bring.

To be clear, I'm not saying that we shouldn't work against injustices in the world because we have inner freedom. That is a particularly insidious argument that Christians have made for far too long: stay a slave, or stay in an abusive marriage. Don't complain, because you're free on the inside. That is not what I mean.

I want to take a minute and talk to the white folks reading this: white people, we especially need to renounce the "stay where you are because Christ makes you free" argument, because we especially have been the ones to use that argument and benefit from it. We need to face the painful ways that we're complicit in the systems we condemn. It's like that Ugandan gentleman told me: white people pay money for stupid things. We need to have the courage to take responsibility when those stupid things aren't about endangering ourselves and our bodies but about pushing other people out of the raft and into the rapids.

That means having the often painful conversations and doing the difficult work of admitting that as white people in a world that values whiteness, we've benefited from the oppression, exclusion, and suffering of our sisters and brothers of color, and we need to work actively against such racism.

Of course we find all kinds of reasons in addition to race to push others out of the boat. Here's a youth group story about pushing others out of the boat. As I mentioned before, I worked at a large church in the heart of Silicon Valley, one of the wealthiest areas of this country. Right across the railroad tracks was East Palo Alto (EPA), one of the most dangerous, poorest urban areas of our country. These two communities are the stuff of stereotypes—two totally different worlds literally separated by the railroad tracks.

Our high school ministry decided that we wanted to reflect kingdom values by reaching out to kids from EPA, so they'd know youth group was a place where everyone belongs. One way we did so was by getting connected with a home for teen mothers. My STRIVE group started babysitting for them, and over time we got to know them well. Eventually the church started providing childcare at our trips and midweek youth gatherings so the teen moms could come.

One day the mother of one of the Silicon Valley girls pulled another leader aside to complain about the presence of teen moms at youth group. She said, "Do you want good kids to look at that and see that you're condoning sexual immorality? Stop letting teen moms come, or I won't let my daughter attend this church anymore." (She used language I won't repeat.)

When I heard about what had happened, I was livid. I wanted to say, if kids can't hear that they belong no matter what at *church*, where can they hear that? Is that not the message of the gospel?

She was pushing those girls out of the raft.

We all know people like this in the church today, don't we? These are the Christians who give other Christians a bad name—those who emphasize morality and legalism over grace and forgiveness; those who value being righteous and right over being humble and hopeful.

Jesus had some opinions about those kinds of people. Take the parable about the Pharisee and the tax collector in Luke 18:10–14 (NIV). To some who were confident of their own righteousness and looked down on everyone else, Jesus told this parable:

> Two men went up to the temple to pray, one a Pharisee and the other a tax collector. The Pharisee stood by himself and prayed: "God, I thank you that I am not like other people—robbers, evildoers, adulterers—or even like this tax collector. I fast twice a week and give a tenth of all I get." But the tax collector stood at a distance. He would not even look up to heaven, but beat his breast and said, "God, have mercy on me, a sinner." I tell you that this man, rather than the other, went home justified before God. For all those who exalt themselves will be humbled, and those who humble themselves will be exalted.

I like Eugene Peterson's translation of Jesus's final point in verse 14: "If you walk around with your nose in the air, you're going to end up flat on your face" (Luke 18:14 MSG). When I heard about that Silicon Valley mom at our youth group, I wished she could see that she was being like the Pharisee in Jesus's parable. Her nose was in the air, and eventually she was going to end up flat on her face before God.

And I was really thankful that I wasn't like her.

Then I realized it. There I was, thanking God that I wasn't like that sinful woman. There I was, throwing her out of the boat. She's the kind of Christian who gives me a bad name. She doesn't belong at my church.

Jesus's teachings must always begin with us. I learned in that moment that, like the Pharisee in the parable, I needed to pay attention to myself. I don't mean to say that what that mother said was acceptable. What I'm saying, rather, is that her behavior and her heart were not my responsibility. I needed to reorient what was going on in my heart.

If our Christianity focuses on identifying what's wrong with others, on throwing others out of the boat, then we've taken a wrong turn. We're no longer following Jesus.

Far too often in the church, we say every kid belongs unconditionally at youth group. But when it comes down to it, we find all kinds of reasons to exclude them. Our intentions might be good. But we're threatened, hostage to our biases and fears. We're not free. And we're not brave.

Paul's notion of being *autarkēs*—being content in the knowledge that our selfhood is sufficient, that our strength comes from the Spirit who created and unites us—is a freedom that expands our hearts so that everyone is welcome. Not all behavior is acceptable, but everyone belongs no matter what. That kind of freedom facilitates work against injustice because it means we're resilient. We're defiantly joyful in the face of challenge and adversity.

On the other hand, so much suffering and pain come from the absence of unconditional love and belonging. Young people know this intimately. The researcher I mentioned before, Brené Brown, has interviewed middle and high schoolers all around the country, and they say things like "Not belonging at school is really hard. But it's nothing compared to what it feels like when you don't belong at home,"[3] like when teens don't live up to their parents' expectations or parents are embarrassed because their children aren't as cool as the parents want them to be. What's really hard is when parents don't pay attention to their children's lives, or when they don't like who their children are or what they like to do.

Young people long to know that they're worthy of love and belonging. Period. No matter what. When they find that, the result is joy.

Here's how I define joy: joy is a deep inner sense of delight and well-being.

Just before Paul discusses *autarkēs*, he declares, "Rejoice in the Lord always; again I will say, rejoice" (Phil. 4:4 ESV). The word translated "rejoice" here is *chairo*. There are two important dimensions of *chairo* that get lost in English translation. First it is related to "charisma," the

---

3 Brené Brown, *Daring Greatly: How the Courage to Be Vulnerable Transforms the Way We Live, Love, Parent, and Lead* (New York: Avery, 2015), 232.

Greek word for gift. Rejoicing—that is, having joy—is a gift. And what makes something a gift? It's free, not earned. There are no strings attached. God's free gift is that we are worthy of love and belonging—apart from circumstance—simply because we belong to the God who loved us first. No matter what.

Second, *chairo* is related to well-being. It's actually used as a greeting in Greek: "Farewell," says Paul. "Be well." *Chairo.* Rejoice.[4] Joy comes from knowing that, as the fourteenth-century mystic Julian of Norwich put it, "All will be well, and all will be well, and all manner of things will be well."[5] No one and nothing can take that well-being away (Rom. 8:38–39).

Importantly, this does not mean that all is going well. Some think joy is about things going well in life. You get the promotion, you buy the house, you and your family are healthy. But that doesn't ring true in my experience. Some of the most joyful people I've ever met have been in truly dire circumstances—people who suffer from poverty, illness, and prejudice but who nevertheless know how to love.

It's countercultural, because our culture has conditioned us to believe that power, prestige, and popularity will make us happy. We breathe in that message for so long and in so many ways that it becomes habitual. Letting go of those messages is counterintuitive and often difficult. But it's also necessary.

When I went rafting on the Nile, our guide gave us very clear instructions. He said, "When you fall out—because you will—when the raft capsizes, you will want to hold onto your oar. You will want to fight the rapids, to swim hard to the top and fight for air. But you have to let go." It was counterintuitive, but the way to survive, he told us, is to let

---

4 *Chairo* was used in greetings (welcome, good day, hail to you, I am glad to see you) in the imperative mood implying a wish for wellbeing or happiness to the recipient (Mt 26:49). Chairo is used in the introduction to a letter (Ac 15:23; 23:26; James 1:1). Chairo is translated "Hail!" several times in the Gospels (Mt 27:29, Mk 15:18, Lk 1:28).

5 Mirabai Starr, *The Showings of Julian of Norwich: A New Translation* (Charlottesville: Hampton Road, 2013), xiii.

go—let go of the oar and let your body go limp; trust that the water will carry you and spit you out downstream. He was right.

Joy similarly depends on letting go of who our culture tells us to be, letting go of the fight to earn our worthiness, to get to the top, and instead trusting that the Spirit of love will carry us where we need to go.

Throughout the Bible and Christian tradition, we have example after example of people like Paul who rejoice in the midst of things not going well. One of my favorite definitions of joy is Karl Barth's: joy, Barth said, is the "defiant nevertheless."[6] This seems honest to me.

Joy isn't the absence of suffering and pain. It's the defiant nevertheless that says: I may have lost my job, or lost my spouse, or lost my reputation. Things are not going well. Nevertheless I'm *autarkēs*. I'm sufficient through the one who gives me strength. I'm loved and worthy of belonging. No matter what.

Joy is the defiant nevertheless that says: I was bullied at school today, or I was rejected by my dream school, or I might not make my parents proud. Nevertheless I trust that I'm *autarkēs*. I'm sufficient through the one who gives me strength. I'm loved and worthy of belonging. No matter what.

This kind of joy reverberates out and changes lives far beyond what we could ever imagine. Remember the STRIVE group I mentioned before? Fast forward a few years. One of the girls, Kate, is in her second year of medical school on the East Coast, and she's excelling. She's found her calling. One day she got a call from one of the teen moms for whom our group used to babysit (we'll call her Jay). Kate and Jay have stayed friends, despite their drastically different life paths. Jay didn't go to college. She has two kids from two different dads, and she's pregnant with her third. She's addicted to drugs, and the state is putting her children, including the soon-to-be-born infant, into foster care. On the phone that day, Jay said that the only person in the world she trusts to raise her children is Kate.

---

6 Karl Barth, *Epistle to the Philippians* (Louisville: Westminster John Knox, 2002), 120.

So Kate adopted them. Think about this: she's in her second year in medical school, all the way across the country, without family, and she adopted her friend's three children. People told Kate she'd never finish medical school. People told her she was throwing away her future, her happiness, and her independence.

But Kate was far too free and far too brave to believe them. She's an ob-gyn now, with twins of her own, raising an amazing family where everyone is welcome. Everyone belongs. Her life is hardly easy. Nevertheless Kate is one of the most defiantly joyful people I know.

Like Kate—like Paul—we can be either hostage or host. We can be hostage to fear, worrying about the Bad Places of this life, or we can be free enough and brave enough to host the Spirit of peace and joy in a world that desperately needs it.

My sister, Brynn, is a pastor at a church in Salem, Massachusetts, where the Salem witch trials were held in the seventeenth and eighteenth centuries. Today Salem is a headquarters for the occult, Wicca, and modern-day witchcraft. A few years ago, my sister's church hosted a dinner and invited a group of international students from nearby Salem State University. They didn't yet have their own building, so they rented out a theater space downtown. When they arrived the night of the dinner, they learned that occultists had rented out the space downstairs to practice rituals of dark magic.

At that point Brynn's community had some choices. They could sit upstairs and pray against darkness; they could try actively to stop the rituals; they could quietly leave and go elsewhere. Instead they spontaneously invited everyone to join them for dinner: this group of Christians, college kids from all over the world, and practitioners of the occult all shared a meal together. My sister describes it as a sacred time, full of joy, where they built relationships that continue today. All because instead of being hostages to fear, they were hosts. Later, reflecting on that night, Brynn said: "After all, the name of our city—Salem—stems from the Hebrew word 'shalom.'" Peace. Wholeness. Well-being.

That's what our youth need to hear. They don't need to hear they should chase happiness, be omnicompetent, or avoid being weak and needy. They need to hear that who they are in themselves is sufficient. They need to hear they can be *autarkēs* not just when they're already peaceful or happy but also in the suspended life raft moments. Indeed in any and all circumstances. That's when they'll find the freedom and strength to live courageous and meaningful lives, to stand alone when they need to, to ask for help when they need to, to be free enough and brave enough to belong everywhere and nowhere at once, because they belong to the God who is love.

Isn't that what parents really want for their children? Isn't that what we all want? And isn't that really what this world needs?

The price may be high. But the reward is great. Amen.

12

Idolatry

Looking for Joy in All the Wrong Places

JAMES K. A. SMITH AND KYLE DAVID BENNETT

"There is still a small amount of light in human beings. Let them walk, let them walk on, so that the darkness doesn't close in on them."

—Augustine, *Confessions* 10.33 (trans. Ruden)

Even if our goal is to foster joy and focus on the practices that nourish it, we need to be aware of cultural conditions that inhibit joy. To foster joy we need to recognize the hurdles and barriers to joy. For many, joy almost seems like a luxury—a privilege denied to many by a host of material conditions that inhibit the realization of that blissful rest from anxiety we sometimes name "joy." If joy is elusive, and the light of joy has been eclipsed in our societies, it is mostly because of environmental inhibitors that undercut basic human flourishing: the way poverty gnaws away at peace; the way wealth corrodes contentment; the way racism and sexism deny dignity and protection; or the way inequalities of power generate oppression and vulnerability that devour the psychic margin we need to experience joy. The material baseline for flourishing turns out to also be the material baseline for joy. So if we want joy, we should pursue justice.

And yet, there remain many who can take for granted this material baseline—those for whom these environmental affordances for the possibility of joy *are* in place—who nonetheless experience despair, sadness, and a kind of fundamental, subterranean anxiety that robs them of joy. There is a dis-ease that characterizes youth, reflected in astronomical rates of mental health treatment and increased suicide rates. Dismissing this malaise as "affluenza" is not a response; it is a condescending evasion. But what's the inhibitor here?

If we want joy, we should pursue justice.

We want to consider what might seem an almost scandalous possibility: that *idolatry* should be numbered among the inhibitors of joy. That puts us on the terrain of *worship*: what we devote ourselves to, what we give ourselves over to, what we entrust ourselves to with the hope of satisfaction is at once what we worship and what we want. Our worship shapes our wants, and our wants find expression in our worship. So could it be that one of the inhibitors of joy in our secular age is idolatry, i.e., false worship?

Now, we want to immediately address a likely question or concern: Isn't including idolatry as an "inhibitor" an instance of blaming the victim? To describe young people suffering from anxiety and despair as "idolaters" hardly seems like a constructive or compassionate approach. Isn't this kind of judgment only likely to deepen their alienation and disenchantment?

This, of course, is not at all what we intend by considering idolatry as an inhibitor. The point isn't denunciation; it's diagnostic. Our idolatries are less conscious decisions to believe something false and more like learned dispositions to hope in what will disappoint. Our idolatries are not intellectual, they are affective—instances of disordered love and devotion. Idolatry is caught more than it is taught. We *practice* our way into idolatries, absorbed from the water in which we swim. Hence our idolatries often reflect the ethos of our environments. That's why this isn't a denunciation of adolescents; if anything, it's a critique of we adults and older generations who've created the world they've inherited. If young people have absorbed an idolatry that frustrates joy, it's because we've built an environment that nudges them in that (disordered) direction.

To name idolatry as an inhibitor is not to wag our finger at young people in judgment, but to specify the theological and spiritual nature of this inhibitor. To name idolatry as a source of despair is to remember that some spirits can only be exorcised with prayer and fasting, so to speak. Here is an inhibitor that requires more than a therapeutic or structural response. Indeed, this is precisely why youth *ministry* matters. Youth ministry tackles this challenge on the register of the heart and its devotions, offering young people an unapologetically *theological* diagnosis and, even more important, holding out the spiritual disciplines and worship of the body of Christ as an invitation to give themselves over to the One who gave himself for them. In this sense, being invited into the Spirit-ed rhythms of Christian worship is to learn to love again. And reordering love is capacity-building for joy.

Joy, Love, Worship: An Augustinian Account of the Good Life

We believe that a fifth-century African bishop offers assistance as we grapple with these twenty-first century challenges. Augustine shares a fundamental conviction of the *Theology of Joy and the Good Life* project. For Augustine, there is an intimate connection between joy and "the good life."[1] Indeed, one of the distinguishing markers of the happy life found in God is a joy and delight that could not be achieved otherwise—a rest and contentment that stems from *being found*. The absence of joy—what Augustine describes as a state of "restlessness," a

---

1 Or "the happy life" as he would call it, echoing ancient, particularly Stoic, formulations.

frantic, besetting anxiety—is a symptom that one has not achieved or rightly aimed at the good life. In this sense, Augustine can be read as an ancient theologian of joy, for whom the unique rest that accompanies delight is a marker of flourishing. The "authentic happy life," Augustine concludes, is "to set one's joy on you, grounded in you and caused by you. That is the real thing, and there is no other" (*Confs* 10.22.32). Those found by God find in him "the joy that you yourself are to them."

Augustine's account of joy and the "happy life" provides a framework to understand the existential dynamics of idolatry, because he braids together joy, love, and worship. Appreciating this interdependence of our love, worship, and joy is the way to then understand why disordered worship (idolatry) leads to disordered love which then generates unhappiness and despair.

Like Springsteen, Augustine would say that everybody's got a hungry heart. But what we crave is *rest*. "You have made us for yourself, and our heart is restless until it rests in you."[2] This insight in the opening paragraph of the *Confessions* is echoed at the very end of Book XIII: "'Lord God, grant us peace; for you have given us all things' (Isa. 26:12), the peace of quietness, the peace of the sabbath" (13.35.50). The soul's hunger for peace is a longing for a kind of rest from anxiety and frantic pursuits—it is to rest *in* God. And for Augustine, to find this rest—to entrust ourselves to the one who holds us—is to find *joy*. "In your gift we find our rest," Augustine concludes. "There are you our joy. Our rest is our peace" (13.9.10). Joy, for Augustine, is characterized by a kind of quietude that is the opposite of anxiety—the exhale of someone who has been holding her breath out of fear or worry or insecurity. It is the blissful rest of someone who realizes they no longer have to perform; they are loved. We find joy in the grace of God precisely because he is the one we don't have to prove anything to.

The same phenomenon of human desire is considered from a different angle in *De doctrina christiana*. There Augustine emphasizes that the human heart can't not love something ultimately. To be human is

2 Augustine, *Confessions* 1.1.1.

to be a lover, and to be a lover is to look to something *as* ultimate, as the source and end of the happy life. Thus Augustine articulates this in terms of *enjoy*ment. What you *love* is what you "enjoy" insofar as you look to it for ultimate satisfaction. "Enjoyment," he says, "consists in clinging to something lovingly for its own sake."[3] What you love is what you look to for joy, for ultimate satisfaction that gives rest from your striving.

But here Augustine introduces a crucial distinction, because not everything we try to enjoy can actually yield lasting joy. He points out that not everything *deserves* to be loved/enjoyed in this way precisely because not just anything can actually satisfy our hungers. Thus he articulates the *ordo amoris*, the "right order of love" that delineates a normative account of what *ought* to be loved or enjoyed as ultimate. So he expands his definition of enjoyment: "Enjoyment, after all, consists in clinging to something lovingly for its own sake, while *use* consists in referring what has come your way to what your love aims at obtaining, *provided, that is, it deserves to be loved*."[4] Not everything deserves to be enjoyed in this way because not everything can stand up to the infinity of our longings. Indeed, nothing creat*ed* can bear the weight of our love precisely because their corruptibility means they will pass away.[5] "Among all the things there are, therefore, those alone are to be enjoyed which we have noted as being eternal and unchanging, while the rest are to be used in order that we may come at last to the enjoyment of the former sort."[6] All of creation is to be received as an iconic[7] gift that we "use" in the sense that it points

3 Augustine, *Teaching Christianity*, trans. Edmund Hill, OP and ed. John E. Rotelle, O.S.A. (Hyde Park, NY: New City Press, 1996), 1.4.4.

4 Augustine, *Teaching Christianity*, emphasis added.

5 Most poignant case: death of his friend in *Confessions* IV: loved one bound to die as if we would never die.

6 Augustine, *Teaching Christianity*, 1.22.20.

7 Jean-Luc Marion's distinction between the idol and the icon can be helpful here, *God without Being*, trans. Thomas A. Carlson (Chicago: University of Chicago Press, 1991).

or "refers" us to the immortal, infinite Creator.[8] "The 'things' therefore that are to be enjoyed are the Father and the Son and the Holy Spirt, in fact the Trinity, one supreme thing, and one which is shared in common by all who enjoy it."[9] This right order of love and the distinction between use/enjoyment will be a way to reconsider what's at stake in idolatry.

You Can't Always Get What You Want: Idolatry as Joy Inhibitor

So, for Augustine, joy is the rest that is found when we devote ourselves to the One who, for the joy that was set before him, gave himself for us. We find joy when we look for the satisfaction of our hungers in the Triune God who will never leave us or forsake us, when we find our enjoyment in an immortal God whose love is unfailing. That is rightly ordered love, and it is rightly ordered worship/devotion.

But how does this help us understand idolatry?

First: idolatry, on this account, isn't just a problem because it's "false" worship, on the register of truth, or merely a transgression of a commandment (though it is both). Existentially, the problem with idolatry is that it is an exercise in futility, a penchant that ends in profound dissatisfaction and unhappiness. Idolatry, we might say, doesn't "work," in a sense—which is why it creates *restless* hearts.[10] Idolatry is a constant temptation of the *Christian* life as well. Indeed, as Jean-Luc Marion

---

8 For Augustine this "use" is not merely instrumental; it can be attended with its own, rightly ordered/ranked enjoyment or delight (Augustine, *Teaching Christianity*, 1.33.37, 1.35.39).

9 Augustine, *Teaching Christianity*, 1.5.5. I've put 'things' in scare quotes because Augustine goes on to point out that, of course, God is not a thing among other things.

10 Augustine's account of the restless inquietude of the human heart is the catalyst for what Heidegger would later call *angst*, which has now woven its way into our popular lexicon.

observes, conversion only heightens this trial and the burden of self-hood; see *In Self's Place*, pp. 145ff.

Second, Augustine provides a diagnosis of just what's going on in idolatry: we are enjoying what we're supposed to be using. We are treating as ultimate what is only penultimate; we are heaping infinite, immortal expectations on created things that will pass along; we are settling on some aspect of the creat<u>ion</u> rather than being referred through it to its Creat<u>or</u>. Augustine describes this using the metaphor of a journey: disordered love/worship is like falling in love with the boat rather than the destination.[11] The problem is: the boat won't last forever, and is going to start to feel claustrophobic; and your heart is built for another shore.

But we need to recognize that such disordered loves/expectations are not always consciously "chosen"—not "intentionally," at least. They are often *caught* more than they are taught. Indeed, they are absorbed from the liturgies that we give ourselves over to. Our idolatries are less a manifestation of our conscious rebellion and more like the lazy defaults we fall into.[12] This is why our idolatries and disordered loves/expectations can't be adequately analyzed in terms of individual "beliefs." Instead, it requires something more like an environmental analysis of our culture's *liturgies* (which is exactly what Augustine does in *City of God*).

Disordered liturgies instill in us habits of disordered love and expectation. At root, these disordered liturgies train us to enjoy what we ought to be using; to look for ultimate fulfillment from what is only penultimate; to foist upon aspects of creation what only the Creator could return. And since the earthly city is characterized fundamentally by pride and love of self, that means that most of our disordered

---

11 Augustine, *Teaching Christianity*, 1.4.4.

12 See, for example David Foster Wallace, *This Is Water: Some Thoughts, Delivered on a Significant Occasion, about Living a Compassionate Life* (Boston: Little, Brown and Co., 2009). In this commencement lecture first given at Kenyon College, Wallace points to the invisible (like water) structures of our experience that we take for granted, but which can become idols.

liturgies are variations on a theme of self-reliance and fetishizing our own autonomy. Thus, as Jean-Luc Marion has suggested, the idol is often a mirror that returns our own gaze (unlike the "window" of the icon that we see—and are seen—through).[13] This might go a long way to explain how and why our own cultural liturgies generate a heightened self-consciousness that mitigates joy. It's to an analysis of one of these contemporary liturgies that we now turn.

Contemporary Analysis: Idolizing on Instagram

What are the idolatries young people have absorbed? We'd like to briefly home in on social media as a case study. As parents and youth workers know firsthand, social media is a valued dimension of young people's lives, which is why they spend so much time on their devices.

In our work with high school and college students, we have found Instagram to be a key social platform that young people use and one that seems to inhibit joy in a particular way.[14] There is something about Instagram that grips young people.[15] Prima facie, we could ascribe this to the image-based culture of Instagram. Surely young people must find this attractive. After all, Instagram seems to be the home of the

---

13 Jean-Luc Marion, *God Without Being: Hors-Texte*, Second Edition (Chicago: University of Chicago, 2012), 11, 12.

14 Facebook, Snapchat, and Twitter certainly are used by young people and can have negative impact. But these other platforms seem to be more easily "shed" than Instagram. See, for example, Leah Shafer, "Social Media and Teen Anxiety" in the Harvard Graduate School of Education, December 15, 2017: https://www.gse.harvard.edu/news/uk/17/12/social-media-and-teen-anxiety.

15 On the demographics of Instagram users, see, for example, http://www.pewinternet.org/fact-sheet/social-media/. On the steady increase of Instagram use among young people projected until 2021, see https://techcrunch.com/2017/08/22/teens-favoring-snapchat-and-instagram-over-facebook-says-emarketer/, accessed August 3, 2018.

"selfie."[16] But fixation on selfies (and a simplistic association with selfishness) can distract us from a more fundamental question. Instagram is all about *presentation*, and the most basic question is: what do I want when I present myself in this way? And what does such presentation do to us? Does it foster joy? Or quite the opposite?

When asked if she gets anxious at any point using social media, a student noted that she does, especially when using Instagram. "[I get] anxious about [the] number of likes [I get]," she said. "I have notifications turned off so its only when I check a few times a day . . . [It's a] very low level [kind of] anxiety . . . I usually tell myself it's pointless." When asked what exactly brings this anxiety she answered, "How many of my followers like my pictures, percentage of total [likes], [and] getting more likes than the last picture." Another student put it this way. "I would definitely say that Instagram can have a negative effect on me. I try to follow accounts that are uplifting and inspiring, but I inevitably compare my appearance, my experiences, and my lack thereof to the people and photos I see." The placement of features matters. Likes and comments are the first option viewers have. And one has to wonder what Instagram users are being set up to anticipate and hope for when they encounter the filter feature immediately after they take a photo—the "gatekeeper" they must pass *before they can post* their image or video.

Presentation. Presentation. Presentation.

What's the big deal, though? Aren't there bigger fish to fry in the domain of idols? Instagram is just a mole hill, right? Apparently not. When asked if any of these platforms affect the joy they have in their lives, and if so, how, one student responded, "Instagram—I don't know if I would say my joy is lost in those moments, but I feel inadequate, or rather I feel like I'm not doing enough, I'm not receiving enough out

16 Of course, this "selfie" culture could be taken cynically: Christine Rosen, "Virtual Friendship and the New Narcissism," *The New Atlantis* 17, Summer 2007, 15–31. In Augustinian fashion, we are looking for the longing.

of life. So maybe that is stolen joy." Another said, "both [Instagram and Facebook] affect the joy in my life. I took a year to abstain from social media altogether, and it was a very peaceful and freeing season of my life. I think social media intensifies the opportunity to compare myself and my life to others, making me feel discouraged or lacking when I don't match up. Also people only project their best selves and the life they want to have so I'm constantly comparing myself to an ideal and unrealistic life." Young people clearly experience anxiety, and sometimes anger, when they turn to this platform. And these experiences of anxiety and anger are often movements in response to failed expectations and realized disappointments. They were hoping for more likes than they received. Aiming for more followers than their peers. Comparing those viewing their videos to how many followers they have. On many levels, their interaction with this medium and others on this medium subtly and causally works against the joy that they are ultimately seeking.

The constant pull to present. The ever-present impulse to compare and evaluate. The acutely felt experience of inadequacy after one has unwittingly or wittingly done this. All of this takes its toll on young people. It isn't simply what the user brings to this platform. The cause of anxiety and anger doesn't only lie with young people. It's the dynamic of using Instagram. It's the unique features on offer that invite and encourage these movements. It's exhausting, yet young people have a difficult time walking away from it. They are aware of their restlessness, yet they continue to give themselves over to it. Their restlessness seems to come in two forms. There is the restlessness that comes from constantly feeling the need to present oneself like everyone else and there is the restlessness that comes from seeking affirmation from others through likes and comments. There is the restlessness that comes from posing seventeen times for the same picture before getting it right. Then combing through all of the filters, writing a witty caption, and choosing the right hashtag. And then there is the restlessness that comes from putting oneself out there in the promiscuous picture with "duck lips" and a low tank top that needs to get more than two hundred "likes." This restlessness is rooted in young people's response to felt anxiety and anger.

The anxiety young people experience on Instagram doesn't only manifest itself in online presentation, though. It takes another form. Though keenly felt, this one is not so easily detected. Hear the words of one student. "I get super anxious at times when I'm on both social apps [Instagram and Facebook]. Every time I click on them, I am reminded of the time I'm wasting, sometimes I don't care, and other times I internally freak out because it's almost like an addiction. *I get anxious that I am not present*, but sometimes I remain on the app just out of compulsion. It's kinda scary" (emphasis mine). She continues. "I get anxious that I am wasting my time because while I'm on the app, *I could be paying better attention to the people around me, or the place I am in.* It's really distracting to me also because it interrupts whatever I am doing all the time. I could pick up my phone for a reason like searching something on the web that I need to know for homework, and so forth, and all of a sudden my fingers are clicking the social apps and scrolling, and I lock my phone without even accomplishing my intended task. I get mad at myself sometimes for those reasons, like I don't feel in control because I'm so automatic with technology" (emphasis mine).

While there is the experience of anxiety in presenting oneself on Instagram, as already discussed, there is another form of anxiety young people experience when they aren't presenting themselves online. Yet it is related to *presentation* in general. This we might call the anxiety of "being-presented-as" to others face-to-face when one is online. This "being-presented-as" is not to be confused with the anxiety that some young people experience when they realize that they are missing out on something, typically known as "FOMO." We might throw "FOMO" under the more general category of "being present." This fear of missing out has to do with the unsettling realization that one is not getting all that one could be getting, or doing or experiencing all that one could be doing or experiencing. The anxiety of "being-presented-as" works differently. It is not so much about being present as it about being absent. There are two sides to this "being-presented-as." In one of its manifestations, one is unsettled by the realization that one is not "there" for another even though one is right next to them. She experiences herself divided as she is present to others online but absent to others physically proximate to her. Then there is "being-presented-as" as being roped into the perception or judgment of another. The sense that one is being seen, watched, objectified, and evaluated even.[17] This is the uneasy feeling that one is being judged as one is online.

The anxiety and anger that young people apparently experience on social media, particularly Instagram, should clue us into the idolatrous movements being made on these platforms. Idols are present and idolatry is being practiced. In particular, young people struggle to not give themselves over to the culture of presentation that is invited and encouraged by the features and use of these platforms. They struggle to not pursue perfection and prize affirmation through likes and views. They struggle to deal with not achieving omnipresence when they attempt to be "present" online to friends and sorority sisters who just posted a pic and are awaiting "likes." They struggle to balance between presenting themselves online, "being present" to others offline, and "being-presented-as" while online. Many young people (and their elders!) have fallen into the trap of putting too much faith in themselves, too much hope in others, and too much love in appearance. For all of the satisfaction and enjoyment that Instagram can bring, it can foster just as much dissatisfaction and restlessness. Instead of inviting users to look beyond themselves, by its subtle patterns and practices of "gramming" and the features it offers, users experience the invitation to use this platform as a source of security and relief. Ironically though, as we have been indicating, this platform becomes a source of suffering that at the very least, deters or defers joy, and at worst, inhibits it, during adolescent years and possibly beyond.

---

17 What Charles Taylor calls the dynamics of "mutual display" in *A Secular Age* (Cambridge, MA: Harvard University Press, 2007), 481–85.

Liturgies of Hope

If idolatry—disordered loves and expectations—is a joy inhibitor that generates anxiety and restlessness, robbing young people of the joy that attends that *rest* we find in a gracious God, then only a theological and spiritual response will adequately address this inhibitor. This is how and why youth *ministry* could be a beacon of joy: precisely by retrieving the disciplines of the faith and the liturgical practices of the church, and especially welcoming adolescents into the multigenerational body of Christ, learning how to love, and enhancing capacity for joy/rest.[18] Youth ministers are at the front lines of reprogramming young people's use of platforms.

Youth ministers don't need to be clued into how social media works. They are on the front line of this. They deal with this every Wednesday night as they try to gather middle schoolers for icebreakers or keep high schoolers attentive during Bible study. But if we are to minister to the needs and longings of young people in our congregations, we would do well to carefully consider what expectations a given platform cultivates and if these expectations work against the very joy of life in the Spirit that we are trying to cultivate. We would also do well to consider that we have resources at our disposal—the rich liturgical practices and spiritual disciplines of the Church. We would like to propose icon viewing and meditation as two spiritual disciplines that can help youth resist idolatry in our digital age, and thereby mitigate the anxiety and anger that inhibits their joy. While the Ignatian Examen could help young people pinpoint aberrant desires that they bring to their practice of "gramming" and the Jesus Prayer—or the repetition of a Psalm—might help them calibrate their focus and attitude as they approach social media in general, what young people seem to really need is a renewed sense of what to see and how to see. Icon viewing and meditation are two disciplines that directly attend to these goals.

---

18 See, for example, Dorothy Bass and Don Richter, eds., *Way to Live: Practices for Teens* (Nashville: Upper Room, 2002).

It might seem odd to some to refer to the viewing of icons as a spiritual *discipline*. In prominent streams of Christianity, such as Eastern Orthodoxy or Roman Catholicism, icon viewing isn't a discipline *per se*—it's a given. It's a gift. It's a means to communion that is a part of the Christian's life and worship. But there are basic disciplinary elements (i.e., instructional components) to icon viewing that should be highlighted and appreciated. An icon is seen. One has to look at it. The fact of the matter is the eyes could go elsewhere. Something else could be seen instead of the icon. We could spend our lives looking at other visible things besides icons. So we have to discipline ourselves to look at icons, whether we are at home, church, work, or school. We have to walk up to them and plant our eyes on them. So in this sense, our eyes have to be taught to look. And our feet have to be taught to move toward them. And our minds have to be taught the importance of all of this. We have to teach ourselves this through the process of icon viewing. All the while recognizing that the icon itself teaches us too.

Though visible like other things, the icon isn't just an image. It isn't a portrait or a picture. Whether it's the Pantocrator, John the Baptist, Mary with Child, the Resurrection, or Noah's Ark, an icon points beyond itself. True, an icon does tell a story. And we need to recognize the power in seeing the gospel story portrayed in images, as early Christians like John of Damascus did. Icons disclose what has been done and what is to come. They are alternative visions and visuals of reality that are already but not fully. And seeing this is important. If we hear a language spoken long enough, we'll start to pick up on it. If we eat certain foods long enough, they start to affect our digestive system. If we gaze at certain images long enough, they start to shape our vision of the future and perception of the now. But icons don't merely tell a story. An icon carries the viewer beyond the image (and ourselves) to a vision of truth and reality.[19] An encounter, actually. An icon puts us before the gaze of

19 As Jean-Yves Lacoste poetically puts it, "The things which one uses liturgically [e.g., bread, wine, cup, candles, *icons*] occupy a space which is not that of geometry but a lived space, and a space which envelops us." Quoted in

God. We all live *coram Deo*—before the *presence* of God. But there is a sense in which when we put ourselves before an icon, we put ourselves before the *face* of God. It is a means of putting ourselves before God and communing with him.

Icons don't only disclose. That is, they don't only tell us something. They also reveal. They show us something. They not only make known what is true about this world, for example, they tear down the veil of lies we tell ourselves about ourselves in this world (*re-* 'again' [as in a reversal] + *velum* 'veil'). In an idol one looks as one wants to look and at what one wants to look. But in an icon one is looked at—and possibly in a way that one doesn't want. We may treat it as the object of our observation, but in the end it observes us. We stand before the gaze of God. And this gaze does something to us. We feel the pull to see what it sees—what God sees. God does not see us the way we see ourselves. Icon viewing is the spiritual reversal of interpersonal perception. This is precisely why icon viewing is counter-formative.[20] Accustomed to presenting ourselves in a certain way and bringing the right image before others, particularly on social media, the icon invites the exact opposite. Seen by the one who sees everything as it should be seen, we become aware of how we ought to see and present ourselves. His gaze strips us of our pretensions and feigned presentations. We become aligned with a vision of ourselves as bearers of his image, not our own. Indeed, as we gaze at these icons, we are reminded that we are image-bearing icons who should be pointing to the invisible God and should be looking at others like we are being looked at in this icon.

Icons instruct us in not only what to see but how to see and how to be seen. Meditation works in a similar fashion. The word "meditate" comes from the Greek word *medesthai*, meaning "to care for," and from the Latin word *meditari*, meaning to "consider," "think over,"

Christina M. Gschwandtner, *Postmodern Apologetics? Arguments for God in Contemporary Philosophy* (New York: Fordham University Press, 2013), 178.

20 Jean-Luc Marion, *The Crossing of the Visible* (Stanford University Press, 2004), 66–87.

or "measure." When we meditate, we give care to something. We take in its value and worth. We think over it and orient ourselves toward it. In the Christian tradition, we are invited to meditate on God's Word, which includes a lengthy and detailed account of who we are as creatures and image bearers. We are consistently and frequently reminded that we are broken, disoriented, and even rebellious. And at the same time, we continually encounter God's claim on us that we are his and that we are "fearfully and wonderfully made" (Ps. 139:14 NIV). That we are his children. When we meditate, we consider these words of wisdom, these nuggets of truth—even if we don't believe them. Most importantly, we practice them.[21] We continually tell ourselves the truth by meditating on these words and images. This work should lead us to be less interested and invested in presenting ourselves and proving our worth to others through our poses and postures.[22] We don't have to present a certain image of ourselves. And we don't have

---

21 As a practice, meditation is meant to transform living. Commenting on the view of ancient monks, Jean Leclercq, OSB, writes, "to meditate is to read a text and to learn it 'by heart' in the fullest sense of this expression, that is, with one's whole being: with the body, since the mouth pronounced it, with the memory which fixes it, with the intelligence which understands its meaning, and with the will which desires to put it into practice." Jean Leclercq, *The Love of Learning and the Desire for God* (New York: Fordham University Press, 1961; 1974; 1982), 17. Cp. Kyle David Bennett, *Practices of Love: Spiritual Disciplines for the Life of the World* (Grand Rapids, MI: Brazos Press, 2017), 71–74.

22 Half of the battle is realizing that thoughts can be controlled (to some extent). Hear the plain but nonetheless wise words from "Abba Moses," as recorded by John Cassian: "The mind cannot be free from agitating thoughts during the trials of the present life, since it is spinning around in the torrents of the trials that overwhelm it from all sides. But whether these will be either refused or admitted into itself will be the result of its own zeal and diligence. For if, as we have said, we constantly return to meditating on Holy Scripture and raise our awareness to the recollection of spiritual realities and to the desire for perfection and the hope of future blessedness, it is inevitable that the spiritual thoughts which have arisen from this will cause the mind to dwell on the things that we have been meditating on." John Cassian, *The Conferences* (New York, N.Y./Mahwah, N.J.: Newman Press, 1997), 57.

to long for it to impress anyone. We bear his image, and he does the impressing. Meditation reinforces what we hopefully already believe about ourselves but occasionally forget in the patterns and practices of social media.

Meditation also calls to mind our neighbor and her standing before God. We are reminded of how God sees her and how we ought to see her. Like us, she is broken, rebellious, disoriented. Like us, she too is a child of God. She bears his image. She is "fearfully and wonderfully made," regardless of how she longs to present herself. Like us, she anxiously searches for the right filter and mulls extensively over the right caption. She, too, has the same misguided longings that lead her to pose fifteen times before she gets the right shot to post. She, too, can be enticed by narcissism, prompted to vanity, and inclined toward arrogance. We are all in the same boat. She is not something for us to compare ourselves to or compete against but someone to compliment us. Meditation brings to the fore important truths and realizations about us and our neighbor that ought to form and reform our anticipations and leanings as we interact with others on social media. Like icon viewing, meditation gets us "looking" to God's intended and destined way for interacting with one another. How ought we to portray ourselves on social media? How are we supposed to treat our neighbor? How do we interact with her on these platforms? Which photos do we like? On what are we complimenting her? Are we reinforcing what this platform is inviting or are we reforming the very expectations it aims to fulfill?

What if young people were trained in the fundamentals of icon viewing? What if they were shown how to look at themselves and their world by learning from the one who rightly looks at them in icons? What if they were taught how to meditate and mull over the words of truth that seem to be easy to dismiss or manipulate for our own satisfaction? What if young people brought an awareness of their dignity and worth *in Christ* to everything they did—especially when posting pictures after the party? Let's be clear, though. Icon viewing and meditation are not magical alternatives to looking at "selfies" and thinking about the right caption. Going through the motions of looking at a slab of wood or thinking about Galatians 3:26 will not inevitably make one allergic to false gods. Idolaters are not fixer uppers; they have to be rebuilt from the ground up. Which is why icon viewing and meditation are *spiritual disciplines*, not mere replacement practices. They help us *unlearn* certain ways of seeing and thinking that disconnect us from truly inhabiting the kingdom of God here and now. They take the scales from our eyes, enabling us to see the idols we prostrate ourselves before and the idolatries that get their foot in the door. But they also *correct* our seeing and thinking by reforming and renewing our habits of perception, judgment, and memory.

Conclusion

What would it look like to invite young people into alternative liturgies that might retrain their loves, hopes, wants? What if the path to joy was giving ourselves over to a God who gives himself for us? What if joy takes practice? Then it might be that inviting young people into the rhythms of grace will liberate them from the idols that have captured them.

Interestingly, this arc of redemption is hinted at on that same Arcade Fire album, *Everything Now*.[23] While it opens with the malaise and despair of "Creature Comfort," on a later track, "Good God," that despair is starting to be haunted by another possibility. While the first refrain sounds like cursing—good goddamn—by the end the narrator is wondering, "What if there's a good God? *Damn*." "Maybe there's a good God, *damn*. If He made you."

What if young people will find hope and rest and joy in being reminded that they are made, and that the one who loves them doesn't require a performance?

What practices might foster this? Here are a few concrete practices for youth ministers to implement in worship and discipleship programs.

23 Arcade Fire, *Everything Now*, Sonovox Records and Columbia Records, 2017.

- Teach a series on icon viewing. Introduce students to why Christians of the past used icons to inspire, edify, and educate novices and catechumens in the gospel story. Most importantly, talk to them about communing with God through icons. Provide accessible and helpful introductions to this practice.
- Practice icon viewing during your worship time. Have icons in your worship space. Allocate time during worship to view those icons. But also remind your students that the whole earth is an icon ("The whole earth is a living icon of the face of God" ~ John of Damascus, *Treatise; Seventh Century*)[24] that ought to be encountered and seen a certain way.
- Buy icons for young people in your congregation and give them as gifts for graduation or birthdays. Encourage them to place icons in most frequented rooms in the house (e.g., kitchen, bathroom, bedroom) or at school (e.g., inside locker, inside desk, on the back of a dorm door) and at eye level. Laminated icons could even be used as bookmarks.
- Teach a series on meditation. Begin by making students aware of their thoughts and even thoughtlessness. Have them read Kyle David Bennett, *Practices of Love*[25] to do so, or selections of John Cassian's *Institutes*.[26] Introduce how Christians of the past have practiced meditation in their daily routines.
- Practice meditation during youth group. Show them how to "do" it. One could tie this with *Lectio Divina*. Find a passage related to presentation and have them meditate on it several times. An accessible discussion of *Lectio Divina* can be found in Charles Cummings, *Monastic Practices*.[27] For a more detailed

24 St. John of Damascus, *Apologia of St John of Damascus Against Those Who Decry Holy Images* (London: Thomas Baker, 1898).

25 Kyle David Bennett, *Practices of Love* (Grand Rapids: Brazos, 2017), 59–76.

26 John Cassian, Boniface Ramsey, trans. *The Institutes of John Cassian* (New York: Newman Press, 2000).

27 Charles Cummings, *Monastic Practices* (Minnesota: Cistercian Press, 1986), 1–19.

but accessible explanation, see Michael Casey, *Sacred Reading: The Ancient Art of Lectio Divina*.[28]

- Via email, GroupMe, or social media, give young people weekly Scripture passages or devotional sayings to meditate on during the week. Send them as GIFs or memes. If you have an Instagram page, post these passages or sayings to your feed. Get creative with them (e.g., images from youth group but with these passages or sayings written on them or in the caption). Select passages that not only affirm their dignity and worth as persons but emphasize their life *in Christ*.

28 Michael Casey, *Sacred Reading: The Ancient Art of Lectio Divina* (Liguori, MO: Triumph Press, 1996).

Contributors

Steven Argue is the associate professor of youth, family, and culture at Fuller Theological Seminary and the applied research strategist at the Fuller Youth Institute. Steve coauthored *Growing With: Every Parents' Guide to Helping Parents of Teenagers and Young Adults Thrive in Their Faith, Family, and Future.*

Kyle David Bennett is assistant professor of philosophy at Caldwell University, where he also directs the Spirituality and Leadership Institute, a think tank and training center that focuses on spiritual formation and citizenship in North American democratic society. He is the author of *Practices of Love: Spiritual Disciplines for the Life of the World.*

Kenda Creasy Dean is the Mary D. Synnott Professor of Youth, Church and Culture at Princeton Theological Seminary. She is the author of numerous books on faith and young people, including *Almost Christian: What the Faith of Our Teenagers Is Telling the American Church* and *Delighted: What Teenagers Are Teaching the Church about Joy* (with Wesley Ellis, Justin Forbes, and Abigail Rusert).

Michal Beth Dinkler is assistant professor of New Testament at Yale Divinity School. She is author of *Silent Statements: Narrative Representations of*

Speech and Silence in the Gospel of Luke. Dinkler is also an ordained minister in the Presbyterian Church (USA).

Amanda Hontz Drury is associate professor of practical theology at Indiana Wesleyan University. She is the author of *Saying Is Believing: The Necessity of Testimony in Adolescent Spiritual Development* and *Testimony and Trauma,* forthcoming. She is also the founding director of Examen, a theology program for high school youth, and the Brain Kitchen, a trauma-informed after-school program that teaches children to cook.

Fred P. Edie is associate professor of the practice of Christian education at Duke Divinity School. He is the author of *Book, Bath, and Table and Time: Christian Worship as Source and Resource for Youth Ministry.* Edie's research interests include exploring the relationships between Christian worship and Christian identity and creating rich contexts for the formation of Christians.

Wesley W. Ellis (Wes) is a veteran youth worker and the associate pastor of First United Methodist Church of Toms River, New Jersey. He is also a PhD candidate at the University of Aberdeen. Ellis has served in Methodist, UCC, Presbyterian, and evangelical congregations on both the East and West Coasts of the United States.

Sarah F. Farmer is assistant professor of practical theology and community development in the School of Theology and Ministry at Indiana Wesleyan University. She is the author of *Raising Hope: 4 Paths to Courageous Living for Black Youth* (coauthored with Anne E. Streaty Wimberly).

Nyle Fort is a minister, organizer, and scholar based in Newark, New Jersey. Fort is currently a PhD student in religion and African American studies at Princeton University and a Ford Pre-doctoral Fellow. Nyle has worked in the fields of education, criminal justice, and youth development for nearly a decade in various capacities, including as youth pastor of First Baptist Church of Lincoln Gardens in Somerset, New Jersey.

Christian Gonzalez is the young adult ministries coordinator for the Department of Youth and Young Adult Ministries of the Greek Orthodox

Archdiocese of America. He is the cohost of two podcasts, *Pop Culture Coffee Hour* and *We Are Orthodoxy.*

Pamela Ebstyne King is the Peter L. Benson Associate Professor of Applied Developmental Science in the Thrive Center for Human Development in the School of Psychology at Fuller Theological Seminary. She is also coauthor of *The Reciprocating Self: A Theological Perspective of Development* and coeditor of *The Handbook of Spiritual Development in Childhood and Adolescence.* King is also ordained in the Presbyterian Church (USA).

Alaina Kleinbeck is the director of the Thriving in Ministry Coordination Program at Leadership Education at Duke Divinity. She also serves Duke Divinity School as director of youth ministry initiatives. Kleinbeck has served ministries and organizations in suburban St. Louis, urban Houston, Central America, and Norway. She holds degrees from Concordia University Nebraska and Duke Divinity School.

John Leedy is the associate pastor for Christian formation at University Presbyterian Church and is a Benedictine oblate of St. Meinrad Archabbey. He is also working toward his doctor of ministry degree at Austin Presbyterian Theological Seminary.

Stephanie Paulsell is the Susan Shallcross Swartz Professor of the Practice of Christian Studies at Harvard Divinity School. She is the author of *Honoring the Body: Meditations on a Christian Practice* and, with Harvey Cox, of *Lamentations and the Song of Songs.* Her current research is on Virginia Woolf and religion.

Andrew Root is the Olson Baalson Professor of Youth and Family Ministry at Luther Seminary. He is the author of numerous books, including *Faith Formation in a Secular Age*, *Exploding Stars, Dead Dinosaurs, and Zombies: Youth Ministry in the Age of Science*, and *The Theological Turn in Youth Ministry* (coauthored with Kenda Creasy Dean).

James K. A. Smith is professor of philosophy at Calvin College, where he holds the Gary and Henrietta Byker Chair in Applied Reformed Theology and Worldview. He is the author of numerous books on faith and culture, including *You Are What You Love: The Spiritual Power of Habit, On the Road with Saint Augustine: A Real-World Spirituality for Restless Hearts,* and *Desiring the Kingdom.*

Miroslav Volf is Henry B. Wright Professor of Theology at Yale University Divinity School and the founding director of the Yale Center for Faith and Culture. He has written numerous books, including *Exclusion and Embrace, Free of Charge,* and *A Public Faith: On How Followers of Christ Should Serve the Common Good.* He also served as principal investigator on the John Templeton–funded grant project titled "A Theology of Joy and the Good Life."

David F. White is the C. Ellis and Nancy Gribble Nelson Professor of Christian Education and professor in Methodist studies at Austin Presbyterian Theological Seminary. His recent publications include *Dreamcare: A Theology of Youth, Spirit, and Vocation* and *Awakening Youth Discipleship in a Consumer Culture.*

Anne E. Streaty Wimberly is professor emerita of Christian education at the Interdenominational Theological Center (ITC) and is executive director of the Youth Hope-Builders Academy, a theological program for high school youth. She is the author of numerous books, including *Soul Stories: African American Christian Education* and *Nurturing Faith and Hope: Black Worship as a Model for Christian Education.*

Almeda M. Wright is assistant professor of religious education at Yale Divinity School. She is author of *The Spiritual Lives of Young African Americans* and coeditor of *Children, Youth, and Spirituality in a Troubling World.* She is ordained in the American Baptist Church. Her research focuses on African American religion, adolescent spiritual development, and the intersections of religion and public life.

Vanessa Zoltan is the cohost of the popular podcast *Harry Potter and the Sacred Text* and host of *Hot & Bothered.* She is also CEO of Not Sorry Productions and founder of Common Ground pilgrimages. Zoltan also worked as a humanist chaplain at Harvard University.

Index

CPSIA information can be obtained
at www.ICGtesting.com
Printed in the USA
LVHW010315160620
658200LV00005B/1274

9 781945 935732